Advance Praise for Hand-Me-Down Blues

"Anyone who has experienced the bewildering and frustrating effects of having a depressed spouse, parent, or other family member can use this book. *Hand-Me-Down Blues* offers a new, sensible view of depression, and, more important, easy-to-use, practical suggestions for coping with and changing depression."
—Bill O'Hanlon, co-author of *Love Is a Verb, Rewriting Love Stories,* and *A Brief Guide to Brief Therapy*

"This is the most astute and comprehensive book that has yet been written on depression, and it holds out the greatest hope for depressed persons and their families. Dr. Yapko cuts through the confusion and mystification surrounding depression and places it where it belongs—in the realm of human experience, complex and varied as all human experience is. Most important of all, he provides useful information and guidelines for an antidepressant way of thinking that can be incorporated into daily living. Bravo!

"Every leap forward in mental health comes from individuals like Dr. Yapko who have the courage to challenge the prevailing ideas and popular myths of the time and to speak with a different voice. We owe him a debt of gratitude for his invaluable contribution to understanding, treatment, and prevention of this devastating condition."
—Peggy Papp, director, Depression Project, Ackerman Institute for the Family

"Dr. Michael Yapko is one of the nation's leading experts on the treatment of depression. His thoughtful review avoids simple 'one-size-fits-all' notions that are popular in current American culture, such as 'It's all in your genes,' or 'It's all in your brain.' Along the way, the reader is exposed to a comprehensive and holistic approach for shedding even the most difficult hand-me-down blues."
—Scott D. Miller, Ph.D., co-director, Institute for the Study of Therapeutic Change

"Hand-Me-Down Blues is a refreshing, balanced, and sensible guide for professionals and nonprofessionals alike. Dr. Yapko is realistic about the seemingly conspiratorial quality of today's culture that can disable one's innate problem-solving capacities. He challenges and inspires us to believe we have the power to generate depression-resistant patterns of living and relating, especially within the sanctum of the family."
—Kate Burns, M.S., clinical coordinator, Sharp Vista Pacifica Hospital, San Diego, California

"Hand-Me-Down Blues is a very helpful book for both laypeople and professionals. I am especially impressed with Michael Yapko's ability to synthesize the huge literature on depression in readable fashion, and with his attempts to bust the many myths about depression that prevent people from understanding this complex problem."
—Susan Nolen-Hoeksema, Ph.D., author of *Sex Differences in Depression*

"Dr. Yapko represents a powerful paradigm shift in the treatment of depression in *Hand-Me-Down Blues.* It will help readers open their hearts and minds to developing new ways of coping with life's difficulties. More important, readers will discover many helpful ways to create the kinds of healthy relationships within the family that can help reduce and even prevent depression."
—Consuelo Casula, Ph.D., psychologist, Milan, Italy

"In *Hand-Me-Down Blues,* Michael Yapko thoughtfully and clearly reviews the challenges to the notion of depression as an inevitable family legacy. He provides effective tools of thinking and action which can allow us to create a different—and more hopeful—life story for ourselves and our families. With respect for the reader and without minimizing the very real pain that sometimes exists in life, *Hand-Me-Down Blues* succeeds in illuminating paths to resilience. I expect to frequently utilize this book as a tool that can widen the lens through which problems—and solutions—are viewed."
—Miriam Iosupovici, MSW, Psychological and Counseling Services, University of California, San Diego

Hand-Me-Down Blues

HAND-ME-DOWN
BLUES

HOW TO
STOP DEPRESSION
FROM SPREADING
IN FAMILIES

•

MICHAEL D. YAPKO, PH.D.

ST. MARTIN'S PRESS
NEW YORK

This book contains references to actual cases the author worked on over the years. However, names and other identifying characteristics have been changed to protect the privacy of those involved.

Designed by Suzanne Noli

Library of Congress Cataloging-in-Publication Data

Yapko, Michael D.
    Hand-me-down blues: how to stop depression from spreading in families / Michael D. Yapko.
        p.   cm.
    Includes bibliographical references and index.
    ISBN 1-58238-021-X (alk. paper)
    1. Depressed persons—Family relationships—Popular works. 2. Family—Mental health—Popular works. 3. Children of depressed persons—Mental health—Popular works. 4. Family psychotherapy—Popular works.   I. Title.
RC537.Y3526   1999
616.85'27—dc21

                                                                                    CIP

First published in the United States by Golden Books Publishing Co., Inc.

10   9   8   7   6   5   4   3   2   1

*With deepest love
to my wife, Diane,
and
in loving memory of my father,
Benjamin Yapko*

Acknowledgments

I felt a strong sense of urgency about writing this book. I think it's a critically important topic. Bringing this project from conception to completion was made possible by many others who also thought it important and made great efforts on my behalf. I would like to express my deep appreciation to all of them.

First and foremost, as always, is my wife, Diane. She has a gift for getting to the heart of things (including mine) that is both mystifying and wonderful, and she shares it with me generously and lovingly.

My secretary, Linda Griebel, has been and continues to be the hub of the wheel, the eye of the hurricane. She has gone above and beyond the call of duty many, many times over the years, and is always so good natured about it. I can't imagine a finer, more worthy person with whom to share a professional life.

This book came about as a direct result of a conversation I had with my literary agent, Audrey Wolf. Her perfect record in helping me get my ideas into print speaks volumes about her substantial abilities.

I have been exceptionally fortunate to have the support and advice of many friends and distinguished colleagues throughout my career. I thank them for all they have contributed to me both personally and professionally.

Laura Yorke, my editor at Golden Books, was committed to this project from its earliest moments. Her editorial skill and sincere desire to improve the quality of life for families is a powerful combination. I'm grateful for her strong influence on this work.

The Yapko and Harris families are wonderful and life-defining sources of comfort and inspiration. I am extremely lucky to have a family life that is so filled with all the best that families can provide.

The Horowitz family is my other family. Wendy, Richard, and Megan are incredible lifelong best friends, and we have come a very long way together. Meg ("The Hugbug") is only seven, but she holds the pink slip on some of my proudest feelings.

Finally, I'd like to thank all those inspiring people who walked into my office, sat down, started talking, and invited me into their private lives. These are the people who taught me the most about the many ways that people in distress can rise above adversity and live life with skill and integrity. They have contributed far more than they know.

—MDY

THE POET AT MIDNIGHT

in the small gray times
when life's energy wanes
and the sunshine is as far away
and as badly needed
as the warmth of a lover's caress

my heart feels the ache that comes
only at these special times
as the mice of regret gnaw at my soul
their sharp teeth bring
exquisite pain

I weep for lost dreams, betrayals,
the weakness which kept me from ever
striking out boldly
as others do
reaching for something, I know not what

I know only that my life is strangely
incomplete for its lack
that, in failing to define what was
necessary for me
I betrayed all that makes life livable

secure in my pride
my arrogant belief in my own power
I sold out, too cheaply
for the gilded lead coins
of others' approval

it is in these small gray hours
that I explore the barren wastes
face the limits of my future
the fear of dying
without having lived

Larry Hoppis

THE POET AT 3:00 A.M.

So what do you do
      when the pain comes
            and the tears don't?

Your sinuses throb
      a giant fist squeezes your throat
            they've pounded a stake through your heart

Dive into a bottle?
      Lose yourself in a book?
                movie?
                activity?

Sit and feel sorry for yourself?
      Hate everybody else?
            those who aren't suffering?
               made you hurt so?

Let blackness corrode your gut
      while you strike out
            blindly?

Feel lost?
   futile?
   helpless?

How long can you tantrum
      like a two-year-old
            who has taken a tumble

Before tiring of the display
      getting up
            dusting yourself off
                getting on with life?

When will you
          identify that pain
          understand its cause
          work to heal it?

So your life won't turn into a soap opera

Larry Hoppis

Contents

Foreword

Depression is a depressing subject to think about and even worse to live with. It would be nice to have a clear cause and a brief cure, which are goals sought by Dr. Yapko in this work. As he points out, though, depression has many causes and many possible short-term interventions. Dr. Yapko examines the variety of theories that are current, from genetic and biological causes to the idea that depression is the result of a depressing human situation. His special emphasis is on the family and what might be called "family depression," and he contrasts that with chemical imbalance theories. The official diagnosis of depression is said to currently apply to nearly 20 million people, and the number of people diagnosed with it is increasing. Regardless of whether this increase is caused by biology or by unfortunate social situations, people are suffering. Dr. Yapko makes a strong point that family therapy can be very helpful in treating depression, a point that has previously been understated in comparison to the great attention given to drug therapies.

Family therapy was born in the 1950's as the American family began to disintegrate toward the current 50 percent divorce rate. It has been applied successfully to the whole range of human problems and psychological symptoms, especially depression. The approach is controversial since it tends to offer a different set of premises about problems and how to change them, in contrast with more traditional individual therapies. Traditional psychotherapy assumed that the focus should be on emotions which need to change in order to change behavior. A family approach assumes that *behavior* must change before what we think and feel can change. Therefore family therapy is usually active and directive rather than reflective, and requires families to reorganize. It is also assumed by family therapists that the past need not be the focus of therapy since the present must be changed. One other opposing view was the assumption of individual therapy that symptoms were caused by past misfortunes while family therapists assume that symptoms have a current function and are somehow adaptive to the present social situation. Thus, to change the symptom one must change the social situation. These differences are particularly relevant when applied to the therapy of depression, as readers of *Hand-Me-Down Blues* will discover. Current scientific evidence for the value of active interventions for depression stresses that the approaches described herein not only make good sense—they work.

These key points are well described throughout the book: Therapy must focus on the depression; action must be taken for change to occur; the concern is with the present and not supposed past causes; and the function of the symptom in the social situation must be dealt with. More than one person should be involved in the therapy—if not in the therapist's office, then at least the therapist's thinking.

Dr. Yapko insightfully discusses the different family therapy approaches as well as the systemic emphasis for individual problems. He emphasizes how depression can be relieved with a family approach, as family members are brought together to relieve their distress by learning to help each other and to avoid blame as the whole family reacts to depression. What helps and what does not is presented in detail with many examples to illustrate the ideas. People who are depressed, or who are suffering because of relatives who are depressed, will find this book to be helpful guidance.

Jay Haley
July, 1998
La Jolla, California

Introduction

In 1997, my self-help book *Breaking the Patterns of Depression* was published. In turn, I gave some lectures describing the multiple factors that can contribute to the disorder of depression. After my presentations, I invited members of the audience to ask questions. I was disheartened by how often the very first question, despite all I'd just said, was, "But doesn't it all just come down to your level of serotonin, and isn't that a genetic thing?"

In the wake of growing medical sophistication and the well-publicized advances in our understanding of the intricacies of the body, including the brain's complex functions, there is a growing fascination with the purely physiological aspects of mood and behavior. Most of us have been exposed (to one degree or another) to the biology of mood and behavior through the many media stories on the subject. We've learned that the brain is a fantastically complex organ comprised of billions of neurons or nerve cells whose communications are mediated by numerous chemical messengers called neurotransmitters. Neurotransmitters play a role in *all* experiences, including the experience of mood.

The enormous publicity given to the world's most popular antidepressant drug, Prozac, has made the neurotransmitter called serotonin almost as much of a household word as the name *Prozac* itself, since the two are inevitably linked whenever the biology of mood is discussed. As a result, people have learned that when the biology of the brain goes awry, and there is a chemical imbalance in the brain's level of serotonin, one of the predictable results may be a disease called depression.

But is this purely biological view of depression accurate? With our advanced brain-imaging techniques, can we reliably see depression? No. With our advanced blood chemistry analysis methods, can we reliably identify depression? No. With the steady progress in gene mapping, has a "depression gene" been found? No, but it *has* been found that one *won't* be found. With our growing knowledge of the relationship between certain neurotransmitters and mood, has the availability of new antidepressant medications stemmed the rapidly rising tide of depression? No. (For many individuals, the answer is yes, drugs have helped. But for the tens of millions of afflicted but untreated Americans, the answer is no. And for all those whom the drugs have not worked for, or even made worse, the answer is also no.)

Perhaps the most relevant question is this one: Even if there were a reliable blood test, or if some other reliable diagnostic means to identify biologically based depressions is eventually developed, is the identifying physical marker the *cause* or the *consequence* of depression? People have been led to believe a chemical imbalance is the *cause* of depression, and this not-entirely-correct belief has important implications that we must carefully consider. A primary one is its deemphasis of even more powerful influences on depression, like the social context in which it appears.

IS "HIGH-TECH" THE *RIGHT* TECH FOR DEPRESSION?

Americans typically love technology. We love satellite dishes, the Internet, pictures from Mars, moral debates about the merits of cloning humans with desirable genetic attributes, instant communication anywhere in the world, and any new high-tech gadgets we can get our hands on. We admire technology for the insights it provides us about the workings of the universe, we appreciate the speed and convenience with which we can get things accomplished, and we especially value the increased control it provides over many aspects of life that used to seem hopelessly insurmountable. So, it is little wonder that we look to science for the answers when our lives don't go very well because of sickness, injury, and the often cruel things we do to each other. Some of us go in the other direction, of course, eschewing science and instead redefining human problems in purely spiritual terms. Instead of taking two pills at bedtime, some of us would rather pray for some divine intervention or explore the bad karma from our past lives.

But as deeply as we may feel a longing for simple solutions to our complex problems, we have to face those problems realistically in order to be able to address and hopefully resolve them. To underestimate the complexity of a problem is to guarantee its continuation, despite making valiant efforts that were destined to fail for all they didn't take into account. Likewise, to overstate the importance of one aspect of a problem is to simultaneously understate other aspects of the problem that may also significantly influence what happens. This is a primary issue I address in this book: In plain terms, I believe that depression has been so overly medicalized that it has become a mantra of our culture to state that "depression is a disease caused by your genes and/or a chemical imbalance."

Expert physicians routinely go on television and show us sophisticated brain scans and cite impressive research findings to support this oversold view of depression. In doing so, they hold out great hope for all the millions of sufferers that one day the perfect pill will be developed to cure the world of depression.

That will *never* happen, though, for reasons I will describe in this book. New medications that are stronger, "cleaner" (i.e., have fewer side effects), more effective, and more reliable will undoubtedly be developed, just as they continue to be at this very moment. But the biology of depression is only one aspect of the disorder and it is *at least* as much consequence as cause. Other variables—culture, individual history, family dynamics, social network, range of problem-solving skills, and so on—are all *critical* to the development, continuation, and possible abatement of depression.

Until the distinguished researchers and clinicians of the National Institute of Mental Health and the members of the American Medical Association and American Psychiatric Association actively take the responsible position of informing the public that depression is in part a biological disorder—*but also much more than that*— with the same level of zeal with which they promised the American public that Prozac would make them "better than well," they will continue to do a disservice to the very people they purport to serve. Physicians in general and psychiatrists in particular cannot and should not mislead you, your family, or anyone into thinking that all you have to do is "take a capsule a day to keep the depression away."

DEPRESSION AND FAMILY SYSTEMS

In light of current research, to be truly realistic about depression one must view it more systemically: An individual's experience of depression is but one in a network of interrelated components. In a system, each component affects all the others; as a result, no one component can be isolated and studied realistically without also considering its interplay with the others. Viewing depression simplistically as a disease or as the apparent result of a biochemical imbalance in the brain ignores crucial data that indicate depression is directly and indirectly affected by many nonbiological variables. Consider as evidence the variable rates of depression in different age groups, its differing rates according to gender, its differences in appearance and fluctuations in rate according to culture, and even the effects on depression based on whether you live in an urban or rural environment.

A systemic, or interpersonal, viewpoint holds considerably greater potential to help depression sufferers by acknowledging that there are multiple paths into—and consequently out of—depression. These paths go beyond biology to consider cultural and family factors. In fact, one of the more insightful ways to study depression is from the standpoint of the family and its influence on mood. The family systems perspective has received too little attention in depression literature compared to the biochemistry of mood, although that is beginning to change as more clinicians and researchers begin to recognize strong family influences on the disorder. Mental health professionals have known for decades that depression runs in families. The research data consistently show that wherever you find a depressed individual, there's a considerably better-than-average chance that you will also find depressed brothers, sisters, and parents. Many have interpreted this as probable evidence of a genetic transmission factor, although subsequent research has lent only weak support to that conclusion. The evidence is greater that depression runs in families because of the family interactional patterns I will be addressing in this book.

DEPRESSION IS A FAMILY THING

Depression distorts family relationships, often skewing them in the negative direction of misery loving (yet also hating) company. It splinters families, riding a wave of helplessness and hopelessness when divorce seems like the only alternative. Depression isn't contagious in a strict medical sense, but it surely spreads from one person to another like a virus: One depressed individual can spread doom and gloom to others at least as easily as one cheerful person can spread rainbows and sunshine. Dad's "bad day" (which may have gone on for years) may have exacted a high price in his bewildered wife and children. Mom's feeling "under the weather" (which had nothing to do with the temperature or season) cost Dad and the kids plenty when just coming home meant having to put their smiles away. Parents and children, brothers and sisters, are all related by the common bonds of shared ancestry and family identity. But families share far more than genes and the same name. They share experiences and they form value-laden judgments about those experiences. In short, they share to one extent or another a way of seeing and responding to each other, themselves, life, and indeed the universe and all its daily offerings.

With whom did you live out significant portions of your personal history? Who translated society's expectations into your formative daily experiences? Who formed your earliest relationships? Who taught you your personal habits of thought and behavior through their very presence? Your family did—and it *still* does—all of these things and more. Not *only* your family, of course, but your family provides the foundation for your personal development on many separate but related dimensions.

WHY I WROTE THIS BOOK

I am a clinical psychologist with nearly a quarter-century's worth of experience in treating depressed individuals, couples, and families. I am also a depression researcher and the author of three previous books on the subject of depression, two of which were exclusively for my professional colleagues. Depression is a critically important topic to me for many reasons: first, approximately 18 million to 20 million Americans currently suffer the pains of depression; second, each depressed individual is directly and indirectly affecting the lives of spouses, siblings, and children, expanding the number of adversely affected people by *at least* a factor of three; third, depression hurts our entire culture by people's socially destructive or simply inadequate attempts to cope with it. For example, alcoholism and drug abuse plague our society, and undiagnosed, untreated depression is a common underlying factor of both disorders. Domestic violence and child and spousal abuse are also common outgrowths of depression. Divorce, breakups, custody fights, and a thousand other pressing social problems are common consequences of an inability to recognize and manage depression effectively; four, depression is underrecognized by doctors and underreported by patients. What a pity, since *the majority of depression sufferers can be helped.* Depression is responsive to good treatments, and good treatments are available. These are just some of the vital reasons why I want to see depression addressed more realistically and comprehensively.

WHAT THIS BOOK IS ABOUT

I will be describing the family as a powerful system, both for unwittingly teaching depression and for helping to overcome it. I will describe how families can deal effectively with depression, armed with considerably more than just a prescription for medication. Family influences ranging from genetics to collective abilities to perform the tasks of the family (such as parenting and group problem-solving) will be considered relative to depression's onset and course.

I assume that you are reading this book because you and/or a family member you care about are caught in the grip of depression and you want some help in breaking free. I will offer you a different, and I believe a more realistic, interpretation of the reasons for the growing rate of depression in American culture and in other cultures that adopt or share our Western ways. (Cross-cultural studies show that as other societies around the world westernize, their rates of depression typically go up.)

The evidence is clear that depression is *not* exclusively—or even mostly—about genes, biochemistry, or disease. In this book I will shift the focus away from drugs as the total solution, to *families* as a key component of what must be a multifaceted solution.

The ideas and methods in this book for helping yourself and others come from the enormous body of clinical and research literature that has been amassed in trying to answer the question: What works in the treatment of depression? The evidence is overwhelming that therapy—including family therapy—is at least as effective as medications, and in some ways is even *more* effective.

This book is divided into three sections. Part I considers the nature of depression, including its biological and social underpinnings, and introduces you to a family systems perspective. Part II presents the core aspects of hand-me-down blues: how you derive depression from your family of origin, unintentionally introduce its negative influence into your marriage, and unwittingly pass it along to your children. Part III presents ideas and methods for curtailing depression's influence in your family, offering you ideas both for self-help and for participating in family therapy if so desired.

The careful reader will notice that I make frequent use of case examples (with the names and identifying data changed, of course) and often repeat myself when I present key concepts. Twenty-some years of doing therapy with depression sufferers have taught me that when I'm teaching new ideas and skills to people struggling with depression, saying something only once and expecting someone to get it is simply not realistic. Saying something important in a variety of ways and then expecting someone to grasp it is considerably more reasonable.

The fact that depression occurs at higher rates in families of depressed individuals provides a window through which to view some of the most important aspects of depression. These are the focus of this book. I hope our evolving a broader systemic view will help curtail the widespread and growing burden of depression that now threatens to slowly suffocate our most valuable resource—the family.

Michael D. Yapko, Ph.D.
Solana Beach, California
July, 1998

PART I

Depression in Perspective

Depression: Parts of the Puzzle

They are ill discoverers that think there is no land, when they can see nothing but sea.

Francis Bacon

When Jimmy's teacher called for another parent–teacher conference, Mary was more than a little annoyed. To be interrupted at work with a personal matter she felt surely could have waited until she was home was irritating in itself. But having to muster the resolve to face yet another teacher telling her about Jimmy's shortcomings, which she knew only too well, was an instant energy drain. Mary's mind began to wander, and she found herself wishing she was someone else living a totally different life—a life without a soon-to-be ex-husband who nagged her endlessly about her shortcomings as a woman, wife, and mother, a life without a withdrawn, impossible-to-talk-to—yet obviously angry—preadolescent son, a life without a detached and secretive daughter, and a life without a supervisor at work who had no inkling of how to supervise. Mary's whole life had been spent wishing she was living a different life, for one reason or another, so this was hardly a new feeling.

Mary had tried many times to talk to Jimmy. He was unresponsive to her repeated efforts. When her frustration with him neared the destructive level of wanting either to hurt him or abandon him altogether, she just gave up trying. "His father thinks he's such a genius—let him figure it out," she decided. To have to call Jack now and tell him his son's teacher needed to see them both about Jimmy—again—was more than Mary could take. She knew she'd be blamed (as always) for whatever Jimmy did—or didn't—do. It wasn't a question of whether she'd be blamed, just how much. And that was directly correlated to how much Jack had to drink that day.

Mary left a curt message on Jack's voice mail telling him when the meeting was, and so began the evolution of feelings of intense dread about the meeting, the anxiety over what more she'd be told she did wrong, the guilt over Jack's placing the blame on her, the fears about what would happen to Jimmy, the despair and doubts about continuing to live this way, the terror that she might have to, and on and on. Her stomach turned sour, and a familiar nausea set in. Mary sat alone and cried, and then went to her supervisor and received permission to go home early because she wasn't feeling well. She went right to bed, her well-established place of refuge. From there, she scheduled another doctor's appointment about her fatigue, headaches, and nausea. Maybe a test would find something wrong this *time.*

At the same time, unbeknownst to Mary, of course, Jack was in a bar drinking to excess as usual while complaining to anyone who'd pretend to listen about the "raw deal" he got in life. Meanwhile, Jimmy was sitting in the school counselor's office, effortlessly maintaining an utterly vacant look on his face while the counselor continued to talk at *him about how important it was to develop personal discipline. And asking him why he couldn't be more like his sister, Judy, only eighteen months older, who got great grades in school without all the discipline issues. (Of course, the school counselor didn't know that Judy was at a friend's house, scared that the home pregnancy kit she had just bought would deliver the kind of news that could change her life in just a few minutes.)*

A typical American, turn-of-the-millennium family?

Mary is on the edge—again. And she's home in bed. Jack is out getting drunk (again) and bending the ear of anyone who will listen to his well-rehearsed litany of examples of life ripping him off. Jimmy is somewhere off in his own private hell, and he isn't checking in with reality and picking up his messages. And Judy, a mere child, who always seemed to be doing so well, is about to face a set of complex, emotionally charged decisions with enormous life consequences without the benefit of a mom or dad or *anyone* who could help her choose wisely.

Let's call them the Smith family. To say that the Smith family is in serious trouble is an obvious understatement. Here we have four very unhappy people whose lives will be and already are forever linked in a number of complex ways. Each individual contributes directly and indirectly to the family as an entity and, in turn, each is affected by that family.

How might we explain the afflictions of the Smith family? Perhaps we should simply say that Mom is a wimp, Dad's an alcoholic jerk, Son is a space case, and Daughter is a slut. Fine. We have the simpleminded judgmental labels handy, we've used them, and now what? Ignore them and hope they go away?

Perhaps we could be more insightful and compassionate. We can say that Mom is obviously depressed and overwhelmed with serious problems that she cannot possibly manage alone, Dad is totally detached and unable to provide empathy or support because of his alcoholism, Son is hostile, withdrawn, and unable to cope with the emotional abandonment of his parents, and Daughter is desperately looking for love but mistaking sex for love. Now we have some psychological jargon added to our appraisal of the Smith family.

As another alternative viewpoint, perhaps we can consider the social and cultural context of the Smith's difficulties. Mom has been victimized by a sexist culture that disempowers women and leaves them too helpless to fight back; Dad has faced lifelong pressures to be a financial success, climb the career ladder, and suppress his feelings about having to compete all the time, thereby causing him to be nonempathetic and emotionally unsophisticated; Son has been told he must be "the man of the house" now that Mom and Dad are divorcing, and so he hides his fear and uncertainty behind a veneer of false bravado; Daughter hit adolescence and was confused by the mixed cultural messages of "strive to be a strong independent woman" but "you have to be popular with the boys for anyone to think you worthy." Okay, this level of analysis makes it clear we need more social activists. Will *they* help the Smiths?

There's a simpler level of explanation for the Smith family, of course, if you're a biology fan. Mom is pre- or postmenstrual and is perhaps premenopausal, too. Besides, "everyone knows women are more likely to suffer from depression—it's genetic or chemical or something." Dad has a gene for alcoholism and "everyone knows it's a disease and if he'd just face up to his disease and join Alcoholics Anonymous and work the program maybe he'd recover." Son and Daughter have Mom and Dad's genes, of course, which explains their problems. So "they'll just have to learn to play the cards life dealt them and manage the inherited diseases of depression and alcoholism with medications that will correct their chemical imbalances." Is medication really the answer for each of the individual members of the Smith family? Change their individual brain chemistries and collectively have a restored and happy family? That *is* a simple, appealing answer. . . .

But as you can appreciate, the problems of the Smith family *aren't* going to be solved by taking some magic pill or listening solely to social activists, psychologists, or simplistic labels. As we'll discuss in this chapter, the reality is that there are many complex factors that can combine in various ways to create the different kinds of depressions manifested by each of the Smiths. The depression of the Smith family, as individuals and as a family unit, colors their every thought, decision, and action. They are in pain, and they need help. But will they get the help they need?

WHAT IS DEPRESSION?

Are the Smiths—Mary, Jack, Jimmy, and Judy—depressed? Would *they* describe themselves that way? These questions are simple and direct. The answers, however, are not.

Depression is likely the most common emotional disorder affecting Americans. Somewhere in the neighborhood of 18 million to 20 million Americans are suffering from clinically significant depression at any given moment. It is widely assumed that this figure represents an underestimate because many of the people who are depressed don't know they are depressed, and many more do not and will not characterize themselves in this presumably unflattering way.

For those who do not know they are depressed, it is not merely because of self-deception or a lack of intelligence or insight. It is because depression can take many different forms and can easily be camouflaged by other symptoms. Some people wouldn't claim to be depressed, yet they have physical symptoms that lead them to make frequent visits to doctors, who can never seem to find anything wrong with them (Mary Smith?). Some wouldn't say they're depressed, but they are aware of how little life matters to them and how nothing they experience seems to bring a sense of satisfaction or pleasure for more than a moment, if at all (Jimmy Smith?). Some wouldn't say they're depressed, but feel so terrible about themselves and so desperate for approval or acceptance that they'll do almost anything to get it, things they end up hating themselves even more for having done (Judy Smith?). And, finally some wouldn't say they're depressed, but they would say life has been unfair, it always will be unfair, and so drinking (eating, smoking, etc.) provides the only moments of well-deserved comfort (Jack Smith?). A variety of other symptoms, physical or behavioral, can easily mask an underlying depression.

There are at least two reasons why many quietly suffering individuals may not think of themselves as depressed. For some, it represents a character flaw: "If I were a stronger person, if I weren't such a wimp, I wouldn't feel this way." For others, it's a "tar baby"—touch it and either you'll never get away from it or you'll never successfully get it off of you. The fear is that by acknowledging it instead of avoiding it, they'll enter an arena in which they'll fight a never-ending battle. So they tough it out and keep going, typically leading productive but unhappy lives. They meet their obligations but always feel like they're barely staying one step ahead of a life implosion.

Neither the character flaw or tar baby perspectives is correct, of course. But depression has a long history—as long as there has been sufficient human consciousness to experience and recognize it—and an associated long history of myths, including the new ones being propagated even now. Depression *isn't* a character flaw. It *isn't* a reflection or consequence of personal weakness. It *isn't* an inevitable, lifelong affliction that must passively be accepted as one's unfortunate destiny. And, it *isn't* just a problem that unfortunate individuals develop because of some neuro-chemical accident.

CHARACTERISTICS OF DEPRESSION

Depression is a complex, multifaceted disorder. Technically, the mental health profession characterizes it as a mood disorder. But it is much more than that. Depression can and does exist on many different dimensions of experience and in many different forms, and there are various diagnostic types and subtypes. New conceptual formulations and appellations are being developed all the time, each progressive incarnation appearing in the ever-expanding catalog of psychiatric disturbances, the *Diagnostic and Statistical Manual,* or *DSM,* currently in its fourth edition, hence *DSM-IV.*

DSM-IV lists the following as the defining characteristics of what is known as *major depression:* 1) depressed mood most of the day nearly every day for at least two weeks; 2) a significantly diminished interest or pleasure in all, or nearly all, daily activities; 3) an appetite disturbance leading to either significant weight loss or weight gain; 4) a sleep disturbance manifested by either too much or too little sleeping; 5) either an agitation or restlessness or slowing down that is evident to others (and not just self-observed); 6) a nearly ever-present sense of physical fatigue or loss of energy; 7) feeling excessively guilty for little or no reason and/or feeling worthless as a human being; 8) impairments in the ability to think clearly, concentrate, and act decisively; 9) repetitive thoughts about suicide, death, dying, and perhaps even actually attempting suicide.

When five or more of the above symptoms have been present for at least two weeks and the symptoms are not attributable to drug side effects, an illness, or an obvious related cause like grief following the death of a loved one, then major depression may be diagnosed.

What complicates matters, however, is that for the majority (not all) of depression sufferers, there are other symptoms that may be at least as hurtful as those of depression (like anxiety), or other illnesses may mask the depression altogether (like cancer). This is clinically known as *comorbidity,* the coexistence of other disorders that may need to be treated first or in conjunction with the depression. As a result of the high incidence of conditions comorbid with major depression, it is all too easy to either miss the symptoms of depression altogether (thereby leaving it both undiagnosed and untreated), or to greatly underestimate the complexity of the problem and thereby try simplistic solutions that *won't* work because they *can't*—at least not long-term.

DEPRESSION AND MANIA

Major depression is also known as *unipolar disorder* because it involves only one pole, or side, of the mood disorder continuum. There is another disorder that also involves depression. It's called *bipolar disorder,* commonly known as manic-depressive illness, because it involves both poles of the mood continuum: depression at one end, and mania at the other. Mania is characterized by an extreme emotional upswing, generating an emotional high that features a greatly enhanced sense of self-esteem (grandiosity) such that the person feels he or she can do *anything*, reckless impulsivity (such as spending money wildly, hopping planes to wherever the whim takes one, or engaging in casual and careless sex), inability to slow down racing thoughts and behaviors, and being unable to sleep, perhaps for days, and even becoming psychotic. Such manic episodes may seemingly be triggered by external events, but more often they are generated internally.

It's a myth that for every down there's an up. Someone may correctly be diagnosed as bipolar when he or she had even *just one* manic episode many years ago and numerous depressive episodes in the years since. It is an important diagnostic distinction to make, because the bipolar diagnosis carries with it a substantially different treatment plan than does a diagnosis of major depression. The evidence is quite strong that bipolar disorder is largely a product of biology gone awry, and medication is considered an integral component of a comprehensive treatment plan.

Due to the larger influence of biology in bipolar disorder, some of the points made throughout this book will simply be less relevant to bipolar individuals. However, genetics and biochemistry aside, the social implications of bipolar disorder are every bit as profound as those of unipolar disorder. Bipolar individuals have families, too. They have sisters and brothers, dads and moms. How anyone handles his or her disorder— *whatever* it is—meaning how and to what degree a mood disorder influences the quality of one's interactions with others, is the foundation of this book. *It bears repeating, though, that there are significant distinctions on all levels between unipolar and bipolar disorders, and that I will focus almost exclusively on the relationship between families and the disorder of major depression.*

A MULTIDIMENSIONAL VIEW OF DEPRESSION

While *DSM-IV* categorizes depression as a mood disorder, it is clearly more than what is suggested in that one-dimensional appraisal. Depression can affect your mood to be sure, evidenced by feelings of sadness and a loss of humor, but it can also affect you in many other ways, perhaps even more profoundly. Depression can affect your *physiology,* as in sleep and appetite disturbances, reduction of sex drive, or physical agitation. Depression can affect your *behavior,* as in crying spells, anxious behavior, and excessive drinking or drug abuse. It can affect your *thinking* (cognition), as in the inability to concentrate, think things through, and make reasonable decisions. Finally, depression can affect your *relationships,* leading you to abuse, ignore, or withdraw from others, passively accept others' abuse or inappropriate treatment of you, and engage in foolish, inappropriate, or reckless relationships.

Depression is clearly a multidimensional disorder. Its potentially negative impact on every aspect of your life is what makes depression so serious a problem. The pain and distress it causes in the lives of people we love and care about, the staggering impact on the economy (estimated to be more than 50 *billion* dollars due to lost productivity, the costs associated with accidents and injuries, and the expenses of medical and psychological therapies), and the loss of life from those people who judged suicide to be their permanent solution to their temporary problems, are all ways depression is terribly costly to us.

Any one of the dimensions of depression I have described could be the focus of relevant books describing clinical research and practice. In this book, however, I focus almost exclusively on depression from the unique standpoint of the *family.* This perspective affords us a broader range of considerations about the nature of depression and its treatment. After all, for every individual suffering depression directly, others suffer along indirectly. Families are hurting all over America because depression is impairing their ability to cope with the demands of life. Yet depression cannot only be reduced in families, we can also encourage families to think and act preventively. These are my primary goals. But we can't really do these things by only trying to fix individuals and assuming families will then fix themselves.

PARTS OF THE FAMILY DEPRESSION PUZZLE

The range and quality of human experience is impressive, at least to most of us. It's nice the way the human mind can appreciate its own complexity, isn't it? We are, at the simplest level, biological creatures—

comprised of tissue, bones, and blood. We are also *psychological*, sentient beings, capable of insight, skilled at problem-solving, and able to create great masterpieces of art, literature, and scientific achievements. And we are *social*, each of us individually linked to complex societies and moved deeply by love and the need to be loved, and by the need or desire to have and raise families. We join or form groups for any number of reasons that bring us into a meaningful association with others.

These three dimensions—biological, psychological, and social—largely define us. They represent the foundation of *all* experiences, good or bad, including depression. Individually, each dimension offers a glimpse of one facet of whatever we happen to be looking at. It is, however, a glimpse through a narrow lens that inevitably precludes seeing a total picture.

Our biology is an inescapable part of who and what we are, and can't be excluded from the field of consideration when we're trying to understand ourselves. Even the most extreme among those who believe we are totally a product of our environments would have to concede that, if this were truly so, it would mean we would have been biologically endowed to be sensitive to environmental influences.

Likewise, we cannot escape our own individual psychology, which encompasses our perceptions, thoughts, feelings, spirituality, motivations, information processing, cumulative learnings, and life choices. Brain and mind are forever indivisible, and each features in all we do.

Our social connections—our families, friends, intimates, acquaintances, colleagues, mentors, heroes, enforcers, cultural icons; in short, all those people in the world out there—are also inevitable influences. Even the exceedingly rare human who chooses the life of a hermit is reacting to the social sphere of human existence. There is no escaping the influence of others. We learn a common language, a shared set of standards for conducting our lives and interactions with others (what we can and can't say, what we can and can't do, how we should and shouldn't live our lives), and we share a common culture that exerts pressure on us even beyond that placed on us by our families.

It has become a well-established viewpoint within the mental health profession to approach most, if not all problems (even seemingly physical ones) from this combined biological-psychological-sociological, or *biopsychosocial*, perspective. It is clear to all but the most extreme advocates of a particular viewpoint that each dimension is comprised of many, many factors, some or all of which can combine in an almost infinite array of possibilities that generate the remarkable diversity of human experiences. In the realm of complex human behavior, the simple days of "single cause—single effect" are all but over. Let's briefly consider each dimension with regard to depression.

THE BIOLOGICAL DIMENSION

Unraveling the mysteries of the biology of depression has been and continues to be the object of extensive clinical research. The benefits of such research are already well known to the millions who have been helped by antidepressant or other psychoactive medications, like Prozac and Zoloft. Yet the human brain is so enormously complex, with its billions of microscopic neuronal connections and mystifying neurochemical interactions, that despite many impressive recent advances in the neurosciences, much more remains unknown than known.

What isn't known yet in the realm of biology is crucial to evolving a realistic perspective about the key questions of depression: Is depression the *consequence* or the *cause* of genetic and biochemical processes in the brain? (Or is it merely an "innocent bystander"?) And, as a corollary, can the genetics or biochemistry of depression be reliably identified and altered, and thereby allow us to eliminate or even prevent it? In other words, can we alter the biology of depression for our individual and collective benefit?

These are difficult questions that to date have not yet been answered. No specific depression gene has been identified. No specific biochemical imbalance has been identified as the reliable trigger for depression in all or even most people. No specific biologically based test (like a brain scan or blood test) has been developed that can identify the presence or absence of depression in an individual. No specific physiopathway has been identified that fully explains how antidepressants like Prozac work, or why they can work on disorders other than depression. No one knows why the same drug that makes one person better makes another person worse, or why the newest drugs have no higher success rates than the older ones.

Despite the lack of specific genetic or biochemical knowledge of the intricacies of depression, enough is known to develop biologically based treatments with a proven value. Medications can and do help reduce depressive symptoms for more people than not, at least temporarily. But in our zeal for rapid cures within a technological or scientific framework, have we asked too much of our scientists? Is it realistic to believe that a complex phenomenon like depression can or will be reduced to a mere chemical equation? Can we place blame for our depressions on our family's genetic and chemical makeup? This question in particular, and many of its implications will be discussed at length in the next chapter.

THE PSYCHOLOGICAL DIMENSION

What can we say about the mind-set of depression sufferers? The psychology of depression is easy to appreciate but not so easy to understand. All of us suffer the hurts and disappointments of life, and so all of us know something about what it is like to feel depressed. But most of us don't *stay* there. We somehow endure the down time, but we eventually become aware of its weighty burdens lifting from our souls and psyches. How and why it lifts in some people and not in others is not clear.

There *are* important insights into depression, however, that have been offered by psychology. Three psychological models have enjoyed the greatest empirical support for their theories and associated treatment methods. They are the cognitive, behavioral, and interpersonal models, each discussed briefly below.

The Cognitive Model. The cognitive model of depression focuses on cognitions, or in plainer language, thoughts. Depressed individuals often make identifiable—and correctable—errors in the way they think about themselves, others, and life events. In a literal sense, so much of what depression is about is the fact that people think hurtful things ("nobody loves me"), interpret life in self-destructive ways ("life is so unfair") and then make the mistake of *believing* themselves. In cognitive therapy, clients are first taught to recognize their particular patterns of thinking errors, called *cognitive distortions,* and the associated underlying beliefs, called *schemas.* Next, clients are taught to actively challenge their thoughts and beliefs by setting up deliberate "experiments" to test their validity. The point is to challenge self-limiting ideas and strive to make them more realistic, rather than just passively accepting them and then sinking into despair or depression.

The most relevant features of the cognitive model for our focus on depression in the family have to do with two particular variations of the cognitive model: the *attributional style* model, and the *learned helplessness* model. The latter was originated by experimental psychologist Martin E.P. Seligman, Ph.D. Seligman did research highlighting the principle that many individuals, when exposed to aversive (painful) and uncontrollable (inescapable) stimuli in the laboratory, would form a broad and erroneous conclusion (called an *overgeneralization*) that when they were being hurt, there was nothing they could do about it. When circumstances later changed, and escape from the painful stimuli *was* possible, their previously established belief of helplessness was strong enough to prevent them from even attempting to escape. They had, in effect, learned helplessness, and were so entrenched in that erroneous viewpoint of powerlessness that they endured further pain needlessly. Many suffered depression as a result.

At its simplest, the attributional style model of depression involves identifying the qualities of our causal explanations for events that take place, whether it's someone's behavior or a life occurrence. It appears basic to human nature to construct explanations or stories that we tell ourselves and others about why things happen. For example, as a child you might observe that Dad is gone a lot and when he is home, he's often tired and not very attentive or emotionally available. What you tell yourself about *why* Dad is that way has enormous implications for your mood and outlook. If you tell yourself that Dad doesn't really love or care about you or else he'd spend more time with you, then you will predictably feel hurt, rejected, angry, and resentful. Your ongoing exchanges with Dad might then be curt and angry, or whiny and demanding. If, on the other hand, you attribute Dad's absences and demeanor to how very hard he is working to selflessly provide for the family, and how inspiring and honorable it is that he will exhaust himself for the well-being of the family, you'll likely feel affection for him, and protective of him, maybe even to the point of feeling guilty if you need to bother him with one of your "trivial" problems. Your exchanges might then be superficial and polite, or perhaps distant and evasive. To the extreme, you may even feel like you were a burden to the family, and feel self-loathing as a result. As a third possibility, you might recognize that Dad is busy trying to provide for the family, and realize you can have *some* of his attention when you want or need it, but not always at the exact moment you'd like. By being patient and accepting, you can have a deep and satisfying relationship with Dad based on what is realistic, not just what is ideal. In other words, the relationship can still be close and loving even though you'd want more time with Dad. When you don't take his work hours personally, the relationship won't be filled with destructive resentment.

Your routine formation of attributions (explanations) about the meanings of life events are patterned; they are repetitive, stylistic ways you have of seeing and responding to the things that happen in your life. They are the heart of your feelings about yourself, your family, and your life. And, most important, *how your attributional style is formed and developed within the family* is critical to understanding and overcoming depression. Later chapters will expand on this and other key family-based issues that are associated with the cognitive model of depression.

The Behavioral Model. Your behavior is what you do. It reflects what you strive to seek or avoid, reflects your personal values, and leads to gradations of success or failure in achieving its intended outcomes or goals. Assessing behavior isn't nearly as complex a task as trying to sort out the nonobservables, like thoughts and feelings. You can *see* behavior, you can *measure* it, and you can *observe its consequences.*

The things that you *do* are every bit as important as the things that you *think.* After all, your thoughts are your own private domain. No one knows what you or anyone else is thinking (save your money and skip calling the psychics); people can only *infer* what you're thinking or feeling from the observable actions that you take.

The core tenets of a general behavioral model are quite simple: People strive to obtain rewards and avoid punishments. Consequences of behavior serve to increase or decrease the likelihood of that behavior being repeated, depending on whether it was rewarded or punished. "Wrong" behaviors can unintentionally get rewarded (such as giving lots of extra unnecessary attention and support to a depressed person who uses it to reinforce staying depressed); likewise, "right" behaviors can unintentionally get punished (such as honestly confessing to breaking Mom's favorite vase and getting grounded anyway and ignored for the honesty).

Behavioral therapy of depression strives to teach and reinforce behaviors that are inconsistent with depression. For example, it might strive to teach successful strategies for managing stress, creating plans for fun things to do and carrying them out, defining ways to behave skillfully in important interactions, and so forth. The behavioral model places a huge emphasis on *action:* Effective action is vital to managing depression in the family, as we will see later.

The Interpersonal Model. *Interpersonal* means "between people." Our most basic human needs get played out in the world of relationships. Your ability to love, to tolerate frustration, to empathize and be compassionate, to communicate and be open to others, to endure potential threats to your personal sense of security, to accept others' choices that differ from yours, and many other such relationship skills all predispose you to relationship successes or failures, in *and* out of the family. The interpersonal model focuses on developing these skills and many others as well.

Good relationships are essential for good mental health. The depression data make it abundantly clear that people who are involved in positive, healthy relationships are much less likely to suffer depression. The data also make it absolutely clear that the loss of such relationships (through death, divorce, or abandonment) is a reliable trigger for depression for most people. No amount of *any* antidepressant medication can teach the kinds of relationship skills that are known to be effective in reducing depression in families. In that sense, the dominant model evidenced throughout this book is an interpersonal one that not only embraces family psychology, but also the sociology—the larger social context and its influence on the family—of depression, discussed briefly in the next section, and in greater detail in chapter 4.

THE SOCIOLOGICAL DIMENSION

The rates of depression have been steadily climbing in all age groups over the last few decades. Those in the baby boomer generation are nearly ten times more likely to be depressed as their grandparents. In recent years, the average age of onset of a first depressive episode has lowered from the mid-thirties to the mid-twenties. Depression continues to strike younger and younger targets. What are we to make of these startling facts about the growing presence of depression in the United States? Is it reasonable to conclude that the "disease" of depression is contagious and rapidly spreading?

There is a more realistic explanation than a depression virus. From studies of other cultures and the kinds of emotional disorders their people suffer, a clear trend emerges: As other societies westernize, i.e., become more like America, their rates of depression typically go up. For those societies where depression is not as prevalent, their internal social structure is significantly different than America's in a variety of ways. There is less emphasis on technology, less emphasis on mindless consumerism, and perhaps most important, less emphasis placed on self and more emphasis given to one's family and community. This lends strong support to the point that culture influences the mental health issues of its members.

TECHNOLOGY'S COSTS AND BENEFITS

In the last few years, our collective attention has been drawn to the old African proverb "It takes a village to raise a child." This quaint but insightful proverb is no less meaningful today than it has ever been; it is only much less realistic. High-tech types like to describe Earth as a global village because of the speed with which we can connect and share information around the world. "Global village" is an oxymoron, however. We may seem to be united by the Internet, but sharing information is not the same as having a *real* relationship. No one in a chat room is going to carpool your kids to school or get your mom to her doctor's appointment. The "global village" isn't capable of raising *anyone's* child.

Why make a link between technology and how we feel? Because while our range of knowledge and our access to information has increased dramatically in the past fifty years, so has the rate of depression. The increased availability of information clearly does not automatically lead us to be either smarter or wiser. It obviously doesn't make us happier, either. The ready accessibility of technology may make it easier (and less personally threatening) to learn some new computer function than to probe for and discuss what's on the mind of your family members, but the net result is a lack of genuine human contact—the sort of connections between people that hold the potential to insulate us from the pains of depression. Technology isn't going to go away, of course, nor do we need it to in order to help ourselves. We have to be more realistic, though, than thinking we can solve the social and cultural issues that cause and exacerbate depression by developing more and better antidepressant medications or computer programs. People will have to become more "tuned-in" to the effects of living in a society where many basic rules have changed from even one generation ago about sex, marriage, dating, divorce, careers, gender roles, money, family, and other such fundamental aspects of life.

POLITICS, MORALITY, MENTAL HEALTH

In the last couple of presidential elections, candidates made broad pitches about being "pro-family." (And now that candidates have successfully gotten themselves characterized as "pro-family"—as if *anyone* is "anti"— it seems a safe prediction that future candidates will continue to portray themselves in this way as well.) What exactly does it mean to be pro-family? In part, it has meant actively viewing current social issues from a purely *moralistic* standpoint. Thus, candidates have railed against the media's glorification of sex and violence, pushing for stricter controls and better guidelines on what we see on our movie and television screens. It has meant politicians taking a moralistic stance about what should and shouldn't be taught in our schools, which social and educational programs should and shouldn't receive government funding, and so on.

People continue to argue about the moralistic approaches to govern-ment, as well they should. After all, whose morals are to be legislated *is* a critical issue. But while some argue the moral implications of social policies, and fight to be defined as more pro-family than their opponents, I would urge consideration of the relevant issues from a different perspective—the mental health perspective.

While the politicians have uniformly been identifying threats to the family as external ones (e.g., the widespread availability of illicit drugs, the casual attitudes toward sex in the movies, and the destructive power of Joe Camel), I believe it is the internal threats from within the family that are even *more* powerful: The absent or even invisible parents ("We see our kids on Saturday afternoons"), the physically present but emotionally apathetic parents ("They get meals and a roof over their heads, what else could they want?"), the psychologically or emotionally unsophisticated family ("How was I supposed to know that telling her she's stupid wasn't going to motivate her to try harder?"), the socially irresponsible family ("Screw the neighbors. Let 'em whine. It's our property"), and, as the primary focus of this book, the *depressogenic* (i.e., depression-causing) family ("Life stinks. This family stinks. Why bother?"). The family that does not know its own power to hurt or heal its members, or does not equip its members to deal skillfully with an ever-changing world, is a family at risk for becoming overwhelmed and, yes, depressed. Some presumably well-intentioned psychotherapists have even contributed to the problem by portraying the family as an expendable commodity on the path to greater personal satisfaction. Encouraging divorce as a means to attain individual happiness and personal empowerment can be a very destructive recommendation.

Social and cultural forces directly and indirectly affect all of us. TV commercials define what we want, movies define what we find entertaining, nightly news defines what we should know about, schools define our creative abilities and educational opportunities, jobs define our daily schedules and economic futures, government defines what we can and can't do, and on and on. Do we have true choices or only an illusion of choice? I believe it's only an illusion if we're oblivious to what shapes our perceptions of ourselves and our very lives. Too many of us *are* oblivious, only reacting to whatever life happens to dump in our laps.

The sociological dimension of depression encompasses many, many factors, including gender inequities, racial and socioeconomic inequities, conflicts in social expectations, and unrealistic cultural values that may do harm to average people who can't possibly live up to them through no fault of their own. These issues, which directly and indirectly affect depression in families, will be explored further in later chapters.

GET THE BIG PICTURE

The biopsychosocial model of depression is a statement in its own right about the extraordinary complexity of the phenomenon of depression. I believe it is imperative that people in general, and depressed people in particular, come to understand and *act on* the knowledge that *depression has many causes,* not just one. Physicians are not doing their patients a favor when they state as the bottom line that depression is a disease requiring medication. This is not so much wrong as misleading. It ignores the other aspects of depression that are also profound influences on its origin and course. Likewise, psychologists are not doing their patients a favor when they seek a simple cause–effect relationship between some childhood or adult psychological trauma that can be identified as *the* cause, simultaneously ignoring the reality of biological factors and treatments. And, finally, sociologists are not doing a society struggling with depression any favors when they attribute it to large scale social inequities and the decline of the traditional nuclear family. Such insights fuel a deep sense of nostalgia for "the good old days" while preventing us from adapting skillfully to a world that will *never* be the same as it once was on *any* level.

But we are a nation of people who typically strive to quickly get to the bottom line on complex issues, and so, more often than not, we get trapped by our own desire to "keep it simple." But we face issues every day that cannot and will not be solved with simplistic appraisals ("There go the liberals again") and simpleminded solutions ("Why don't we just put up electric fences at the borders to keep the illegal immigrants out?"). Depression is clearly not simple to resolve. To focus on one component is to miss the bigger, more accurate picture.

When you focus on something, you amplify it in your awareness. There are plenty of books focusing on the miracles of modern medicine that tell the stories of brilliant scientists striving to find the "cure" for depression. I intend to focus on, and thereby amplify, an awareness in people of a nonmedical, nonbiological aspect of depression that I believe has been terribly underrepresented to the public. I choose to focus on the family, including our family of origin in which we were conceived and raised, for better or worse, as well as the family we create. Families are our deepest emotional connections, no matter how emotionally or physically close or distant we eventually might be. The countless ongoing interactions with our families continue to shape us. They were and continue to be mirrors for seeing ourselves, and they provide the lenses through which we learn to see life.

People may, and often do, say that depression runs in families. And, to be sure, it does. But perhaps not for the reasons we have typically assumed, as you will see. Beyond passing on genes, the family also provides the first and nearly universally most powerful context for conducting social relationships. The family also serves as the vehicle of introduction of its members to the larger society. It *is* your family that provides you with a body and genes and the biology of your very being, but your family does much, much more on many other levels as well. And these other levels play a far more significant role in contributing to or insulating people from depression than most people realize.

Biology matters in depression, but so do families. In the next chapter, we will explore the role of heredity in hand-me-down blues.

A SUMMARY OF KEY POINTS

- Approximately 18 million to 20 million Americans are suffering from a diagnosable major depressive disorder; their suffering directly negatively affects the lives of tens of millions more.
- Depression can take many different forms and can easily be camouflaged by other symptoms. How you and your family members describe your feelings about yourselves and your lives is the first step in evaluating depression's presence and level of severity in your lives.
- Depression isn't about being weak as a person, nor is it an endless abyss of a problem that would be best to avoid. Depression can be treated successfully with skill-building psychotherapy, and sometimes with medications, in a relatively short period of time in most cases. Are you and your family now getting or do you plan to get help?

- Depression exists in a social context; it plays a role in people's relationships, negatively affecting the quality of those relationships, in turn creating more distress and depression. Families are affected by the choices their individual members make. Are you aware of the effect you have on others?
- Depression has a cognitive component; the attributional style and learned helplessness models of depression highlight how frequently people's thought processes involve errors that exacerbate depression. Are skills in clear and rational thinking taught and encouraged in your family?
- Depression has a behavioral component. The things you do may or may not be effective in helping you get the results you want. When your actions yield negative or unwanted consequences, you can easily feel bad, stupid, or worse. Are effective behavioral strategies taught and encouraged in your family?
- Depression has a biological component. Genes and biochemistry *do* play a role in depression, and there are many diseases where depression is often a consequence. Likewise, there are many medications that can produce depression as an unwanted side effect. Have you had a thorough physical exam and discussed your concerns with your physician yet?
- Depression has a cultural component. Depression is manifested in different ways and rates in different cultures. How do your values and cultural perspectives influence your view of yourself and your life?
- Depression encompasses many variables. It will help you in your efforts to overcome depression to know of them.

Is Depression Only About Brain Chemistry and Genes?

There are two ways of "adjusting" a person to his situation without producing growthful change. One is to stabilize the person by the use of medication . . . The other method of adjustment is long-term individual therapy focusing upon helping the person to understand his childhood development situation. Many (people) have been stabilized for years by intensive analysis. Instead of encouraging them to take action that would lead to a richer and more complex life, the therapy prevents that change by imposing the idea that the problem is within their psyche rather than in their situation.

Jay Haley
Uncommon Therapy

Tom called my office and asked to speak to me for a few minutes about his circumstances. When he got me on the line, he described a veritable avalanche of hurtful events taking place in recent months: His wife was leaving him for another man and threatening to take their two young daughters with her; his daughters were taking the news of the probable split badly and retreating from him; he was finding it difficult to concentrate and so his work performance was impaired, potentially harming his career; and on and on. After spilling his guts about all the terrible things he's trying to cope with, he said, "The reason I'm calling you is to find out what medication you think I should be on for my kind of depression." Tom said, "I just figured once I got on antidepressants, I'd feel better and think more clearly and do more of what I should do. My mom was depressed, too, when my parents divorced, and so I just figured it must run in the family. You know, bad genes . . ."

IS DEPRESSION GENETICALLY BASED?

It has been known for quite a long time that there is a higher incidence of depression in families of depressed individuals. Simply put, where you find one depressed person, you are likely to find more depression sufferers who are biologically related, *if* you look for them. Is this evidence of a "depression gene" in the family? To a limited extent, the question is badly worded. From our growing knowledge of genetics, it is increasingly clear that the idea of a single gene being responsible for a complex set of behaviors, perceptions, emotional responses, or thought processes in *any* aspect of human behavior (not just the phenomenon of depression) is no longer tenable. No single specific depression gene has yet been identified, nor is there much of chance that one will be. However, there is growing evidence that genetics *do* play a small but significant role in depression in ways about to be described here.

Two young but rapidly developing fields have paid a great deal of attention to the issue of the influence of genetics on behavior. One is aptly titled behavioral genetics. The other is evolutionary psychology, the study of the evolution of human psychological traits. These two fields share a basic premise, that our genes are ultimately responsible for our personalities, psyches, temperaments, and behavior. A third related area is modern biological psychiatry, which is primarily interested in the implications of genetic and neurochemical influences on behavior, thought, and emotion. Specifically, biological psychiatry places great emphasis on psychopharmacology (the use of psychoactive medications) and other *physical* treatments (such as electroconvulsive therapy, or ECT) in treating the brain anomalies (such as the presumed chemical imbalances of relevant neurotransmitters) that are thought to underlie most psychological disorders, including depression. Biological psychiatry has recently evolved a preferred name: clinical neuroscience.

What does the current research in these fields indicate about the influence of genetics on depression?

GENES AND DEPRESSION

As you can imagine, it is a complex line of research to try and disentangle to what degree depression is a product of family genes versus a product of family environment. Quite a few studies have addressed variables like temperament, mood, and personality in general, but relatively few have made depression a specific focus. Of those that have, no clear or specific conclusions can yet be drawn as to the exact degree of influence of one or the other, so mixed are the statistical results. However, a general conclusion *can* be drawn from these studies: *In general, environmental factors are more influential in the onset and course of major depression than are genetic factors.* How do we know this?

It would be helpful to know how genetic studies are conducted in order to appreciate the insights they offer. There are two primary ways to study the influence of genes on behavior. The first is the adoption study, which involves infants that have been adopted who, later as adults, are studied in terms of their beliefs, behaviors, diagnosable disorders, and the like, in comparison to their adopted and nonadopted biological siblings. The second approach is the twin study, which compares identical and fraternal twins. Identical twins develop from the same egg (hence the term *monozygotic),* and each twin therefore carries the same exact genes as the other. Fraternal twins come from two different eggs *(dizygotic),* and so are only as similar genetically as any other pair of siblings. Fraternal twins have approximately half the genetic similarity as identical twins. Both kinds of twins obviously shared the same prenatal environment, although there may be actually some slight differences in this regard for identical twins since they do not necessarily share the same attachment to the placenta.

Whenever a condition being studied—in this case, depression—has a higher rate of occurrence in identical twins that are reared apart (if one is adopted, or for some other reason, perhaps), and there is a later opportunity to compare them, it then becomes possible to identify the extent to which the differing environments have influenced the condition under consideration. In other words, having the same genes operating in different environments makes it more plausible to assume that observable differences are attributable to environmental causes.

The next relevant issue to consider is whether a gene *causes* a particular phenomenon or is merely *correlated* (meaning a measurable relationship exists between them) with it. Earlier in the field of genetics, the working hypothesis was that single genes caused specific disorders. In fact, the highly publicized Human Genome Project was, in part, founded for identifying such links. Researchers ambitiously hope to delineate the specific functions of each of the more than five thousand human genes identified so far. To date, they have identified the specific chromosomal locations of nearly two thousand genes, and have successfully cloned more than six hundred genes, thereby revealing their functions with considerable precision. Since there are approximately four thousand diseases thought to be genetically transmitted, a primary goal is to identify, clone, and hopefully replicate healthy genes that can be infused and used as a "gene therapy" to treat such disorders. Very, very few diseases—only about a dozen—have a known specific gene as their underlying cause. (Huntington's disease and cystic fibrosis are examples of the single gene–single disease model for which researchers have been able to identify a specific DNA transmission.)

What has emerged with remarkable clarity in the study of genetic influences on complex behavior is that the "one gene–one disease" model is largely disproven. In fact, the inescapable conclusion of genetic research is that *multiple genes even occupying different chromosomes can give rise to the same traits or disorders.* It is simply erroneous to talk about a depression gene that is the sole or even primary cause of anyone's hand-me-down blues.

A single gene or multiple genes may be correlated with a trait. For example, there may be a high correlation or strong relationship between sales of lemonade and accidental drownings: Lemonade sales are highest when the most drownings occur. Does drinking lemonade *cause* drowning? No. Another factor may be related, namely temperature: On hot days, more people are drinking lemonade, and more people are also swimming. With regard to depression, while there is a higher incidence of depression in families, the family genes appear less to *cause* depression than they do to *correlate* with depression. The family genes are, metaphorically speaking, the "higher temperature" leading to an increased thirst for lemonade and desire to swim.

Regarding the correlational relationship between genes and environment, some prominent researchers suggest that there are three such gene–environment correlational types to consider:

1. *Passive correlations,* in which parents transmit genes that promote a certain trait, like depression, and then construct a child-rearing environment likely to support the child's genetic predisposition (for

example, generally providing a critical and negative atmosphere but especially so when the child is viewed as difficult);

2. *Evocative correlations,* in which the presence of the genetically acquired predisposition to particular traits evokes reactions from others that reinforce these traits; thus, a child predisposed to depression displays a depressive behavior or demeanor (such as being irritable or withdrawn) that evokes responses from others that inadvertently reinforce depression (such as being ignored or excluded);

3. *Active correlations,* in which people actively seek out experiences that fit with their genetically influenced traits; thus, a depressed person expecting hurt or rejection actively (but not necessarily consciously) seeks out difficult relationships that are more likely to fail that serve to reinforce depression.

What is the growing evidence for a gene–environment *correlation* for depression over a purely genetically based *cause* of depression?

To answer this all-important question, let us now look to the research that is specific to the genetics of depression. There is a 1.5 to 3 times greater likelihood of depression occurring in the other nuclear family members of a depressed individual. Studies of fraternal twins indicate that if one of the twins is diagnosed as depressed, there is an 11 to 20 percent chance of the other twin being diagnosed as well. Studies of identical twins indicate that if one of the twins is diagnosed as depressed, there is as much as (but not more than) a 50 percent chance of the other twin being diagnosed as well.

Of three major adoption studies conducted which were specific to major depression, only one found significant genetic effects; the other two studies concluded there was greater evidence for environmental effects on depression's onset. Of three major twin studies, the best evidence suggested a range of 42 to 50 percent genetic influence on the onset of depression. *The major studies represent a consistent view of depression as caused by many factors, and not all of them are of equal influence.* The genetic influence is at most 50 percent, and it is the conclusion of the majority of researchers that the strongest predictors of depression are: one, stressful life events; two, genetic factors; three, previous history of depression; and four, individual coping styles.

What can we reasonably conclude, then, about the relationship between one's genes and one's depression?

1. Complex experiences like depression are almost invariably a product of genes *and* environment, and not either factor alone;

2. The research indicates that genetic influences can account for anywhere from as little as 11 percent to as much as 50 percent of the variance in depression; this represents a significant, but far from overwhelming, degree of influence;

3. The genetic evidence has been *at least* as powerful in pointing to environmental influences on depression as it has been in its suggestion of genetic influences;

4. It is as inaccurate to state that depression is *not* heritable as it is to say that it is;

5. Depression is *not* caused by a single gene that has been identified as the culprit; rather, depression in *some* cases—not all—appears to be a product of complex interactions between multiple genes;

6. Our inherited neuronal connections determine the range of what we can learn and experience, affecting the *probability* that depression will occur rather than causing it directly;

7. The greatest probability is that any genetic influences that are important will operate through specific personality, psychological, and cognitive features rather than on a global phenomenon called *depression*. (To illustrate this point, consider *perfectionism*, a pattern that is closely associated to depression. While no perfectionism gene has been found, it is nonetheless a strong trait that shapes people's experiences. On the level of personality, it typically leads people to be impatient and judgmental. On the psychological level, perfectionism typically leads people to be sensitive to criticism and filled with self-doubts. On the cognitive level, it usually leads people to see things in all-or-none terms of success or failure and involves the distorted thought that perfection and universal acceptance from others is even possible. So, if there was such a thing as a perfectionism gene, it would show up in these specific ways, and not just as a global label.)

8. A gene–evironment correlation means *variations in genetic expressions are systemically associated with varying environmental circumstances.* Simply put, as conditions change, so do genetically influenced

responses. This is the most well-supported model for understanding the phenomenon of depression in general, and from a family systems perspective in particular.

Despite the best scientific evidence to date that genes account for only a portion of depression, only half at most, articles suggesting a "happiness gene" proliferated recently when some excitable researchers concluded there is an inherited "happiness set point." These researchers have hypothesized that there is a genetically determined mood level that may shift slightly up or down, but stays essentially the same over time, regardless of the quality of life events. Given the complexities and stability of personality, including the patterning of *learned* thought processes that are enduring throughout life without interventions, it is no wonder that one's outlook generally remains stable over time. But, the simplistic notion of a happiness gene is not supportable given the abundant data indicating that heritability of *any* complex trait is only partial. Media attention was also given to researchers who claim that other complex traits are also genetic—including thrill-seeking, the propensity to divorce, and yes, even the amount of television you watch each day! You can—and should—be skeptical about such reductionistic views of complex behavior. Genes may help define the broad region within which we live, but it is now clear that the environment is a powerful force in shaping our specific address. It is *not* a one-way phenomenon of genes influencing experience. It's a two-way street, for we now know that experience influences genes, too. Genes matter, but are they destiny? *Absolutely not! You are more than your genes.*

THE CHEMICAL IMBALANCE OF DEPRESSION

In the same way that there are those who would reduce depression to bad genes, there are those who reduce depression to bad chemistry. And, like those who argue for the genetic model of depression, there *is* certainly some supportive evidence for the notion that brain chemistry matters. But is depression simply a chemical imbalance that is best treated with antidepressant medications?

The notion of a complex, multidimensional disorder like depression being a neurochemical screwup is appealing. It makes it a medical problem and thereby holds out hope for a medical or pharmaceutical cure. This is, arguably, the most potentially damaging part of the exclusively biochemical, intrapersonal viewpoint. It separates individuals from the relationships that define them: from the marriages and families that influence them, and from the larger culture that teaches them what is true or not true, good or bad, right or wrong.

The big push for this popular biochemical imbalance view came about just over a decade ago. The famed antidepressant Prozac was released in January 1988, amidst a great deal of hoopla. It was touted as a wonder drug that would revolutionize the treatment of depression. Well, it has. But not for the reasons most people would expect. *Prozac does not have any higher a success rate in treating depression than the older drugs it has replaced.* It is a "cleaner" drug, however, meaning it, and the many newer drugs released since Prozac, have fewer troublesome side effects. As a result, patients will demonstrate a higher rate of treatment compliance, meaning they are more agreeable to staying on the drug. Stay on it, and it has a better chance of working. Prozac and all the newer antidepressants do not not fully warrant the wild enthusiasm and noncritical acceptance they have received. They can and do alter mood for some—but not all— people. They can and do make dramatic differences for some—but not all—people. They can and do save the lives of some—but not all— people. All antidepressant drugs, however, are ultimately providing a means of chemical management for those lucky enough to have the drug work for them. (Many are not so lucky.) And even when the drugs do provide a therapeutic benefit, the short-term, positive results do not insulate the patient from painful relapses. In fact, the rates of relapse are significantly higher in those patients who only take antidepressant medications in comparison to those who also receive competent psycho-therapy. *All* of the medications also produce undesirable side effects, including some that go beyond merely annoying and into the realm of hazardous. Furthermore, there is growing evidence that many people actually experience unpleasant withdrawal symptoms of sorts when they discontinue taking them even with the newer drugs that are widely touted as nonaddictive.

I would agree with the evolving premise that *no depression is either purely biological or psychological.* Depression clearly has physical symptoms and may even have physical causes (like certain diseases or the side effects of certain medications), and likewise, depression also has clearly psychological symptoms and causes. Having said that, the key question is a variation of the "chicken or egg" paradox: Does negative life experience cause depressing chemical changes, or do the chemical changes cause depression? The answer is *both:* There is a circular, *systemic* relationship between neurochemistry and life experience. It is not a simple, linear cause–effect relationship of low serotonin causing depression. The evidence is unequivocal on this point: *Environment affects the serotonin and other neurotransmitter levels in our brains.* Life experience matters at least as much as genetics and neurochemistry.

Stephen Suomi, Ph.D., is chief of the Laboratory of Comparative Ethology at the National Institute of Child Health and Human Development. His primary research is on the relationship between serotonin levels and behavior. In the April 1997 *APA Monitor,* Suomi said, "The most important message our research can make is that experience is as strong or stronger than anything that is inherited." Dee Higley, Ph.D., is also a primate researcher at the National Institutes of Health. In the same article, Higley states flatly, "Just because a trait runs in families doesn't mean it can't be influenced by the environment. Our research is a prime example that low serotonin is likely a mix of genetics and environment."

How does environment and life experience affect neurotransmitter levels? It is too complex for anyone to fully understand, but therapeutically speaking, in the same way that a vulnerable organ in the body (like a heart) genetically predisposed to weakness might be subjected to ongoing stress that leads to permanent changes, the affected brain may evolve a sustained pathological level of functioning to cope with environmental stress. For example, serotonin might be depleted over days, weeks, or months as someone deals with ongoing stress. The brain adapts to that new lower serotonin level, and then when the stress ends, the brain does not "kick back" to its original level—it has adapted pathologically.

Can therapy really affect the brain in the same way as medications do? There is growing evidence that it can. In his book *Brain Lock,* Dr. Jeffrey

Schwartz provides compelling evidence, in the form of brain imaging, that obsessive-compulsive disorder (OCD), which, like depression, is thought to be mediated by serotonin, is responsive to both therapy and medication. In fact, the before and after images of the brains of people receiving therapy look *identical* to those of people receiving medication. It is reasonable to conclude that good therapy can stimulate the same or similar neural pathways as medication. And, more important, such therapy doesn't have side effects that range from irritating to maddening, nor does psychotherapy pose the higher risk for later relapses that medications as the sole treatment do.

If simply raising the concentration of serotonin (or any other neurotransmitter) in your brain would reliably eliminate depression, then drugs like Prozac would provide a relatively uniform effect across people. They don't. In fact, some people actually get *worse* on such medications. Likewise, it is a statistical flip of the coin whether the first such antidepressant drug one tries will even be helpful.

What is of greatest importance to me as a clinical psychologist and marriage and family therapist, however, is how carefully conducted therapy and the deliberate creation of experiences can lift depression *at least as successfully as medications can.* The studies comparing the effectiveness of psychotherapy and medications make it clear: Psychotherapy is at least as effective as medications, and in some ways may even outperform medication. Psychotherapy may even function in similar ways to medication.

I want to state flatly and unequivocally that I happen to favor the use of antidepressant medications in treatment. Given all I've said, that might well surprise you. (It shouldn't, though, because as you may already be discovering, I am a fan of what *works.*) Medications can and do provide at least *some* benefits to the majority of the people who use them. They can raise the floor on depression (so you don't go so low), improve sleep and appetite, decrease agitation and rumination, increase energy, and lift your mood. They can help someone improve enough to engage meaningfully in therapy when severe depression has limited the sufferer's ability to engage in the process. (Statistically, though, the majority of depressions are mild to moderate, not severe.) To their credit, medications typically work more quickly than psychotherapy does, which is a strong advantage when symptoms are extreme or even hazardous. However, if and when medications are employed in treatment, they *must* be provided responsibly and with more realistic and meaningful insight than just saying "It'll stabilize your neurotransmitter levels." Care must be taken to help the depressed person—or family—understand that depression is much more than merely biology gone awry.

There are clearly many, many factors influencing one's experience of depression and one's response to medications. The chemical imbalance theory has been vastly oversold, and with a disorder as complex as depression, it is not doing any patient a favor to state as the bottom line that their mood *is* their brain chemistry. *You are more than your brain chemistry.*

GENES, NEUROCHEMISTRY, ENVIRONMENT: WHAT'S THE DIFFERENCE?

All of the endeavors we make to improve our lives are based on the underlying premise that we *can* improve our lives. We attempt to change all kinds of experiences, from trying to heal ourselves of cancer to cutting down on sweets. As noted psychologist, researcher, and author Dr. Martin Seligman points out in his forthright book *What You Can Change . . . and What You Can't,* it would help us to know what clearly falls in the realm of changeable and what doesn't. Considerable amounts of unrealistic self-blame, self-condemnation, deep personal insecurity, and guilt could be prevented from arising with such knowledge.

The larger question, though, is my concern here. Why should anyone try to learn new skills or make deliberate efforts to change in *any* arena if he or she is convinced that effort is futile, because the problems all stem from seemingly uncontrollable factors like genes and biochemistry? In the realm of philosophy, the debate over what is known as *biological determinism* is as rowdy as ever. Even in the realm of psychotherapy, there are colleagues of mine who have taken the position publicly that we are basically life support systems for our genes; they claim we are simply living out a predetermined life that even maps out what brand of tuna fish we'll buy in the grocery store and the most likely name of our as-yet-unknown spouse.

Surely, the other extreme, being told that "if you have the right attitude, you can cure yourself of cancer" can be highly appealing. The underlying belief that you can do *anything* if you just approach it correctly tends to foster an error in perception known in the mental health profession as the "illusion of control." Such thinking is a fairly recent development in our collective psyche, spawned and nurtured by the so-called self-help movement and New-Age consciousness. This represents unbridled optimism that makes people feel good. But the other side of the tracks is where depression tends to live: in the neighborhood of passivity, defeatism, apathy, negativity, self-*no*-help.

Does it help or hurt people to believe that they are neurochemically defective, and that their problems can be readily solved with a prescription and some luck? Certainly, the "miracles of science" regarding the new drugs to treat depression have received plenty of attention. Prozac has been on the cover of *Newsweek* and many other national magazines. Pharmaceutical companies have spent—and continue to spend—billions of dollars each year to convince us that depression is a brain disorder their drugs can quickly and reliably correct. *But there is no advertising equivalent for the healing value of families, communities, or good relationships.*

Perhaps this book can start to correct that omission.

You are more than your genes, and you are more than your biochemistry. Your life matters, and the choices you make and the experiences you actively seek—or passively accept—can define your mood and quality of life at least as much as what you may well have thought were inevitable hand-me-down blues.

A SUMMARY OF KEY POINTS

- The fact that depression runs in families has been known for decades, prompting research into the hypothesis that depression is genetically transmitted. Adoption studies and twin studies are the primary means for sorting out genetic from environmental influences on disorders like depression. Can you simply assume that if depression runs in families that there must be some genetic cause? The answer is no.

- Genetic research has suggested that depression is not caused by a single gene, that the influence of genetics on depression is moderate at best, and that environment plays a critical role in the disorder of depression. Your genes are *not* your destiny, nor are they your only legacy.

- Contrary to the common notion that biochemistry runs experience, it is equally true that experience influences biochemistry. It's a two-way street. The critical idea in this book is that you can deliberately create positive experiences for you and your family that will favorably influence neurochemistry.

- Antidepressant medications have proven themselves to be valuable allies in the treatment process, offering certain distinct advantages as a form of intervention. However, they do not and *cannot* teach the kinds of skills in thinking clearly and relating positively that can be taught in psychotherapy. Such skills are shown to have a greater ability than medications to reduce depression and even prevent later relapses.

- Comprehensive interventions may involve therapy and medication in combination. You can consider medication as an option (not a mandate), but also realize that much more is required of you to manage depression well in yourself and your family, specifically learning and applying key antidepressant concepts and skills.

Depression from a Family Systems Viewpoint

3

When we try to pick out anything by itself, we find it hitched to everything else in the universe.

John Muir

Joey had always been a good kid. He was friendly and quick to smile, reasonably polite to others, respectful of adults, honest in his interactions, conscientious about whatever he did whether it was schoolwork or household chores, and generally eager to please. He was also sensitive to criticism, reluctant to express hurt or angry feelings, and naive in how readily he believed others, even when they were exaggerating, or worse, telling lies. You'd think he'd have caught on and grown more skeptical or cynical over time, but Joey didn't. He was a nice kid.

When Joey was fourteen, though, he changed. The changes were not dramatic at first, just little things like spending more time alone in his room, listening to music with headphones on, and looking at magazines. He didn't spend anywhere near as much time with his friends playing or going places as he did being alone. He wasn't as quick to smile, and his answers to people's questions were growing ever more abbreviated. His grades at school were also starting to slip just a little, and when a couple of his teachers noticed that he seemed more distracted and less responsive in class, his response was simply to agree and say he'd try to do better. If there was anything weighing on his mind, he didn't say anything about it, despite having a variety of opportunities to do so.

After a while, the changes grew more obvious and dramatic. His grades deteriorated and his demeanor alternated between withdrawn and hostile. Attempts to probe him were met with a "shields up" impenetrability.

Joey's parents were called in for several parent–teacher conferences. Asked by the school counselor if anything was going on with Joey that they knew of, both claimed quite sincerely that they could think of nothing. Asked if he might be doing drugs, they were shocked at the thought and instantly dismissed the possibility because "he's just not that kind of kid—he's very naive, you know." Joey's dad lamely offered the perspective that perhaps it's just about being fourteen because "you know how traumatic a time puberty can be, with his raging hormones and all." Joey's mom, making a considerable reach, said, "Maybe it's the music he's listening to."

Joey was taken to the doctor. Findings were negative, but the doctor felt sure that Joey had a biochemical imbalance that a course of antidepressant medications could correct. Unwilling to jump to the same conclusion, Joey's parents reluctantly took him to a psychologist. There was nothing to report from the initial sessions beyond the fairly obvious fact that Joey was depressed and that he wasn't very communicative.

Everything came into sharp focus in the fourth session, though, when Joey asked as innocently as he could, "If a guy knew that one of his parents was having an affair and he knew that if he told it would wreck his parents' marriage and then there'd be a divorce and his whole life would be ruined, but his parents are arguing all the time anyways, do you think he should just act as if he doesn't know, even if it's all he ever thinks about . . . and it's driving him crazy? I mean, shouldn't they just work it out themselves?"

Joey's depression is, in large part, a reflection of what's going on in his family. He carries depression that is, in essence, a family burden. What if Joey had been pressured into taking antidepressants? How would that have even remotely addressed the legitimately burdensome issues he was wrestling with? How could anyone who attempted to figure out Joey's problems have possibly known there was anything else going on that might account for his depression when he was noncommunicative and his parents were unwilling or unable to reveal what was happening to them? It is tempting to simplify matters at such times and reach a purely biological conclusion that it must be all about brain chemistry.

Let's go a step further. What if—after many weeks of following the prescribed drug regimen—he didn't improve, what would his doctor and parents conclude then? ("The medication isn't working for Joey so let's try a different one because each person's chemistry is different and hopefully he'll respond better to another drug.")

As you can tell, the "biochemical imbalance" theory of depression, just like the genetic transmission theory, is of very limited value in cases such as Joey's. And, to be sure, cases like Joey's represent the preponderance of cases of depression—good people who are sinking because they face circumstances—such as failing marriages, family crises, deteriorating health, or job-related difficulties—they are ill-equipped to effectively manage. They become overwhelmed, despairing, and depressed in their efforts to just stay afloat on the stormy seas of life.

As I described in the first chapter, it is clear that depression is a biopsychosocial disorder: Biology, psychology, and sociology *all* contribute in some way to the disorder of depression. Having encouraged you to think of depression as a multidimensional disorder, I must also state my perspective explicitly: By carefully considering the family's contributions to causing, maintaining, and resolving depression, I, too, am focusing primarily on only one dimension of a multidimensional disorder. That is *not* to say that the family environment or family dynamics are more (or less) important than neurochemistry, or are more (or less) important than cultural influences or individual history and psychology. I believe such evaluations about the hierarchy of influences can only be made in the context of specific cases. I want people to be aware of the family as a significant ingredient in the depression formula, and to take family issues into account whenever trying to figure out how to help.

COMING BACK TO THE FAMILY TO OVERCOME DEPRESSION

Surprisingly, throughout its entire history psychotherapy has advocated philosophies of separatism and reductionism. Western medical science was founded and gradually developed over the centuries on the separation of mind and body.

Similarly, the earliest psychotherapies separated brain from mind, conscious from unconscious, hypothetical parts of the mind from each other, mind and brain from behavior and emotions, and on and on. Remarkably, throughout the first six decades of therapy's first hundred years, practitioners successfully separated individuals from their families and culture. *Families did not feature in the treatment process at all!*

In the absence of holding direct discussions with a patient's family members, the early field of therapy successfully separated individuals from the larger network of which they were a part, and thereby defined all problems as entirely intrapersonal (intrapsychic), i.e., the product of one's own personality defects, unconscious conflicts, and other such "the pathology is within the person" explanations.

In the latter half of psychotherapy's first century, some bright and observant individuals noticed that their patients usually had families, and pushed the psychotherapy field to expand its focus to include families. Thus, the field of family therapy emerged, and once it did, therapy has never been the same. Psychotherapists developed theories about, and ultimately, obtained confirming evidence for, their theories when their expanded field of vision included interpersonal (social) variables in understanding and treating people's problems, such as cultures, communities, families, coworkers, and friends. The *systemic viewpoint* emerged as a more realistic one in its recognition that many forces, both *within* and *between* people, shaped the life experience of a person.

The view of the family as a system of interrelated parts, once articulated by the pioneering family therapists such as Jay Haley, Salvador Minuchin, Virginia Satir, Carl Whitaker, and Murray Bowen, became one of the few "truths" of the therapy field. When that larger perspective spread into other related fields, like medicine, it no longer seemed as reasonable to focus on only one aspect of a problem or illness without taking into account other relevant variables. Just providing treatment of a disease without treating the whole person is no longer considered viable in any general medical practice.

As a result of this profound shift in perspectives, therapy became more socially relevant, multidimensional, and ambitious. It also became more self-conscious of its role as an instrument of social consciousness and social welfare. Family therapists no longer wanted or tried to make therapy a secret process (as it had historically been) that would take place in the absence of an expanded accountability to families and society. Family therapists came to include as many influential others in the treatment process as might be appropriate or feasible in a given case, incorporating their expanding awareness for the complexities of multi-component systems. They learned along the way that while individualistic or one-dimensional therapies may be intellectually and pragmatically easier, they too often ran the risk of oversimplifying the problem to the point of actually preventing its successful resolution. Individual therapy can and does work very well most of the time, but there are many times when a family therapy approach would be more valuable.

It bears repeating that depression takes place in larger social, political, economic, and family contexts. Each of these deserves careful consideration, of course. But in focusing on the family component, it becomes clear that it is the foundation on which individual perspectives are built. The family is the proving ground for trial-and-error attempts to learn, grow, communicate, relate, plan, and *live.*

What you learned and what you didn't learn has made you what you are. What your genes and biochemistry predisposed you to learn and experience and to absorb from those experiences, and how your family pushed you or didn't push you to your limits in a million different ways dictates your range of possibilities.

FAMILY SYSTEMS

When I introduced the term *systemic,* I offered the general definition of a system as multiple, interrelated components comprising a whole; thus from a systems viewpoint, each part of the system directly and/or indirectly affects every other part of the system. One of the chief implications of the realization that no one is fully separate from the larger system of which he or she is a part is that an individual's symptoms can be seen as a reflection of something going or having gone wrong in his or her larger network. Isolating the part (individual) that seems most obviously to be the problem and treating it as if it is the entire problem may make for a convenient scapegoat, but may divert attention away from other relevant variables contributing to the problem.

To help us better understand the concept of systems, an easy and common illustration is a biological ecosystem. Consider the fragile relationships between plants, animals, and their native habitats. Farmers concerned about losing their crops to insects begin to spray chemical insecticide on their fields to destroy the invaders. Rain eventually washes the now insecticide-laced soil into streams, lakes, and rivers. Fish in the water absorb significant levels of the toxic chemical and either die or simply become toxic food to the larger predatory fish or birds that consume them. The birds absorb the toxins and can no longer reproduce at all, or lay eggs that are not viable to develop because their shells are too soft. Bird populations dwindle, and the number of small rodents, insects, and other creatures that were controlled by the bird population now proliferate. Trees and plants that, in order to reproduce, had their seeds spread by birds through their droppings, diminish. As the foliage diminishes more land erodes in the rain, clogging streams and rivers, killing even more marine life. And on and on . . .

As you can see, each component of the ecosystem affects every other component to one degree or another. Similarly, each component of a social system affects the others, as do the interrelated components of any system: political, educational, family, military, research, business, *whatever.*

Let's make it more personal. Obviously, I don't know the specifics of your particular life. I don't know *if* you work, or what kind of work you do if you do. I don't know your age, if you're single or attached, richer or poorer, socially well-connected or alone and lonely. From a systemic perspective, what are the various components of *your* life? These include the quality and quantity of your past and present interactions with your parents; the past and present influences on you by your siblings (if any) and vice versa; the range and quality of your formal schooling and informal educational experiences, past and present; the past and present influence of relatives, friends, mentors, critics, and all those who contribute to who you are in some way; the type of environment (rural, urban, suburban) you live in now and the one you grew up in; the size and makeup of your community; the values your family and community encouraged and still encourage you to adopt; your religious upbringing (if any) and current practice of faith and the philosophy and approaches to life it may have instilled in you; the political mood of the times you grew up in and the current political mood; the social consciousness of the times you grew up in and the current social consciousness you share with others; the ideas and lifestyles you were and are exposed to through other people and the media; the experiences you actively sought and continue to seek out or avoid and all those that "just happened"; and many, many other such formative influences.

You are more than any of these individual components, of course. You are a multifaceted, complex human being that can act on or react to any thoughts, feelings, or situations that you choose to. The key point, of course, is that with so many different components comprising the system that is you, to focus on any one part alone, out of relationship to the other parts, is to miss the bigger picture.

Whether you realize it or not, and whether you care to acknowledge it or not, you are also part of a larger system, namely your family. Alive or dead, in touch or out of touch, your family system is as inevitably a part of you as you are inevitably a part of it. Understanding its role as one individual component of a larger system provides another window through which to see and better understand depression. The interactional sequences between a family system's components can generate many different consequences. Depression just happens to be one of them.

Approaching the treatment of depression from a family systems perspective involves a number of underlying assumptions. To begin with, a family system is defined as *two or more related people.* As you can no doubt appreciate, these people don't have to be in daily or even regular contact in order to affect each other's lives. Sometimes the people who most influence our daily lives are people we no longer see and haven't seen for decades. In that respect, it is fair to say that *the whole of the family is greater than the sum of its parts.* Family relationships involve complex, shared connections that trigger responses in each other well beyond just simple isolated causes and effects. These include things like family roles, rules, expectations, significant memories, and all such things that we carry within us as representative of our family experiences.

I have made the point previously that depression has many causes and that searching for *the* cause is typically a futile endeavor. Consider Joey from this chapter's opening vignette. Was his depression caused by his secret knowledge of a parent's affair? We can speculate about many other causal or contributing factors. Perhaps if he had a more direct style of confronting the offending parent he wouldn't be depressed. Or maybe if he had a stronger ability to set the issue aside as none of his business he wouldn't be depressed. Or if he had a better support network and an ability to better verbalize his feelings he wouldn't be depressed. But it's not quite so simple as his parent having an affair causing his depression. The relevant point regarding a systemic approach is that a family system generally features a *circular causality* rather than a linear one. Simply put, behavior is typically both the cause *and* the effect: "I did this because you did that, but you did that because I had done this, but the reason I did that was because of what you did before when you . . ."

Similarly, in a family systems perspective, there is generally no "right" or "wrong" way to feel or behave in an absolute sense. Unethical or immoral considerations aside, I'm referring to the individual choices people have a right to make, like whether to pursue a college education, whom to marry, or whether to seek a job promotion. Instead, the focus is much more on behaviors that do or do not yield desirable results. One of the things I especially appreciate about this perspective is that it depathologizes people. Instead of labeling people or their behaviors with terms denoting illness, an individual's behavior is considered in terms of whether it helps or hurts the larger system of which it is a part. Does the behavior hit or miss the target?

To isolate the individual and treat the problem as if it's only his or hers alone denies completely the role of other contributing factors and effectively isolates the symptomatic person as the "sicko" in the family. *Behavior in general, and symptomatic behavior in particular, is influenced and perhaps even maintained by the larger system in which it occurs.*

One of the most fundamental of all concepts associated with a systemic approach is the observation that *all behavior has message value.* Whatever you say or do, and likewise, what you don't say or do, communicates information to others. Simply put, *one cannot not communicate.* What often surprises people during the family therapy process is how clearly others heard them without their ever saying a word. So, for an example, what does it say to others when you don't make time to be with those you profess to love? Or when you don't do something you said you'd do? Sometimes the biggest problems a family faces revolve around their inability to communicate well, such as when a parent offers the mixed message of saying "I care about you" while acting utterly apathetic to the child's needs or concerns.

A family system is dynamic and ever-changing. Each family faces lots of challenges and must successfully accomplish many developmental tasks in order to be a healthy place for its members. Healthy families accept the inevitability of change (children get older, interests change, friendships dwindle and new ones evolve, family members die, people marry, and so forth) and adapt more readily when changes occur by regularly revising their patterns for acting and reacting. Less resourceful families may get stuck, unable to flow smoothly with change, and become symptomatic as a result.

Depression often reflects the individual's and family's unsuccessful attempts to cope with changes and demands. One-dimensional solutions aren't often effective in changing multidimensional problems.

With this in mind, it is vital to take more into account than just your mood or outlook on life, or those of whoever you care about and are trying to help. Telling a depressed person to cheer up, look at the bright side, and all the other trite (and often even foolish) things we tell people, may be well-intended, but they hold little potential to help. Depression is more complicated than that. That's also why blaming someone for his or her depression ("You're just wallowing in self-pity," or worse, "You must enjoy your depression") is an insensitive act. The depressed person is undoubtedly dealing with many different factors, both internal (thoughts, physiology, feelings) and external (other people, job and family stressors).

Furthermore, when someone has been slotted into a position within the family that somehow is hurtful or restrictive, and he or she feels powerless to change things, depression can often be the result. In the next section, we'll consider how a family might contribute to depression in its members.

FAMILY TRIGGERS: FOR BETTER OR WORSE

There can be a universe of empty space in between people's intentions and the outcomes they actually generate. Did you intend to end up where you are right now? Or did you get there by way of some things happening that you didn't expect, weren't prepared for, or couldn't handle? Whoever it was that first said "Life is what happens to you when you have other plans" knew what he was talking about.

Was it your parents' intentions that your life turn out as it has? What did they want for you? And what did they want *from* you? As we've seen, two of the core tenets of systems thinking are the maxims "one cannot not communicate," and the closely related "all behavior has message value."

Consider these maxims in relation to your parents' intentions in raising you.

As a child, you were exposed to the behavior and communications of your parents and other significant influences. You could not help but be influenced by their actions and reactions as they interacted with you, doling out rewards (smiles, approval, support, contact) and punishments (anger, rejection, confrontation, withdrawal) as you did whatever you did.

Your parents had power. Power, in the psychological sense, means the capacity to influence. Your parents had considerable power to influence you by providing you first with experience and then feedback about that experience. They chose, intentionally or otherwise, to encourage or discourage your spontaneous behaviors, interests, reactions, style of thought, emotional responses, and all the other parts of you these processes influence.

It is generally harder for people to understand that although the influence was more obvious in the direction of parent to child, you influenced your parents' reactions as well. From the moment you were born you cried and smiled a lot (or didn't), engaged with others a lot (or didn't), slept easily (or didn't), traveled easily (or didn't), and so on. You provoked, quite unintentionally of course, countless reactions in your parents. Was it a good fit between you? What happens when an impatient mother has a finicky eater, or an emotionally unexpressive father has a child hungry for eye contact, a smile, a hug and a kiss? Babies, children, teenagers, young adults, *people* trigger experiences in other people. In an interaction between people, each response is caused by, and becomes the cause of, other responses.

There are people in your life who can bring out the best in you. When you're with them, they make you feel lighter, happier, funnier, more energetic, smarter, more enjoyable, better. Likewise, there are people who bring out less than the best in you. They make things heavy and burdensome, lead you to feel negative and full of complaints, bring up feelings of insecurity or inadequacy, and worse.

When I say people can make you feel better or worse, I don't mean it in quite the way you might think. It's true, no one can make you feel *anything* if you're not amenable. But to be sure, when you have an emotional connection to another person you are vulnerable to their influences. You were, and most likely still are, vulnerable to your family's influences, whether you see them a little, a lot, or not at all. And, in turn, each member of your family system is vulnerable to *your* influence, whether you have realized it or not. Again, it says just as much when you don't call or visit as when you do.

The key point, of course, is that it is an illusion to view yourself as a victim of others. When you were a child, you were vulnerable and *could* be victimized to a considerable extent through violence, neglect, sexual and emotional abuse, and the like. As an adult, you can be victimized by others' insensitivity, manipulations, and abuse of power. But to be a victim means doing nothing to actively change the circumstances on your own behalf. It implies you are powerless to change either the circumstances if possible, or to change your reactions to the circumstances if they are truly unchangeable.

In doing family therapy, I routinely work with people who feel helpless to do anything about their lives. So often the triggers for their depressions are their too narrow views of how their family "should" be, how their spouses "should" treat them, how their kids "should" behave. Instead of learning how things work, striving to see how others see things and make decisions, and how the family functions as a system of interdependent parts, people too often get wrapped up in how they feel or what they want. Thus they miss the opportunities to "do something different" that will actually make a difference. Reacting to yourself and ignoring what's out there is a reliable path to making costly mistakes. These hold lots of potential for depression.

It seems strange, in a way, to have to write a book describing the influence of one's family on depression. While it is currently fashionable to blame one's parents for all sorts of problems one might develop, a simplistic "blame the obvious source" strategy does little to differentiate the *actual* influence of parents from their *imagined* influence. Such blame does little to empower people to understand their vulnerabilities and learn to transcend them. On the contrary, once one begins to fan the flames of anger and blame, the fire can quickly spread out of control and consume all in its path. Labeling one's parents or family as "toxic" and teaching full withdrawal from them as the desirable solution can unwittingly perpetuate the very problem it purports to help: It suggests helplessness. It would be better to strive to develop ways to deal with each other *within* the boundaries that define family.

When people say things like "I'm depressed because my husband does this to me, or doesn't do that to me," I want them to know they're not just passive receptacles for whatever life happens to dump in. They can influence what happens next. You are not just triggered; you are also a trigger of your own experiences, those that enhance you and those that diminish you.

IS FAMILY STRUCTURE A "CAUSE" OF DEPRESSION?

We tend to categorize families according to their structure, such as whether they are the traditional *nuclear* type (biological parents and children), *blended* or step-families ("yours" and "mine" from previous marriages or relationships blending to make "ours"), *single parent* families (a separated or divorced mother or father living alone with primary custody), and *extended* families (comprised of combined generations—grandparents, for example—or combined family units, such as aunts, uncles, cousins, living together). Each structure has its assets and liabilities under different circumstances (consider Joey's nuclear family dilemma in this chapter's opening vignette). Each type of family structure progresses through developmental stages and each faces its share of challenges. It has become clear from research that *any* family structure holds the potential to be helpful or hurtful to its members. In other words, it is less the *type* of family structure and more the *quality* of the atmosphere and interactions, the level of family skills in communicating and problem-solving, that dictates what the family system and its members experience in their relationships to one another.

While the content of each family structure may vary—meaning the different names, faces, roles, and positions people occupy in the family hierarchy—the system only functions as well as it is able to meet the demands it faces. In this respect, I am actually less interested in *what* specific problems families face, and much more interested in *how* families go about trying to resolve their problems.

Someone once wryly observed that "life is one damn thing after another."

He or she may have been having a bad day, but it's true that problems are ever-present. There is nearly always something troublesome going on that needs to be handled in a timely and effective manner. But what if individuals and families don't do "timely" and "effective" very well? A pattern or symptom may evolve that is quite unintended (intentions versus outcomes), such as aggression, withdrawal, or even depression.

What is *your* family structure? Is it your family of origin, or the one you've created, or both that you're considering? What specific and unique challenges does it pose for your family as an integrated unit, and for each of the members as individuals? How do you know when things are going well or badly for your family as a unit—is it merely the absence of conflict or tension, or is it the presence of identifiable positive things? Your carefully considered answers to these questions and the many others I pose throughout the book will help you begin to identify the ways you and your family can play a significant role in fostering—or preventing—depression in yourself and other members of your family.

I mentioned family atmosphere, the quantity and quality of family communication, and family problem-solving skills as more predictive of how people feel than whether their family structure is nuclear or blended. The implication is that while a family structure may not be readily changeable, the patterns of interaction within the family usually are. Consequently, the family that unwittingly predisposes any member(s) to depression through its unintentional mishandling of key aspects of its own development is known in some professional circles as *depressogenic,* or depression-causing. But like genetics or biochemical influences, a depressogenic family is only a partial explanation for depression's onset. A family system may predispose one to depression, but it is also true that anyone has the potential to self-create an environment that minimizes the probability of depression as a response.

SHEDDING BLAME AND TAKING RESPONSIBILITY

It is tempting to try and identify specific causes that can account for specific effects. And often it is possible to do so because many things *are* sequenced in a linear fashion where "this" causes "that." (Flip a switch and the light will go on.) But when dealing with something like depression, family problems, social problems, and other similarly multidimensional problems, it can actually be counterproductive. People attempt to ascribe blame to something (like a biochemical imbalance) or someone ("My parents did this to me") and they are more likely to be wrong than right. It is a far more difficult and sophisticated skill to be able to say, "I don't know the cause of my depression" than it is to just make something up and then believe it.

Fortunately, however, ascribing the blame is unnecessary in order to recover. As we've seen, from a systems perspective it doesn't much matter who did what to whom or what triggered what. By recognizing that each component directly or indirectly affects every other component, we can create deliberate and well-reasoned changes in a system. In other words, if you change what you do, those around you will likely change what they do as a result. Their new responses guide your new responses and your new responses influence theirs, and so on.

I will provide many examples as we go on, of course, but a quick and simple illustration of the point may help. One couple I worked with that I'll call John and Mary was forever angry at Mary's sister, Alice, because she invariably showed up late for dinner whenever she was invited. Her lateness "made" John and Mary feel hurt and resentful; they felt disrespected and devalued. Despite their direct and gentle expressions of irritation, Alice didn't listen or change her tardy behavior. I asked what they did when Alice was late, and they said they angrily waited for her to arrive to begin eating. They'd complain a little, but the dinner event continued to center on Alice's arrival. This was an easy one. I told them to go ahead and eat on time, and clean up and put the leftovers away and carry on with their dinner as if Alice weren't coming. John and Mary looked shocked that I could suggest something so rude, but agreed nonetheless to try my recommendation. The next time Alice showed up late, fully expecting that her arrival signaled the start of the meal, she was flabbergasted to find that everyone had already eaten. She was told to "help yourself to the leftovers in the fridge." Interestingly, though she started to protest, she caught herself and said nothing. The same exact thing happened again the following week. Again, shocked silence from Alice. A very interesting thing happened the following week, though.

Alice showed up on time. John and Mary made a point of acknowledging her timely arrival, expressing their happiness to be able to enjoy her company over a leisurely dinner for a change.

Alice hasn't been late since.

Did Alice need to be blamed as the bad sister in order to improve things? No, she didn't. Did John and Mary need to stew in their anger, feeling victimized by Alice's insensitivity? No, they didn't. They were willing to do something different, and their system of interaction changed for the better as a result.

The point surfaces repeatedly throughout this chapter that you are influenced by, *and you influence,* others. So often in the course of the therapies I conduct I am struck by the pervasive sense of helplessness in the people I see. They are absolutely convinced they are being wronged by their wives, husbands, kids, parents, bosses, and the universe itself. Helplessness is a core component of depression. Helplessness defines one as a victim, unable to change one's circumstances to any significant degree.

But when you understand that you have the capacity to influence—the definition of power—you can be far more willing to test out the range and quality of your power to improve things. You can be more willing to run little experiments and find out what happens if you try "this" instead of just doing "that" again. If John and Mary hadn't been willing to experiment with their dinner situation with Alice, they could easily have just gotten angrier, and then withdrawn, and stopped inviting Alice altogether. They might well have choked an otherwise decent relationship to death. They took the *responsibility* to try something different. They took the *initiative* to develop a new plan and endured the discomfort of trying it out. They took the *risk,* and won the gamble. Risks are inevitable in life—the idea is to take *intelligent* ones on your own behalf and on the behalf of those you love and care about.

Just as placing blame on others typically does little to overcome depression, so does regularly placing blame on yourself. It is important to recognize in each specific situation where the responsibility lies for taking positive, problem-solving action. Consider the differences between blame and responsibility. Blame merely says who is at fault, but offers nothing constructive by way of response. Responsibility is positive in its recognition that you have the power to act. In one respect, depression itself reflects an abuse of that power when it stems from the self-deception that "there's nothing I can do." I am encouraging you to take responsibility for yourself. You *are* in a position of influence in your relationships with others. To deny it or avoid using that influence constructively by staying stuck in "blame mode" is to abuse your power.

MORE THAN ATTITUDE, WHAT ABOUT FAMILY SKILLS?

Families are inevitable. Our current political climate is one professing to be pro-family, and there is a parallel societal call to be more family-oriented. I suppose that notion for most people simply means more time spent together as a family. If it is a family blessed with good communication skills, high mutual regard, sensitivity, support, good problem-solving opportunities as a group, and an atmosphere of affection and caring, then the emphasis on family values might be a good thing. But being pro-family in words only and not in deeds just creates more time for people who happen to be related to each other to get tangled up in messes beyond their ability to effectively manage. "Can't we all just get along?" is a nice but utterly futile sentiment if not accompanied by the specific skills necessary to get and keep a system running well.

Families are not only inevitable, they are *vital* to every individual's development. We as a society may treat families as if they are expendable while saying otherwise (as we will see in the next chapter), but they are not now nor will they ever be expendable. Families will survive, but I want them to *thrive*. This book is about strengthening the family system in the specific ways *known* to reduce depression in its members.

In promoting a systemic viewpoint, I know I run the risk of making depression seem even more complicated and overwhelming. It's a risk because when depressed people or those prone to depression get overwhelmed, they may give up. Please don't do that! The other side of the coin is that a deeper, broader, and more realistic understanding of depression substantially increases the likelihood of successful recovery. The more you know about all the components of the system called "your depression," the more you can skillfully aim your willingness to do something different in a direction that will yield positive and lasting results.

A SUMMARY OF KEY POINTS

- You are a system in your own right, composed of multiple, interrelated parts (biological and psychological). Likewise, you are also part of a larger social system that includes your family, community, and culture.
- Depression occurs in a social context, including the family. You cannot think of depression as only a biological illness and realistically hope to overcome it on that basis alone.
- Blaming your parents as the cause of your depression is too simplistic to be entirely true. It does little to distinguish real influences from imagined ones, and suggests you have no choice in how you think, relate, and feel. You do.
- Early psychotherapies treated all problems as only individual ones. Current psychotherapies recognize the systemic and multidimensional nature of people's problems and employ methods like family therapy to go beyond the individual.
- A family system is defined as two or more related people. Family relationships involve complex shared connections that trigger responses in each other well beyond just simple isolated causes and effects. Thus, the whole of the family is greater than the sum of its parts.
- Family interactions are characterized as having *circular causality,* suggesting mutual influence on events such that A causes B, but B also causes A. From this standpoint, it becomes both undesirable and unnecessary to strive to find blame when someone is hurting. "You made me do it" or "You made me feel this way" are not useful viewpoints when you're trying to overcome depression.
- All behavior has message value. Everything you say (or don't say) and everything you do (or don't do) speaks volumes to others about you and what matters to you. Often people's problems come about from absorbing unintended messages from oblivious others.
- Depression often reflects the individual's and family's unsuccessful attempts to cope with the demands that he, she, or they face.

- How family members interact with each other matters much more in terms of how people feel than the type of family structure. Thus, family systems approaches to treatment of depression focus much more on teaching specific skills for improving relationships.
- You are influenced by others, and you influence others. You have more power than you may realize to change situations and people's responses. It is vital you learn how to use that power well.

Is Our Culture Hurting Our Families? 4

The means by which we live have outdistanced the ends for which we live. Our scientific power has outrun our spiritual power. We have guided missiles and misguided men.

Martin Luther King, Jr.

When Jennifer entered her final trimester, she and Kent began the Lamaze natural childbirth classes. Most of the other couples in their neighborhood who already had children declared emphatically that "it's the only way to do the birthing process." Jennifer wondered why everybody seemed to take drugs all the time except when they really needed them, like when giving birth, but she and Kent were persuaded by their circle of friends that the birth of their child would somehow be less than optimal if it wasn't done in the Lamaze fashion.

When Brandon was born, Jennifer and Kent had his room decorated by a professional, even though it was small and they really didn't have the money. The decorator was instructed to make the room "a designer showcase" that would make all the neighbors go green with envy. Brandon doesn't remember it, of course, but the room was instantly filled with every noise-making, light-flashing, cuddly feeling state-of-the-art piece of childhood paraphernalia that anyone could imagine.

When Brandon was four months old, Jennifer returned to her full-time job in retail sales. She and Kent had found a suitable day care center, one that was well prepared to accommodate the early morning drop-offs and late afternoon pickups that were often necessitated by Kent's and Jennifer's often unpredictable work schedules. Kent's position as a products buyer for his company often took him out of town for days at a time, but both he and Jennifer hoped that eventually he'd be home more with his family. Kent was sure that climbing the career ladder was much more important than changing diapers.

When Brandon was one year old, one of Jennifer's friends asked her if she had begun the flash card intellectual stimulation program that would increase his chances of becoming academically gifted. When Jennifer professed ignorance on the subject, her friend told her that she should be showing Brandon flash cards every day of words, simple math equations, geographical maps of the world, and other such information. She said Brandon should already be walking and talking, like her own daughter had at one year. Jennifer suddenly felt insecure about whether she was doing enough as a mom, and wondered whether she should get Brandon a tutor. Kent didn't think so, but he said they should reconsider in six months or a year if Brandon didn't catch up.

At two years, Brandon was doing some walking and talking, and Kent and Jennifer decided he should be enrolled in classes to learn a second language, develop greater eye–hand coordination, and develop artistic creativity. They exercised him, ran him through nightly flash cards, and found a myriad of other ways to accelerate his learning. When he gave correct answers or performed admirably, his parents beamed. When he didn't, their disapproval was obvious.

In first grade, Brandon was placed in a gifted student program. He was doing fourth-grade-level reading, third-grade-level math, and his parents' drive for him to succeed grew ever-more intense. He was pushed to do his homework every night, of course, but was given additional enrichment exercises to do by either parent, depending whose night it was to police him. His interactions with his parents could be characterized as regular "pop quizzes," opportunities to demonstrate his growing knowledge base to his eager-to-be-proud parents.

When he wasn't studying on his own or with one of his parents, Brandon was given over to the omnipresent baby-sitter, the television. He was allowed an hour for every hour he studied, and could watch whatever he wanted, within reasonable limits. This was viewed as his leisure time, and it provided welcome relief from parental responsibilities for Jennifer and Kent. Brandon paid an unusual amount of attention to the commercials, and regularly lobbied his parents for the newest toy or gadget that he felt he deserved for having done so well on the latest test. Jennifer and Kent thought it a reasonable means of exchange between them, and filled his room with all kinds of items that could only have been meant to buy Brandon's ambition.

With few changes over the years, this was the family routine. Push Brandon to excel and get top grades. Punish him in one way or another when his grades weren't the best, attacking him by attributing it to his laziness or his lack of focus. Push his teachers to push him in his classes, demanding they treat Brandon as a genius-in-the-making and therefore entitled to more attention than the other students. Get him into every program that seemed like it might give him an edge over others, whether he wanted to be in it or not. Describe other kids to him as his competitors, and theirs as the performances to beat.

From all outward appearances, Jennifer, Kent, and Brandon were leading the lives of the smug, upwardly mobile. When they talked to their friends and relatives, they spoke endlessly of the work they were doing and the steps they were taking to get faster promotions, more money, more recognition, more respect, more . . .

They moved to bigger houses, drove more expensive cars, took pricier vacations, ate at better restaurants, and bought fancier toys. And, they somehow understood perfectly well what Brandon meant when, as a teen, he said he couldn't go to school wearing such "uncool" shoes (even though just a couple of months ago they were very "cool"). They threw some money at him and told him to go get some new ones that would perhaps be more . . . enviable.

The pressure on Brandon to produce top grades never let up. Over the years of his growing up, there were countless fights about his study habits, his childish need to have fun at the expense of what really mattered, the do-or-die of getting into a university that would make his parents proud (and yield job offers), and on and on. Kent and Jennifer inevitably fell back on the almost unbeatable mantra, "We only want what's best for you. . . ." Brandon winced quite involuntarily whenever they said that to him.

At the end of Brandon's first semester at the university, everything seemed to come tumbling down on him. He was taking some hard classes and was not doing well in a couple of them. He tried to study harder, but would lose focus as he wondered what his parents would do if he didn't bring home A's. He actually went to the university counseling center and talked to a counselor there a couple of times about his debilitating anxieties about school and the growing sense of hopelessness that he could not succeed there no matter how hard he tried. The counselor asked him what would happen if he didn't get perfect grades, and the look of horror on his face shocked the counselor for its intensity. Brandon thought the counselor must be dense to not understand how his parents would disown him—or worse—if he didn't get on the Dean's List right away. Brandon described how he had been punished and was even hit a few times when he was growing up for bringing home anything less than top grades. He heard himself tell the counselor what he had never before quite put into words: "No matter what I do, it'll never be good enough. I'm not good enough, and I'll never be good enough." Brandon's despair flooded the room.

When Kent and Jennifer found out some days later that Brandon had dropped out of school, they were stunned. When they arrived at his college dormitory to pick him up and bring him home, Brandon couldn't even make eye contact with them. Despite having rehearsed a more sensitive approach, Kent's first words to Brandon were "How could you do this to us?"

Consider the state of the world today. If you look for the good things happening out there, you'll find them: people volunteering, pitching in to help others out in a crisis; ongoing peace talks; scientific and technological breakthroughs that can provide us with both conveniences as well as truly lifesaving innovations; people showing creativity, kindness, courage, and integrity. People *can* do some great things.

Likewise, if you look for the bad things happening out there, you'll find them: genocide and torture, prejudice and violence, babies born drug-addicted, and teens that literally kill for a thrill or just for some fancy running shoes; parents abandoning their children because they just weren't convenient anymore; political and religious leaders misleading; science and technology run amok while bypassing the moral question of whether we should be in favor of doing something simply because we can; and people retreating into the pseudo-safety of their own private worlds, detached from and apathetic to others.

The oldest and greatest struggle in the entire history of humanity is good versus evil. Optimists believe that good will triumph, and their vision of "world peace" and "all things being right in the world" is an inspiring, desperately needed one. Looking at the glass of life and seeing it half full is a comforting perception. But . . .

But the rate of depression is rising in all age groups. But teenagers are the fastest-growing age group of depression sufferers. But many children Brandon's age and younger are already suffering from depression and worse, and too many of them have already formed the impression that life stinks. Most kids just don't use that kind of language yet to say so. Instead they tend to either withdraw or act out.

In this chapter, we will consider the role our culture plays in shaping our shared experiences and perspectives. Specifically, we will consider the question posed in this chapter's title: Is our culture hurting our families? From a systemic point of view, the problems that we face both as a society and as an integral component of a world population are the larger-scale problems that filter down to the family and its individual members on a smaller—but no less serious—scale.

The fact that there are many great things about America doesn't entirely counterbalance the fact that there are many things that are hurting us emotionally as a society and are damaging to our families. Consider the ironies:

- We get stuck in traffic jams and complain about overpopulation, but in our crowded world people are dying of loneliness. So they meet anonymously over the Internet or take out classified ads in newspapers to market a product called themselves.
- We love the idea of the world as a "global village" and respect the notion that "it takes a village to raise a child," but when was the last time you socialized with your neighbors, let alone discussing important family and community issues?
- We love the idea of increased personal freedoms to do *what* we want *when* we want, but become enraged when someone else does something that hurts us while he was doing *what* he wanted *when* he wanted.
- We love being told to "nurture our inner child," yet we miss the unintentional harm such a perspective can impart to us when we are told it's our parents' fault for creating a dysfunctional family. How exactly does being told we are victims empower us? How and when does one stop being the "adult child of a 'fill-in the blank'"? Can we change when we are taught to think of ourselves in unchangeable terms?
- We love being told we can have it all, but we can miss the fine print in the deal that says "every choice necessarily precludes other choices, so choose wisely."
- We readily adopt mindless sayings like "All things happen for a reason" and "Where there's a will there's a way," and never see the dangers of believing we can know the reasons for all things or that we can accomplish anything if we're just properly motivated.

You cannot escape the influence of the larger culture in which you and your family live. Unless you first realize and then develop a realistic and effective set of strategies to manage this fact, you can too easily deceive yourself (and others) into thinking that depression is only about serotonin levels, or bad genes, or dysfunctional families.

CULTURAL SHIFTS: CATALYSTS FOR DEPRESSION

Epidemiology is the study of the prevalence of various diseases and disorders. Epidemiological surveys give us a reasonably accurate insight into just how relatively rare or common a particular disease or disorder is. It's how we learn things like how rapidly diseases spread and even where they are most likely to be found. It's a way to keep a finger on the pulse of the country, so to speak.

The epidemiology of depression is particularly illuminating, though troubling, because the research yields several important insights. First, as previously mentioned, the rate of depression is growing in all age groups. Second, the rate of depression in those born since 1945, the so-called baby boomers, has increased by a factor of nearly *ten* over their grandparents and by a factor of *three* over their parents. To see such a marked increase in so short a time is truly alarming. Third, as societies westernize, their rates of depression tend to go up. What these data suggest very strongly is that there is something about America's very culture that is depressogenic (i.e., depression-causing). What cultural depressogenic factors can *you* identify that might account for the rising rates of depression?

Gene pools and biochemistry are unlikely to change so radically in so short a time. In sharp contrast, however, American culture has gone through swift and dramatic changes almost overnight. Here, in the much heralded new millennium, I doubt it has escaped *anyone's* attention that the pace of our lives is faster, the number of demands on our time and energy (all the things you have to do just to keep up) is greater, the complexity of life decisions is deeper, the amount of information available to us is far greater than the amount of time we have to try and absorb it, and the rules keep changing about what's "supposed to" matter to us and how we're "supposed to" conduct our lives. It is, of course, possible to fill volumes describing these extraordinary cultural shifts, but I will focus on those that I consider the most influential on the escalating rates of depression.

Technology and the Now Orientation. As I stated in chapter 1, I believe technology in its many varied forms has been a blessing, a curse, and the primary culprit at a cultural level for the rising rates of depression in individuals and families. That may seem, at first glance, to be an extreme statement, but let's consider the message value of technologically driven behavior.

Technology is not a one-dimensional phenomenon, subject to a polarizing appraisal that suggests it is good or bad. Technology makes countless vital functions possible, ranging from an early diagnosis of cancer that saves an individual's life to a satellite's discovery of an evolving hurricane that saves an entire community's life. But, technology also makes terribly unnecessary and destructive things possible, like ever more destructive weapons of war and a new electronic forum on the Internet for pedophiles to spread their child pornography.

Technology has as its primary benefits the characteristics of speed and convenience. The postal service, now referred to by many as "snail mail," has given way to E-mail, an instant worldwide communication capability that was sheer fantasy only a few years ago when faxes seemed nothing short of miraculous. Microchips make our refrigerators and ovens "smarter." (No one likes a dumb oven.) Cellular phones make our rides home more profitable both in business and social terms. In countless ways, both small and large, technology runs us. The everyday applications of technological intelligence are impressive, and yet I believe we clearly have more technology than we have the wisdom to manage it.

The emphasis on speed and convenience inevitably warps our perspective and places us at risk for emotional disturbances like depression in ways people rarely consider. The desire for more convenience in life, and for more instant gratification of our needs, is not unreasonable, of course, if whatever we're trying to do *can* reasonably be accomplished easily or instantly (like sending E-mail). But what happens if we apply the standards of "it's gotta be fast" and "it's gotta be easy" to a context where such criteria are not only inappropriate, but are actually *damaging?* You can't get a good-quality academic education in the next three days. You can't meet someone, fall in love, marry, and raise a happy and healthy family this weekend. You can't climb the career ladder to the top this afternoon. You can't convince your child you are a responsible and loving parent by tomorrow evening. You can't convince your spouse you deserve another chance to be trusted over dinner tonight.

These may sound like unrealistic examples to you, yet I have heard countless variations of every single one of them over and over in my many years doing therapy. Many people have come to truly believe that they can have whatever they want or solve any problem instantly if they just push the right button. As a result, people want things *right now,* what I'm calling the *now orientation.* By wanting an instant gratification *regardless of whether the context even permits one,* people don't develop a key life skill known as *frustration tolerance,* or, more simply, patience. Low frustration tolerance means a minimal ability to accept and tolerate the amount of time it takes to do something, or to bring a goal to completion. Young children often show poor frustration tolerance in lots of ways, such as when they knock down the stack of blocks built only partway because they don't have the patience to build it up higher, or when they lose interest in the details of the story and want you to "just get to the end." In adults, low frustration tolerance shows up in essentially the same way, only in more adult situations: getting angry at the bank when the line moves too slowly; feeling rageful or victimized at the grocery store when someone in the ten-items-or-less line laid down twelve items; scrapping the work agenda for the day because the computer took too long to boot up; going to your child's recital and hating it because there were too many other kids besides yours to have to watch performing; and much more serious examples, like becoming violent in an argument or drinking too much to escape everyday frustrations or problems.

I believe the single greatest technological instrument shaping our collective consciousness as a culture is television. Television has reached nearly 100 percent saturation in American homes. Almost every home has at least one. Research indicates that the average American watches somewhere between four and seven hours of television per day. Four to seven hours *per day!* The majority of American households also have cable television and videocassette recorders; thus the actual amount of television viewing time may even be greater. (And, all the while, people complain they don't have enough time.)

Television can bring us vital information even as events occur. It can amuse and entertain us. But those are the mere surface aspects. Beneath the surface, where our attitudes and beliefs are formed (most often without our even realizing it), television is encouraging us to be chronically dissatisfied with ourselves and our lives. How can we be truly happy without washboard abs? Or another collection of disco hits from the seventies? Or a bigger, better, newer (fill-in-the-blank)? Television tells us twenty-four hours a day to want more than we have, creating in many a perpetual state of dissatisfaction and a propensity toward materialism. So, we work harder and longer hours in order to buy ever more stuff. Are we happier as a people for that effort? The statistics on depression (and other psychological disorders as well) make it clear we are not.

Television leads us to make comparisons. How's my weight compared to the buff model demonstrating the exercise equipment? How's my marriage compared to the cute couple in the "how to have a dazzling marriage" infomercial? How's my job satisfaction compared to the enthusiasm of the "wonderfully employed recent graduate of this state-of-the-art training program"? How's my life compared to those people in the soap operas and the movie of the week who seem to lead much more interesting, albeit often dysfunctional, lives? The problem is, far too many people actually come to believe that what they see on TV is real. They make comparisons on the basis of next-to-zero real information and inevitably come up short. The result is more dissatisfaction, perhaps even self-loathing.

Television continuously reinforces the idea of instant gratification, and as a direct consequence, fuels our low frustration tolerance. We are continually shown, one program at a time, that complex problems can be created and solved in thirty or sixty minutes, minus the commercial breaks, of course. Commercials show our problems being solved in thirty to sixty seconds with *no* breaks. More money is spent in this country on advertising than anything else—more than on defense, education, health care, *anything*. And the reason for all the money spent on advertising is simple—it works. It shapes our buying behavior very predictably. We usually didn't even know we wanted something until an ad told us we could have it *now.* Pharmaceutical companies used to advertise only to doctors in medical journals. No longer. Now they advertise their drugs in *Time, Newsweek,* and *People* directly to you, the potential consumer. Prozac became the most popular antidepressant in the *world* because advertising works—*not* because it's a miracle drug for curing depression.

Television fuels impulsivity. The message is clearly and unabashedly the proclamation that *what matters the most is right now, this moment.* Advertising relies on our absorbing the message that this product or service will instantly change our lives for the better, fueling the impulse to buy or do it. It encourages us to make the decision to buy impulsively by hurrying us with "the first one hundred people to call" or "if you call in the next ten minutes you will get this bonus gift." The undiluted message is "do it now."

It does not seem to be human nature, nor is it actively taught in schools, to think beyond the moment. The mental health profession in this sense has unintentionally contributed to the problem with its overwhelming emphasis on the value of people's "feelings in the mo-ment." Clients are taught to recognize and respond to their feelings and to live in the here and now. People have been encouraged to focus on their own personal gratification, and not on the longer-term value of delayed gratification or the social (community and family) benefits of considering the needs of others. Writers of some self-help books even try to lead you to believe you can have it all. Such philosophical orientations fuel impulsivity, a characteristic that is already too abundant in the world. The impulsivity of our society permits the use of mind-altering drugs with little regard for the possibility of future addiction or dependence. Impulsive sexuality helps spread potentially fatal sexually transmitted diseases. Impulsive spending creates burdensome debts both for our government and for individuals who have charged to the limit (or beyond) on their credit cards. Perhaps the most unsettling example is found in the now orientation that is being applied at a planetary level. We recognize that rain forests, for example, are a primary source of our planet's oxygen, and that they are virtually irreplaceable, and yet we continue to cut them down at the current rate of more than fifty acres a minute. (Gee, I wonder if *that* will be a problem one day.)

By focusing on now and not later, we can't teach impulse control and thereby reduce violence, drug abuse, and prevent children from having children. We can't increase people's interest in long-term investments like a good education or a healthy body when people feel that delayed gratification, or working toward a goal, is the equivalent of self-deprivation. The outlook for our planet, our country, our families, and ourselves is bleak if we don't start to emphasize from early childhood onward that we can insightfully choose courses of action that will eventually yield positive consequences. We can and should teach people to think systemically in terms of cause and effect and multidimensionality, and not just in terms of what seems good right now, for ourselves exclusively.

How many individuals and families become depressed through circumstances that could have been avoided with just a minimal amount of foresight? For me, it's one of the most difficult parts of doing therapy—empathizing with suffering that could have been prevented with even just a little bit of thinking ahead. But who in our popular culture encourages people to delay gratification or set aside their impulses rather than act on them?

Television unwittingly reinforces one of the most troublesome patterns related to depressive thinking, called *global thinking.* Global thinking refers to the tendency to get a general understanding of something but not grasp the relevant component details. Metaphorically, you can globally see the forest yet not see the individual trees. Television doesn't just encourage global thinking—it *demands* it. Television commentators (so-called talking heads) tells us what we just heard in the President's speech tonight, and what it "really" means. Newscasters air the stories that will boost ratings, not promote a true understanding. In dramas, we see actors play out intense and dramatic situations, but we see none of the real consequences. Real life isn't portrayed—there are only programs that say they're portraying real life as an excuse to show us more graphic violence, reveal more nudity, and amplify the sensationalism that increases viewership. Such programs teach the American public very, very little that is helpful, and show us *a lot* that is harmful. The global style of thinking that television encourages in viewers virtually prevents the critical thinking that the pundits tell us is our responsibility to exercise. They're right—we *should* be more critical, but critical thinking isn't likely to be learned by watching television. Viewers only learn to respond to global images and superficial ideas.

Global thinking shows up in real people's lives when they divorce and abandon a family because they "just want to be happy." It shows up when they brood over their fourth beer that they "just want to be successful and make lots of money." It appears wherever one has lofty goals with no clue as to how to reach them, or problems to solve with no idea as to how to solve them. It appears wherever critical, detailed, systemic thinking is absent.

I could say much more about television, technology, and the now orientation that is choking us with the consequences of poor choices we have made and continue to make as a culture. I'm sure there will be some readers who will (globally) conclude, "Yapko must be a political conservative. He's attacking the liberal media." You'd be wrong, however, if you concluded that. To me, it's not so much an absence of morality in the media (although that concerns me, too) as it is *the effect on our national psyche.* Our mental health problems have increased in direct proportion to our viewing habits. The more we have become passive, couch-potato receptacles for whatever junk gets beamed into our brains, the worse our ability has become to be innovative and timely in our responses to our problems at *any* level: as a planet, country, community, family, or individual. The now orientation that is embraced so readily by Americans who are dazzled by quick fixes and techno-gadgets gives rise to the global thinking pattern that makes mysticism and spirituality so appealing, if impotent, a means to solve problems. (Did you know that the "psychic hotline" was last year's top grossing infomercial, raking in hundreds of millions of dollars from people foolish enough to call up and ask life-determining questions like "Should I marry Bill?" This is *not* critical thinking. It's wasted money, usually by people who don't have much money to waste.)

I would never have predicted that any of the television networks would have bothered to respond to criticism about their raison d'etre, but much to my surprise, in August 1997 the ABC network took out a full-page ad on the back cover of *TV Guide* with the headline "TV is Good." They described television as an "innocuous pleasure" and a "harmless habit." They offered no intellectual perspectives about its merits. On the contrary, their appeal was *entirely* emotional: "TV binds us together. It makes us laugh. Makes us cry . . . Can any other medium match TV for its *immediacy,* its impact, its capacity to entertain? . . . Let us celebrate our *cerebral-free nonactivity"* (italics mine).

I'm sure ABC intended their proclamation to be amusing, but if it was meant to be funny, somehow the humor escaped me. It was much too close to the truth.

Many of the most troublesome patterns of thinking and behaving that can lead to depression are societally acquired. We *all* need to address them if we truly want to do something meaningful about it for ourselves and our families. Unless we learn to notice and respond to deeper meanings of cultural fads, fashions, and trends, we can become absorbed in them to our own detriment, with depression as a result.

Breakdown of the Family. The breakdown of the traditional nuclear family has routinely been blamed for nearly all of society's problems. This ignores the fact that many of society's problems *preceded* high divorce rates. Specific to depression, though, I believe the breakdown of the family *is* a significant variable in depression's rising rate, but probably not for the reason you might expect. Most people recognize the need for emotional stability and predictability in the earliest years of life. There has long been a presumed, if not well-documented, link between serious losses (like divorce or death) and later depression. Is depression *inevitable* in later life when children are pushed through their parents' divorce? No, depression is not inevitable—it's just more likely. People assume it is the emotional trauma of the divorce itself that echoes throughout the rest of the child's life, and that may well be the case. Custody fights, arbitrary and inconsistent visitation schedules, parental inaccessibility both physically and emotionally for all sorts of reasons (such as withdrawing because they are dealing with their own hurt and anger while also struggling to rebuild their own lives), and other undesirable changes forced on children are traumatic.

But I think it is the *helplessness* children feel that is the most debilitating aspect of divorce preceding later depression. Helplessness is a core component of most depressions. People typically just give up when they are depressed, succumbing to the paralyzing belief "Why bother? Nothing I do will make any difference anyway."

Picture this real-life scenario: Mom and Dad sit you, as a six-year-old, down and tell you (as sensitively as they can), "Honey, we want you to know we both love you very much. But Mommy and Daddy don't love each other anymore, and we can't live together. We love you and we always will, but Mommy and Daddy are going to live apart now. You're going to stay here in the house with Mommy and go to the same school and have all the same friends and everything will be just the same except Daddy is going to live in another place nearby and you'll get to see him all the time and you'll still be Daddy's little girl (boy) but he'll just be living someplace else. . . ."

Can you hear this child's world crashing? *All behavior has message value.* What are some of the messages? 1) When two people have a family they can break it up if they choose to; 2) When you care about something as much as your mom and dad, you can be devastated when it's taken from you because *there is nothing you can do about it;* 3) When a relationship is in trouble, you can end it; 4) People can hurt you terribly, even while they're telling you they love you; 5) You have no control over some of the biggest decisions in life that will directly affect you.

Divorce isn't always a "bad" thing, of course. Sometimes it's the best choice to make among several poor ones. But just as in my consideration of lowbrow television, it is not a *moral* judgment as much as it is a *mental health issue.* How do the decisions we make and the standards we set as a society affect the emotional well-being of our society's members?

I am also not suggesting that the traditional nuclear family is the best or right type of family to have. The so-called family values debate has missed the mark on this issue by a wide margin. Wishing or actively lobbying for the traditional nuclear family is *not* time well spent. Families have already changed irreversibly. As I stated in chapter 1, there are already many, many different family structures, and the irrefutable fact of their diversity is not the salient issue. It has become clear that *any* family structure has the potential to provide either a healthy or unhealthy environment for its members depending on the way it functions.

Consequently, it isn't the breakdown of the traditional nuclear family that is to blame for depression so much as it is the inability to recognize that the family, *whatever* form it happens to take, is crucial to our ability to survive and thrive. We need to get off the moral judgment question of "Is is *right?*" and instead ask, "Does it *work?*" Diversity of family structures and of subcultures within our society is an established fact.

Let's strive to bring out the best in us all—something that won't be achieved by moral condemnations or a nostalgic wish for things to be "just like they were." It's such a shame that when people aren't quite sure how to move forward they think they can find the answer by looking backward. It simply isn't a good strategy very often, and that's especially true when dealing with depression.

Cultural and Personal Ambiguity. Most people have heard of the well-known psychological test called the Rorschach inkblot test. The clinician shows the patient a series of cards containing inkblots and asks the patient to describe what he or she sees. Of course, the cards mean nothing—each is simply what is called an ambiguous stimulus. An ambiguous stimulus means there is no objective basis for assigning meaning to it. Thus the patient offers a subjective interpretation, or *projection* in psychological terms, as to what it means to him or her. Since the projections can't be judged right or wrong according to some objective criteria, the qualities of the patient's projections are simply analyzed for what they might reveal about his or her "issues" or personality structure.

Ambiguity is a risk factor for people prone to depression because of their tendency to make negative projections that serve to hurt them. Seeing the ambiguous stimulus of the future as a time when "only bad things will happen," or seeing the lack of a prompt return phone call as "He doesn't care about me" are simple examples of hurtful projections in response to the ambiguities about what the future holds or why someone didn't return a phone call.

Our culture is filled with countless ambiguities or uncertainties that make life ever more difficult for families. When it is unclear what the best or the right thing is to do in a given situation, people then project what seems to them to be the best choice. Depending on the quality of their strategies for making choices, meaning how they gather and weigh information and carry their choices out, people can easily end up someplace they really didn't want to go, and possibly become depressed as a result.

Consider the following examples of situations where there are no clear answers as to what is right or best to do, and how whatever choice one makes therefore has the potential to enhance or diminish one's quality of life:

- Should Mom work or stay at home? Should she provide financial relief by bringing in an income, or emotional support by being involved with and available for the kids? Either can seem critical, but can be in conflict with each other.
- Should Dad take the promotion and the much-needed associated pay increase that would ease some family financial pressures even if it means he has to travel and spend more time away from the family?
- Should we push our child for better grades? Or will that pressure stress him or her too much and lead him or her to think that grades are all that matter to us?
- Should we bring our elderly parents, who are too frail to care for themselves, to live with us and crowd ourselves? Or should we get them into a senior community that can provide less personal care but more diverse possibilities and cause less disruption to our lives? Are we selfish and irresponsible if we don't have them live here? Are we being foolish martyrs if we do?
- Should we adopt a child from another race and give a deserving child a chance of having a loving home, or will it harm the very child we want to help by raising him in a racially confusing environment?
- Should I be honest and tell our teenager that I'm leaving his mother because she had an affair, or should I cover it up and say I'm leaving for other reasons in order to protect his mom's reputation? Should I be honest and maybe hurt their relationship, or should I try and protect their very important relationship with a little less than truthful explanation?
- Should we raise our child in my religion, or yours? Why? Should we try and raise her in both religions? How?
- Should we encourage our child to take piano lessons, when she hates that idea, because it will teach an appreciation for music and develop a talent? Or, will we hurt our child emotionally by pushing her to do something she doesn't want to do just because *we* think it's important?
- Should I go through my child's drawers because he might be into drugs, or should I just trust my child and respect his privacy as an individual?
- Should I miss the chance to take a great vacation over the holidays with some close friends who worked out a great trip and want to

include me? Or should I spend Christmas with my parents as I do every year and honor the tradition we've established?

The above ten examples of ambiguity are only ten of *thousands* of examples of the complex and emotionally charged decisions each of us have to make day in and day out over the course of a lifetime. They are ambiguous stimuli, requiring us to project a response. Then we live with the consequences.

Our culture presents us with many different options, many more than used to exist. It didn't used to be a realistic choice for most women to have high-powered careers, nor did it used to be an option for most men to make life choices based on what they wanted instead of doing what they were "supposed to." It didn't used to be a realistic option to divorce when saddled with an unhappy or bad marriage. Family planning didn't used to be a reliable possibility. There are *lots* of choices now that we didn't used to have, and *how* we make them and what the results are increase or decrease the likelihood of depression.

Is having more choices *better?* The answer is yes, *if* people have a good insight into the relationships between ambiguity, choices, and consequences. Often there are no clear ways to tell whether a choice will be the right or best one. Some people react to such ambiguity by becoming terribly anxious. Some become paralyzed with indecision. Some flip a coin and make a decision but give no serious thought to possible consequences. Some defer to another's authority and thereby decide to let someone else decide. Some withdraw into self-doubt, despair, and *depression* because "life is too overwhelming." Some simply escape into the fantasy of finding someplace else to live where there won't be any hassles. That's when they find out the hard way that wherever they go, there they are.

Ambiguity is evident when no choice seems clearly correct or more likely to be effective. Trying to take the ambiguity out of the family structure issue by saying that the traditional nuclear family is best is understandable. Though understandable, it isn't much more than a conservative bias at odds with the diversity—and therefore ambiguity—that is a fact of American life. Our task is to learn to better recognize and accept ambiguity as inevitable, rather than jumping to some conclusion for the mere sake of having a conclusion, even if it is the wrong one.

Ambiguity may frustrate the need for clarity in our low-frustration tolerance society, but it is a force to understand and accept. Critical thinking in the face of ambiguity is much more powerful than blind faith or some wishful thinking that things will somehow just magically improve. *We have to learn to tolerate ambiguity, and at the levels of society and the family, get better anyway.*

Global Ecology. Our planet is in serious trouble. I'll spare you all the statistics about overpopulation, acid rain, ozone depletion, water pollution, air pollution, deforestation, toxic waste, chemical contamination, the daily extinction of animal and plant species, and all the associated impending tragedies. On much more personal levels, how much do the ingestion of chemicals in our food, the lack of physical exercise, the ready availability of junk food, the growth of our cities, the shrinkage of our rural environments, and other such ecologically related variables affect our health, including our mental health?

Does the sunrise or sunset influence your day in *any* way? Does a shopping center seem like a better place to spend a day off than a park? What relationship *do* you have to nature? Nature can be a powerful force in shaping consciousness and restoring a healthy balance with our deeper self. Spending time in nature can be one of the most powerful antidepressants there is. Take your family on a short day hike in some pretty place away from the crowds, and see what I mean.

It is simply not possible to hold a systemic perspective and ignore the fact that our culture and our families are dependent on the air we breathe, the water we drink, and the foods we eat. We are, ultimately, biological creatures that are only sustainable in a suitable and supportive ecosystem. This is not about political agendas, as the "ditto heads" who rail against "eco-nazis" and "environmental wackos" would foolishly suggest. It's not about economics and how many lumber mill workers might be out of jobs. It's about a warped world view that says we can impulsively extinguish life and reduce the world's diversity of life on a whim for mere pleasure or profit, with no regard for the eventual negative consequences for the rest of us. When the impulse to achieve personal gain is coupled with a sense of entitlement, other people simply become objects. Dehumanization is the first step toward violence or abuse.

I have a poster in my office by a well-known marine artist whose work I enjoy, Robert Lyn Nelson, that says "Extinction Is Forever." That observation applies to more than the whales in the picture. Global ecology can be a powerful way to help people develop a deeper realization that life is systemic. The choices we make *now* will continue to echo throughout our future on many interrelated levels.

The world is larger than someone's job and short-term financial well-being, and broader-based human consequences are more important than a company's profits. On a more personal level, your family's health is more important than your smoking another cigarette, no matter what excuse you make to justify it while you expose them to the toxic effects of your secondhand smoke. Your family's emotional well-being is more important than working longer hours for a new appliance. Preserving is far more critical than destroying.

* * *

There are times in each person's life that are pivot points: a powerful experience or a significant learning occurs that instantly and forever shapes one's perspectives. You have undoubtedly had many of these in your own life. Whether it was the moment you learned of the death of someone you loved or the early childhood moment during which you found out there wasn't really an Easter Bunny or a Santa Claus, in that moment your worldview made an irreversible change. In the same way, our families have made an irreversible shift. They've had to defend themselves against charges of being dysfunctional, they've had to suffer through the accusations that they are to blame for all the poor choices of family members, and they've had to struggle to find a new relevance in a rapidly changing world.

No wonder people lapse into nostalgic wishes for the good old days. The current cultural climate isn't very family-friendly, when prominent messages are constantly emphasizing individual satisfaction at the expense of family unity or social responsibility. The all-too-common lament is "What can my family do for me?" And if the answer isn't immediately gratifying, then it's "just not worth the effort." Family relationships are too often thought of as expendable in today's New Order. Children sue their parents for perceived injustices, real or imagined. Spouses sue their partners for money, custody, or whatever on their road to seeking greater personal fulfillment.

The cultural climate encourages us to want more, always more, and therefore to be dissatisfied with what we have. The price of these cultural injunctions is that we are more wary, more cynical, and yes, more depressed. Our world has changed permanently. There's no going back to the (illusory) idyllic family of the past. If the family is going to rise to the level of deliberately functioning as an effective antidepressant, instead of being unintentionally depressogenic, it is going to have to work smarter, not harder. Our world is not the same as it was, and now the task before our families is how to live in it without going slowly crazy or giving in to the extremes of cynicism, apathy, and depression.

This book is about the family and its vital role in both the nature and nurture of depression. It is also about the *prevention* of depression in families. The family is under siege from both external and internal forces that threaten to damage it, perhaps permanently. (According to one very prominent family therapist who had an influential series of programs on public television, fully 95 percent of American families can *already* be defined as dysfunctional. I don't believe that, but it does indicate that there are those in positions of influence who have all but concluded that the family is already in its death throes.) The family is simply too important, and too inevitable, to be relegated to a secondary position. But to keep it first and foremost, and to affirm its potential for positive influence, it must be fortified with relevant self-management skills *now* if it is to eventually respond meaningfully to those forces that threaten it. It must adapt and continue adapting as systemic, multidimensional changes keep almost everything in life in perpetual flux.

In the next section of the book, we'll consider more specifically the role of depression in the family. We'll focus first on growing up in a depressed home, then on how depression manifests itself in the quality of one's marriage, how children can depress parents, and finally how depression can unintentionally be handed down to one's children.

A SUMMARY OF KEY POINTS

- Epidemiology is the study of prevalence of a disorder. Knowing who is affected by a problem often gives insights into contributing factors.

Depression is more prevalent in all age groups than it was a generation ago, and much more prevalent than two generations ago. This suggests more contributions as a result of social and technological changes than biological shifts.

- Technology emphasizes immediacy. As people become more reliant on technology, their expectations for immediate results increase, unfortunately resulting in lower frustration tolerance. Some things just can't be done right away, but depression can surface when immediate gratification isn't obtained.
- Television is a powerful influence on our perceptions, values, and style of thinking. One of its most unfortunate characteristics that relates to depression is its fueling of constant dissatisfaction coupled with a sense of entitlement to want and have more. Another is its emphasis on impulsivity by pushing the viewer to "do it now."
- Impulsive decisions hold great potential for later misery and regret. Learning to develop impulse control and how to make important decisions responsibly and with a realistic understanding of the consequences is a vital skill that can prevent many episodes of depression.
- The breakdown of the family is another variable contributing to the growing rates of depression. The family is necessary to the physical and emotional well-being of its members, and when it is broken or damaged the negative consequences on many levels, including depression, can be profound. The structure of the family (such as nuclear family or stepfamily) is less important than its ability to provide support and love to its members.
- Life events don't usually have clear causes and life choices don't usually have one obviously correct path to follow. Life is often ambiguous, and the more choices you are faced with, the more confused and despairing you can get when you are unclear as to what to do. Ambiguity can contribute to depression when you choose negative or harmful ways to interpret or react to life experiences. Learning to deal with ambiguity is critical to overcoming depression.
- Ultimately, human beings are biological creatures who have bodily rhythms and processes just like all other living things. The costs of moving so far away from our own very nature by eating artificial foods and living in artificial environments are difficult to assess, but

the tendency to view nature as something to be conquered for personal gain rather than something to be respected and preserved is clearly at odds with human nature. Families are a basic unit of human experience, too, and its fragmentation is taking its toll on our national mental health.

- The world has clearly changed in many ways, and our mental health rests on our ability to adjust to those changes in a timely and skillful way.

PART II

Depression in Families

Learning Depression from Your Family 5

Children have never been very good at listening to their elders, but they have never failed to imitate them.

James Baldwin

Sandy had assumed all along that she would get pregnant when she was good and ready. Her first priority when she married Jack at age twenty-six was to get her career as an electrical engineer established. She mapped out her life plan with Jack this way: get her career on solid footing, develop some financial security, and spend a few years married without *children to be absolutely confident that before they add the additional responsibilities of children they are good together.*

By age thirty-four, Sandy's life plans seemed to be working out quite nicely. Her career was going well—she was highly regarded both for her ingenuity and innate drive to do her best. Sometimes she was told to "lighten up," "quit taking things so personally," and "stop being so controlling" by her coworkers, but overall she was well-respected. Financially, she was earning nearly six figures annually, and together with Jack's roughly equivalent salary, they made some good investments and began to feel more relaxed about money. Sandy and Jack's marriage started out good and has only gotten better. They do well together, and despite some inevitable differences in style (Jack's lightheartedness is a definite contrast to his considerably more serious, no-nonsense wife), both would describe themselves as happily married.

It finally seemed the right time for Sandy to get pregnant. Sandy hoped it would happen soon after she stopped taking the Pill, but it was not to be. What started out as a playful—"Let's go upstairs and make a baby"—evolved into a much more serious agenda when many months later Sandy was still not pregnant. As was typical of Jack, his attitude was, "Don't worry—it'll happen when it happens." As was typical of Sandy, her attitude was, "We have to try harder . . . we have to keep charts of my ovulations and we have to cut out all alcohol and I should probably stop exercising every day and . . ."

After trying and trying for nearly two years with no success, both Sandy and Jack sought help from medical experts. Jack's physical exam showed that everything was normal, but Sandy's did not. For complex and unchangeable medical reasons, Sandy found out she wasn't physically capable of ever bearing children.

Jack took the medical reasons for Sandy's infertility in stride, but Sandy fell into a deep depression. She cried often and found herself avoiding anything and anybody where the subject of babies might come up.

Jack finally convinced Sandy that adopting a child was a great "Plan B," and the difficult search began. They wrote countless letters and made endless phone calls to the agencies and attorneys specializing in arranging adoptions, even foreign ones. These were entirely unsuccessful, and Sandy's despair grew almost daily. She never understood how Jack always seemed so nonchalant about the lack of progress. It drove her crazy when he'd say, as if to pacify her, "Don't worry, it'll happen in time." She often thought, "He must not really want children if he can be so up at such a down time." Jack wanted to persist, though. Eventually, they placed their own ads in newspapers across the country, although neither of them really believed deep down that anything would ever come of them.

Fortune, however, smiled on Sandy and Jack only a few weeks later. A fifteen-year-old girl who wanted to give up her baby contacted them, clearly realizing that neither she or her fourteen-year-old boyfriend could be parents either now or in the near future. Their families condoned the teens' plan to give up the baby to Sandy and Jack after only two meetings with them. Sandy and Jack seemed clearly able to provide a much better environment for the baby than any of them could on every level—the baby would be loved, cared for, educated, and given every possible opportunity.

The baby boy was born. He appeared to be healthy, and he was quickly given to Sandy and Jack, who were present at the birth. The look in their eyes as they looked repeatedly at their new son and then each other spoke volumes about a dream fulfilled.

After the first few days of getting everyone comfortable with what had transpired, it was time for Sandy and Jack to leave the teens and their families, give them all their gratitude and lots of reassurances, and begin a new life as a family. Jack was elated, but Sandy was strangely quiet and withdrawn. The return home was uneventful. When Sandy unwrapped her new gift and placed him in his crib, she left the room to get him a bottle. He began to cry. Sandy quickly returned with the bottle, and gently stuck it in his face. His only response was to continue to wail. Sandy tried again to get him to take the bottle, but again no cooperation. Sandy became tearful as she tried several times to get him to quiet down and accept the bottle from her. Finally, after a half-dozen attempts, she threw the bottle at Jack, and ran crying from the room while proclaiming, "He hates me. He'll never accept me as his mother."

In the previous chapter, I talked about ambiguity as one of the major risk factors for depression. When a situation you face is ambiguous, there is no single, clear, objective interpretation you can make about why things are happening the way they are. In such situations it is highly typical to form a conclusion (or projection) about what that person must have meant or why he or she acted that way, and then respond on the basis of that conclusion. The danger, of course, is that the conclusion you form isn't really what's going on.

We'll consider Sandy from the vignette above in greater detail later, but she illustrates the process well. She's faced with a crying baby, certainly an ambiguous stimulus while you look for some clue as to whether the crying is due to hunger, a wet diaper, fatigue, fear of something unfamiliar in the environment, or any one of many other possibilities. Sandy attempts to give the baby a bottle, and he rejects it. Why did the baby reject the bottle? That is unknown in a definitive sense, but it doesn't stop Sandy from jumping to the immediate conclusion that his rejection of the bottle she offers him is a rejection of her. Is that a reasonable, well-formed conclusion? It is not.

In this chapter, I consider the need to make meaning out of life experiences, and the influence of families on this process, for better or worse.

THE MEANING OF LIFE

What is the most ambiguous stimulus that people face? Life. Life doesn't have any inherent meaning—each of us gives meaning to our life through the beliefs we adopt and the behaviors that we choose. Why people need to make meaning out of ambiguous life events is relatively clear: The specific meanings we attach to everyday life events, and the global meaning we attach to life itself, not only diminish the uncomfortable anxiety associated with being uncertain, but give life a structure and purpose that guide the course of daily living. Our meanings dictate our actions to a great extent, defining us and our place in the world. Some people need more of this structure and definition, and some less, but *everyone* needs *some.*

Not all subjectively derived meanings or projections are alike, however. Some meanings we form open up to us the world of positive possibilities, while others are so painfully restrictive that people find it hard even to eat, breathe, or function. Some meanings enlighten us, but some lead us into malicious ignorance. Some meanings inspire humane compassion, yet others inspire fanatical terrorism. And, especially relevant to the topic of depression, some meanings create hope and optimism but others lead us into despair and a sense of the utter futility of it all.

The person who views life as a "grand experiment" or the person who views life as a "cosmic affliction" are both making their own projections. The relevant questions for our purposes are, "What is the effect of your projections on depression?" and "Where do your projections come from?"

Depression itself is an ambiguous stimulus, essentially identical in form to a Rorschach inkblot. Thus, it invites projections about its meaning in the same way as any other ambiguous phenomenon of life does. This point is critical to understanding what your own views of depression are and what they subsequently lead you to do. Likewise, depression invites projections from the professionals who attempt to treat it. So psychiatrists trained in medicine (neurochemistry, psychopharmacology) will naturally view depression through the lens of biology, and pronounce depression a disease resulting from a chemical imbalance. Psychologists who are trained to identify the environmental and developmental influences on depression will pronounce depression a long-term consequence of childhood trauma or the product of sloppy thinking or poor relationships. Marriage and family therapists trained in systemic thought who see life from a contextual perspective will see depression as a product of poor marriages, family dysfunctions, and gender and social inequities. All of these perceptions, and others, too, are to some extent true. Each *is* part of the depression story.

ATTRIBUTIONAL STYLES
OF DEPRESSION

The process of making meaning out of ambiguous events is what psychologists call *projection*, as you now know. When the projection involves making a causal explanation, psychologists call this *attribution formation*. An attribution is simply a cause–effect explanation, such as "I believe A made B happen." When life presents us with situations to react to, as it routinely does, before we can react in a meaningful way we first have to make some attempt to figure out what's going on. For example, consider the experience of flying in an airplane. If you encounter turbulence during a flight, do you simply notice there's turbulence and that's all? No, you tell yourself something about the turbulence—you form an attribution about it. If you tell yourself immediately, "That's turbulence, it's normal, nothing to worry about, it'll pass quickly as we move through the area with choppy air, and I'll be fine," then your reaction will be a relatively calm, accepting one. If, however, you tell yourself, "Oh my God! The plane is in trouble. We're going to crash and I'm going to die!" then you will experience a full-blown panic as if your death is indeed imminent. The ambiguous stimulus is turbulence, and you can see how two very different attributions lead to two very different responses.

Researchers have studied the relationship between attributions and mental health, particularly as it applies to depression. There is substantial evidence that most people suffering depression make attributional errors. Simply put, they read situations incorrectly or make negative projections about the situation, and consequently react badly. Instead of looking for and responding to whatever facts may be available to them, they respond to their own projections as if they are true, much to their own detriment. (It may interest you to know that optimistic people also naturally respond to situations with projections or attributions, but ones that are positive and favorable to them. These allow them to feel good even though they may be just as inaccurate—or even more inaccurate—than pessimists.)

Responding to turbulence in the air is one example, responding to turbulence in the family is another. It's the turbulence in the family I am most concerned with, because much like one hysterical passenger who's screaming and in a panic on a plane and consequently upsets almost everyone on the flight, one person in the family can lead the others to view things badly and get everyone else upset needlessly.

The *way* that people form attributions is *patterned,* i.e., repetitive. Identifying the patterns of attributions evident in your family can tell you where you or your loved ones are making errors that not only may be underlying current episodes of depression, but will likely be the foundation for future episodes of depression if they are not adequately addressed.

To illustrate attribution formation at work, let's return to the story of Sandy and Jack presented at this chapter's start.

Sandy has been very deliberate in planning her life. Career, then marriage, and eventually attaining enough financial security to sensibly permit having children. It wasn't part of her plan to be infertile, though. Nor was it a part of her plan to try to adopt a child and be at the mercy of some unknown person who would willingly part with what Sandy so desperately wanted. Sandy felt truly out of control and depression simply became a way of life for her.

By the time Sandy finally had a son to call her own, she was more deeply entrenched than ever in the very patterns of depression that held the potential to unintentionally harm her and the child she most wanted to protect. Sandy's *inability to tolerate frustration* when she wanted her baby to take the bottle led her to try, try again, and then try again, but soon *give up angrily and then withdraw* from him completely. Sandy interpreted his refusal to accept the bottle as the baby *rejecting her as a mother,* an apparent statement from his behavior that she was, for some reason, *personally unacceptable.* Next, she extrapolates this *negative expectation* of personal rejection forward throughout her entire life by proclaiming and apparently believing, "he'll *never* accept me as his mother."

Sandy's patterns of perception aren't just about giving her new son a bottle. They reflect a considerably deeper set of issues. You might remember that her coworkers gave her feedback like "lighten up" and "quit being so controlling" and "don't take things so personally." Now she brings those same emotional, behavioral, and perceptual patterns to the task of child-rearing. If she can't immediately control her child, is it acceptable to give up angrily and withdraw from him? If he chooses something else besides her or what she offers, is it reasonable for her to conclude it's personal rejection? Is the one interaction of the baby rejecting a bottle predictive of an entire future together, justifying Sandy's lifelong negative expectations when an interaction doesn't go very well?

Sandy needs to learn some very specific skills. She needs to learn frustration tolerance; predictably, there will be countless times in the future when her first attempts don't succeed. How many times will he fall down while she's trying to help him learn to walk? How many times will he forget letters when she is trying to help him memorize the alphabet? How many times will he do sloppy homework, even though she tries to help him, just so he can get it done quickly and go out and play? This first interaction with the bottle is the first of *thousands* of episodes with him where she will need the resource of frustration tolerance. Without it, she will be impatient, angry, and hopeless about him, and self-loathing toward herself. Depression in the making . . .

Sandy needs to learn to depersonalize others' choices. She may have cooked spaghetti, but he wants a hot dog. She may have bought him new pants, but he likes to wear the ones with the hole in the knee. She may have signed him up for the soccer team, but he wants to play computer games. If every time he makes a choice she takes it as personal rejection and withdraws, theirs will be a relationship marred by manipulation, defiance, and distance that strangle any feelings of affection. When there is no closeness or acceptance, you have a ripe situation for loneliness, despair, and, yes, depression.

Let's go a step further and consider the interpersonal effects of her patterns—the way they affect her relationship with her son.

Sandy needs to learn not to plan an entire future on the basis of a single interaction. Tragic lives have been formed in just this way. Consider an example illustrating a relationship over time: A son comes home later than expected from school and Mom concludes he can never be trusted. She then clamps down harder, inviting more secrecy and rebellion. He learns to resist, even if he's resisting something that's ultimately in his best interest. He gets a lousy grade on some test, she tells him he'll *never* be a success. He outwardly discounts her appraisal, but secretly takes her prediction to heart and eventually becomes the self-loathing, depressed failure Mom said he'd be. If every time he makes a mistake it results in a dire prediction of eventual disaster, he can easily learn to "do nothing so nothing bad can happen." How do people learn to be passive in life? Now you know at least one of the ways.

Consider carefully all that occurs over the course of life that flows from a single pattern. Sandy's patterns of low frustration tolerance, and a tendency to personalize events and make erroneous attributions and negative and enduring predictions are patterns that, left unchecked, will undoubtedly damage and depress her future. And they will damage and depress her son, whose life with her will be filled with countless examples of the same negative and potentially depressing sorts of interactions.

As stated earlier, the attributions you make are patterned, meaning the style with which you interpret and react to life experiences is repetitive. Research has shown that attributional style is stable over the course of your life unless you deliberately strive to change it. Research has also shown that certain attributional styles are much more likely to lead to depression than others, as I alluded to earlier. Knowing something about your attributional style and how you acquired it quite unconsciously is the first step in deciding whether you want or need to actively strive to change it. If it depresses you or your family, it is a worthwhile goal to learn to think differently about things.

I will be much more specific about the characteristics of attributions, and I will also provide illustrative examples, in chapter 7. Here I simply want to introduce the concept and identify key attributional style patterns in order to provide a glimpse into "how you got this way." As I will discuss in the next section, there is a strong correlation between the attributional styles of parents and children, but it will help to know that although you learned to interpret life experiences along the same lines as your parents, you are also free to choose new alternatives.

The key aspects of attributions concern whether you view key events in your life as *personal* to you ("it happened because of me"), *permanent* in nature ("it'll be this way forever"), and *all-encompassing* ("it affects everything"). When something bad happens, and you see things in these terms, you are at much higher risk for depression than the person who simply says, "That's life, this situation will pass, and so what if it screws up this one thing."

Identifying your patterns of attributions, and those of your family, is a critical step in both treating and preventing depression. Thus, when you think about things that have happened, are happening, or are going to happen, it is critical that you recognize which parts of these experiences are clear-cut and well-defined, and which are ambiguous. For now, just remember that depressing projections are more likely when ambiguity is present.

THE ORIGINS OF YOUR ATTRIBUTIONS

When I titled this chapter, "Learning Depression from Your Family," I wanted to draw your attention to the fact that you are not born with a genetically encoded attributional style. As babies and later as children, we are continually exposed to both the quality of thought and the quality of action of those who are our caretakers. For most of us, our parents were our caretakers, and their influence on us was multidimensional because of those things they actually said and did, as well as the things that we concluded or learned from what they did and didn't say or do.

People learn through direct experience and also through *modeling*. Modeling is learning by observing others' experiences. When you watch someone do something he or she gets punished for, it typically decreases your desire to do the same thing. When you watch someone do something he or she get praised or rewarded for, it typically increases your interest in doing something similar. From the earliest experiences of Mom modeling for you how to eat by opening her mouth when she's bringing a spoon up to yours, you are exposed to countless opportunities for modeling your parents' behavior. More than that, you learn to model their attitudes, beliefs, and perceptions as you watch them interpret and react to the world you share as a family. More will be said about the modeling of attributions in chapter 7, especially in regard to the attributional style you model to *your* children.

Your parents' attributions don't exist in a vacuum. There was an emotional context they created when you were growing up. That was and is a powerful factor influencing your own internal emotional atmosphere, that is, the emotional environment in which you do your own thinking and behaving. In the next section, we will consider the influence of family atmosphere on mood states.

FAMILY ATMOSPHERE

A family has a mood, just as an individual does. When you think of your family mood, past or present, how would you characterize it? Before you answer, a word of caution: When you think about the past, of course, there is a tendency toward what is known as *revisionism.* People tend to revise, even entirely rewrite their past in light of their current feelings. When you're depressed, it's more likely you will only remember the times that were unpleasant. When you're happy, it's more likely you'll readily recall the good times and the bad times will seem less onerous. Your mood also acts as a filter for whether you assign more weight to the positive or negative aspects of your present life. The more global your attributional style, the more likely you are to remember things in the extremes of good or bad. So strive for as balanced a perspective as you can when you start inventorying your life, instead of selectively looking for evidence to affirm how good or rotten you think your family mood was.

Family mood is a global term—it lacks specifics about its salient or defining components. The overall atmosphere created by all the family members interacting with one another can be characterized globally as somewhere between "good" and "bad." More specifically, though, it can be gauged according to where on each of the following continua the family might be placed: positive–negative, friendly–hostile, cooperative–competitive, close–distant, calm–tense, fun–serious. There are many more ways for a family atmosphere to be evaluated, of course, but these represent the fundamental picture.

Let's consider briefly the role of each.

POSITIVE–NEGATIVE ATMOSPHERE

The Johnson family accepted the Gardner family's invitation to dinner. They weren't usually very social, but the Johnsons' son, Gary, had been playing well in school with Barry Gardner, and both sets of parents wanted to encourage the boys' friendship and perhaps develop one of their own in the process.

Brenda Gardner made a nice dinner, but nothing fancy. Jerry Gardner was a nice enough guy who happened to have a strong interest in sports that frequented his conversation. Gary and Barry were busy playing elsewhere most of the evening, but when all were at the dinner table, Gary felt like he was everybody's focus because his mom and dad kept peppering him with reminders about how to sit, how to take food from the serving platter, and how to eat politely.

On the way home, the Johnsons did a thorough review of the details of the evening, a pattern that Gary was all too familiar with. They took turns as they pointed out what was wrong with the Gardners' style of decorating, with their choice of menu, with the way they treated Barry, with the presentation of the food and the way it was cooked, with their interests and values, and on and on. Gary didn't really understand what all the criticism was about, because he thought dinner was great and the Gardners were really nice. But the longer he listened to the litany of criticisms, the more the evening began to seem like it wasn't a very good one after all. When his mom finally turned around in the front seat to face him and ask him if he wanted to play with Barry again, Gary said, "I don't think so. It wasn't really very fun."

If life is a glass of water, what is the effect of growing up in a home where you are routinely exposed to the positive message from your parents that it is half-*full?* And, likewise, what is the effect of regularly being told and shown by example that it is half-*empty?* Optimism and pessimism are based on our projections regarding the ambiguity of life. Either one may be more realistic or closer to the truth at a given moment in time. (In fact, contrary to the common belief that depressed people only see things in a negatively distorted way, there is evidence that in some ways, depressives may actually see some things more realistically than their nondepressed counterparts.) Though optimism and pessimism may equally be projections, optimism feels better. And, the evidence shows, in some ways, optimism *is* better: Optimists generally suffer fewer mood problems, fewer health problems, and are better able to perform their jobs.

Family mood teaches you to relate to your environment, whether internal (such as your feelings) or external (such as the room you happen to be in). Through repetitive family interactions, you learn to selectively notice and react to what you find. There is both the positive and the negative in and around us: Will you be more likely to notice and react to the new flowers on the table or the small crack in the wall you just became aware of? Will you be encouraged to talk about what you learned at school that was interesting, or will you have to defend (again) why you didn't get an *A* on the science test? Will you get praised for how nicely you cleaned up your room, or criticized for the one book that isn't perfectly aligned on the shelf? Will you be shown beautiful places and things in the world, or only the ugly ones you're supposed to avoid? Will you focus your attention on identifying your own insecurities, or will you focus on identifying your strengths?

One of the core components of depression is selectively filtering out the good and only seeing the remaining bad. Your family can readily train you through repeated complaints about life in general and criticisms of you in particular to immediately see the negatives and ignore whatever positives there might be. Depressed thinking typically involves minimizing the positives while amplifying the negatives. And since the world is filled with things both good *and* bad, there is an endless supply of possibilities to feed either perception and justify it in the person's mind. That is a *perceptual habit* learned early on, and parents are most often the unwitting teachers. Parents need to actively monitor their perceptions to ensure they offer a balanced view of reality if they want their children to have healthy attributions to model.

FRIENDLY—HOSTILE ATMOSPHERE

When Henry met Monica, he was smitten with her. She was bright, beautiful, and a delight to talk to. She had one serious drawback, though, as far as Henry was concerned: her two kids from her previous marriage. Monica was equally smitten with Henry, and their relationship soon turned serious. Henry had never been married before, and certainly was intimidated at the thought of having an "instant family." He didn't think of himself as parent material, and wasn't sure he wanted to try to be. He described his reservations to Monica, who understood his feelings, but dismissed them with the assurance that once he got to know her kids and live with them as their new stepdad, everything would work out. She was sure there was no way Henry wouldn't quickly grow to love her kids.

Love superseded reason. Despite only minimal time with her kids, and Henry's persistent feelings he was making a big mistake, Henry and Monica pushed forward the idea of marriage and it soon came to pass.

Monica was wrong. Henry wouldn't grow to love the kids. He was jealous of their closeness and their ability to collectively make him feel like an outsider. He resented the extra time he was mandated to go places and do things that were "kid stuff" he didn't want to do. His initially soft and polite interactions with them soon turned hard and laced with sarcasm and resentment. Monica was so hurt and angry that Henry was treating her kids so poorly that she pulled back from Henry altogether. The anger between them was at a dangerously high level, and an explosion seemed imminent. The kids were living in fear of Henry, shutting up as soon as he entered the room. They hardly smiled or laughed anymore, something they used to do a lot. Monica felt awful that she'd led the kids into this kind of miserable existence.

Neither Monica nor Henry was sure whether to file for divorce now or wait a while longer in hopes of a miracle.

When you engage in any interaction with another person, no matter how brief or superficial, you convey an emotional attitude. How you engage with the person determines whether you are perceived as approachable and friendly. In terms of family mood, whether in the family you've created or your family of origin, does friendliness or hostility tend to be the attitude guiding the interactions?

Depression is certainly more likely when hostility is present, for it's hard to feel good about yourself or your life when you're among people who don't even like you, or so it seems. And if the hostility is allowed to persist past the reasonable amount of time it may take to work out angry feelings over some incident, then what is the message? That the relationship is expendable? It isn't. That anger can divide the family? Of course it can—but it shouldn't be allowed to. That we don't have to communicate sensibly and reach a resolution, a compromise to restore balance? There should exist a clear expectation on the part of everyone in the family that the relevant issues will be discussed in a reasonable manner in order to reach a workable solution. This is how there can be specific disagreements between members that *don't* globally ruin a family relationship (note the role of global/specific attributions when people think the *entire* relationship is on the line in a single interaction). In effect, the message is a clear one that says, "We can disagree and still love and care about each other." If people are led to believe that the whole relationship may fail because of some issue or difference, they will naturally fear confrontations and live with the anxiety that relationships they value and want to be enduring can be snatched away from them. It is a sad thing when family members cut off communication and sacrifice the whole relationship over some divisive issue, and such circumstances often trigger depression.

You can see how growing up in a family where interactions were rude or hostile, and where anger was allowed to fester, could lead to the emotional withdrawal from such painful relationships and to the isolation where depression dwells. Being connected simply has to mean more than being "right." It sounds trite to say family members should be friends, but I think it's more reasonable to at least expect them to be *friendly*. You don't have to be best friends and confidants to express an interest in and appreciation of each person, or to speak to them kindly or respectfully. Parents can and should encourage these behaviors in their family interactions and exhibit good behavior for their children to model.

COOPERATIVE–COMPETITIVE ATMOSPHERE

Nathan had always been described by his parents as "the quiet one." His older sister, Judy, was a junior in high school and dramatic in her ways of drawing attention to herself; her latest pronouncements were needing her own car and being in love with some new guy who is "so much cooler" than last week's boyfriend, who was so much cooler than the one from last month. Nathan's younger brother, Freddie, just entered junior high school and everything he did was the subject of his parents' close scrutiny because "he's at such a critical developmental stage."

Nathan felt he was invisible to his parents. They seemed constantly preoccupied with Judy or Freddie, and sometimes when he was in a room with them he thought they were actually startled to see him, as if they'd forgotten he lived there, too.

He had stopped fighting with Judy a long time ago. Mom and Dad always took her side because "she's a girl" and "she's the oldest," and Nathan knew he couldn't win even when she was clearly wrong, which was a lot. She was definitely "Daddy's little girl." He had lots of resentment toward Judy, but she didn't seem to notice, nor did anyone seem to care.

Freddie was another matter, though. Nathan didn't fight with him in front of Mom or Dad, but when they were alone and out of parental earshot, Nathan would say some really mean things to him. He teased him about his mild acne, his adolescent heroes, his choice of music, and whatever else he could harangue him about. Freddie didn't understand why Nathan was so hostile to him, but he didn't give it much thought, either. He had absolute immunity because he was "Momma's boy."

Whose boy was Nathan?

Each child strives to get noticed, whether through becoming the athlete, the *A* student, the kid with the most tattoos and body piercing, the sensitive one, or the delinquent. (Adults, of course, aren't much different in their needs—or styles—for getting noticed.) What was it like in your family in terms of how and when you would get noticed? Did you have to do something to get noticed, or was just being who you were enough to get attention from others? In terms of family atmosphere, does each member of your family know they will be valued for who they are, or do they absorb the message that they have to compete to get what they need? Have you replicated the style of the family you grew up in?

Competition for parental attention and approval holds the potential to be a losing proposition when parents don't readily provide them. The idea, of course, is to strive to create an atmosphere in the family that is globally win-win, where there isn't a loser, even when somebody loses.

When Mom and Dad argue, for example, and the kids are around (as they often can and will be), do they see their parents argue respectfully in a manner where both have their dignity protected? If so, they can model patterns of cooperation that can lead to a mutually agreeable solution, or at least a solution that both people come to recognize as effective, even if one has to conclude that he or she was right and the other was wrong. If you as a partner make it easy for your spouse to concede (no put-downs or I-told-you-so's), and the relationship quickly continues as affectionate and respectful, the spirit of cooperation emerges. The message is, in essence, "Our relationship continuing in a healthy way is more important than me winning the argument at your expense." Remember, *all behavior has message value.*

The spirit of cooperation and the ability to function effectively in a marriage and a family system are traits that can be nurtured in many ways. All of them share the common denominator of placing the well-being of the marriage and the family ahead of personal gain. Now you can get another glimpse of why I emphasized in the the last chapter the destructive potential of our "me first" cultural perspective. When pursuing individual satisfaction regularly overtakes any sense of social responsibility, it hurts the culture, the family, and the individual. There *are* ways of pursuing individual satisfaction that are not antisocial. For the sake of our collective mental health, I hope people will look for them.

CLOSE–DISTANT ATMOSPHERE

When his dad died, Stan's brother, Martin, called him with the news. It was the first time they had talked in months. They liked each other well enough, but they lived on opposite coasts, and each had his own busy life.

At the funeral, Stan saw relatives he hadn't seen in many, many years. He had quick interactions with each back at his mom's house afterward. People expressed their condolences and offered to do whatever might be helpful, but nothing was really needed.

After everyone left and the house was quiet, Stan had his first truly private moments with his mother and brother. Over coffee at the kitchen table it turned into a storyfest, swapping stories about Dad.

Stan had talked to his dad every Sunday, but the conversation was always a little hurried because his dad inevitably had something else to do. He didn't bother to tell his dad the details of his family goings-on or what was happening at work. Nor did he ask his dad about his life or his feelings—just whether he was doing okay.

Sitting and listening to the stories coming from Martin and his mom, it hit Stan like a ton of bricks that for all he knew about his dad, he really didn't know him. On the heels of that thought came a question that instantly brought tears to his eyes when he realized the answer was no: Did he really know his mom or his brother?

People who are married tend to suffer less depression than people who are single, particularly if the marriage is a happy one. People who have a strong social support system (good friends) fare better in life in many ways than people who do not. Close relationships have a healing quality to them, *if* they are healthy ones.

Too often, a family is just a bunch of folks with the same last name or address. They may occasionally eat together, or go to the mall together, but not much more takes place between them.

Closeness doesn't just happen. In contrast, distance *does* just happen, unless individuals are actively striving for closeness. Do you call your family members just to say hello and talk about lighthearted things, or only if something heavy is going on? Do you share the smaller details that give others a better sense of what your life is really about? Are you a good listener? Do you give off the message that you're too busy and don't have the time, or that you're mostly available? How do these questions apply to your parents?

It is remarkably easy to forget to call and say hello, to forget to send birthday and anniversary cards, to work instead of going to your child's soccer game or school play, to stay wrapped up in all that's going on with you and rarely step outside your own immediate concerns. As we saw in the last chapter, our culture encourages the notion that it's okay, even desirable, to stay focused on your own needs. Psychologists even tell us we have a *right* to have our needs met and to be the center of our own universes. Maybe so, but the larger issue here is what kind of effect such self-absorption has on others. (I mentioned earlier the full-page ad the ABC network took out in *TV Guide* to convince us "TV Is Good." Recently, while driving, I saw an ad on a bus from ABC that simply said "You can talk to your wife anytime." The message: Your wife can wait—your favorite TV show is on *now*. You can safely predict that the ad irritated me.)

Closeness has to be constantly nurtured. It dwindles away if it isn't. Such nurturing takes time and energy. It opens up avenues of potential conflict ("I'm trying harder than you so why don't you try harder?"). But emotional closeness is too essential to our well-being to simply let slide.

CALM-TENSE ATMOSPHERE

Terri panicked when she couldn't find her dental retainer. She had only taken it out for a little while to eat something and was sure she'd put it someplace safe, but it was missing now and she knew there'd be hell to pay. She'd lost another one a few months ago, and her parents reacted as if she'd said she was pregnant and on drugs. They raged at her for what seemed an eternity about her carelessness, her irresponsibility, her lack of respect for their money and how hard they worked, her lack of appreciation for all they had sacrificed for her in order to get her teeth fitted with braces, and on and on. Terri felt so guilty that she'd tried to make herself invisible so she wouldn't draw any more of their ire. Just going home and having to be around them was so monumentally difficult. They picked on every little thing she did, and constantly made her feel as though she was a stupid and careless person. She could feel her whole body tense up by just coming in the front door.

Deep down, she knew she wasn't stupid and careless. She took excellent care of her belongings, always putting away carefully the things she used whether they were her own clothes or the family's kitchen utensils. But if one of her parents happened to notice a sweater on a chair in the two minutes before she had gotten around to putting it away, she'd get called a slob. If they happened to ask about her homework and it wasn't completely done yet, even if she was well on her way to completing it, she was told she wasn't taking her schoolwork seriously enough. This despite her excellent grades.

As Terri got older, she found more and more excuses to spend time at the homes of friends. She felt different at their homes, and liked the fact that for some time, at least, she could relax a little and not have to worry about the next thing her parents were going to throw at her.

As I hope you've come to appreciate, the quality and intensity of an emotional response is directly related to attributional style. Global attributions (*"everything* is terrible") will generally lead to much stronger emotional reactions than will specific attributions (*"this* is terrible"). What is the effect on children when they grow up in homes where *everything* is a big deal? When Mom and/or Dad are volatile and unpredictable in their reactions, or are prone to judge things negatively (as discussed in an earlier section), and when punishments can be random (i.e., depend on what mood they're in) or severe, it is hard to find the family environment one that you can relax in. On the contrary, there is an ever-present anxiety that you'll say or do something wrong. Living with that anxiety is awfully tiring. Preventing it in such contexts may not be possible since it comes from a generally realistic fear of humiliation, rejection, or even physical punishment. Managing it with alcohol, drugs, or avoidance can start to seem like a good way to kids (and adults, too) to get some relief. Such short-term coping strategies too often become long-term problems.

It is a wonderfully different experience growing up in a family environment where you are told in a thousand ways that you're loved even when you make mistakes, and that you're respected even when you make choices others wouldn't make (as long as they're openly discussed and they have a plausible rationale to them, thereby teaching critical thinking skills). It's so calming when something bad happens and you watch your parents go into a problem-solving mode rather than an emotional hysteria or a blaming, rage-filled attack.

What was your family environment like when you were growing up? Did you live in fear of making mistakes, or were you confident that whatever mistakes you might make, you were still going to be loved and accepted? How does your own background influence the ways you feel about and treat others in your family now?

Anxiety is often found hand-in-hand with depression. As discussed in the section on comorbidity in the first chapter, it is the statistical likelihood that where you find depression you'll also find anxiety. Anxiety arises for all kinds of specific reasons; globally, it's generally about the fear and dread of what terrible things *might* happen. (Terri, who lost her dental retainer in this section's vignette, illustrates what I mean.) People who *aren't* typically anxious may also anticipate in a general (not specific) way that something bad might happen. But, they do two things very differently than those who are overcome by anxiety: They don't imagine a disaster as *imminent,* nor do they believe it will (globally) overwhelm them and ruin their entire lives.

Families can model and teach effective problem-solving skills to reduce anxiety in their members. Families can address specific problems rather than doing a Chicken Little routine ("The sky is falling!"). Families can provide a foundation of love and acceptance that minimizes the common fear in kids that they'll be abandoned if they don't act "right." Families can be consistent and respectful even in the way they dole out punishment. Families can do things together that minimize anxiety and global self-condemnation and maximize closeness.

FUN—SERIOUS ATMOSPHERE

Dinner was always an event at the Morris home: three kids, two dogs, and the expectation that no matter what the meal consisted of, it was second fiddle to the playful banter between everyone. It never seemed to matter how hard the day was for anyone, or what else had yet to be done that evening. Everything stopped when everyone piled into the kitchen to do their share of preparation. This was valuable "catch-up" time and "get in the mood to have fun" time.

At the table, Mom and Dad would ask each child in turn to describe his or her day and significant insights, and each story prompted good-natured jibes and jokes. If the humor turned caustic or sarcastic, which it didn't often, Mom and Dad would step in and demand an immediate apology. Time together was safe and loving. Afraid they'd miss some of the fun, no one hurried away even after a meal was finished.

Even when times were tough for someone, he or she could still somehow maintain a sense of humor about it and the deep conviction that his or her family would be there for them. It never changed, even when the kids were grown and gone. Family get-togethers were frequent and fun as ever.

When Grandma and Grandpa Morris were asked how they'd raised such a loyal, fun, and loving family, Grandpa answered this way: "Someone wise once told me that if I ever had to choose between losing my leg and losing my sense of humor, that I should lose the leg."

Kids pick up quickly on their parents' moods. If your mom and/or dad was depressed, you already know how hard it is to come home cheerful from school. When you walk in the front door, the unspoken message is "You better wipe that smile off your face because things in this house are no damn good." Kids are remarkably diplomatic. (Ever try and get an eight-year-old in a custody hearing to actually say whether he or she would rather live with Mom or Dad? It's often easier to get shaving cream back in the can.) They don't want to offend, and they pick up that "happiness is irrelevant or disrespectful; suffering is the way of things around here." How would you describe the emotional atmosphere in your family of origin? Did you have fun with and enjoy each other's company? Or did you try to find ways to avoid each other because there was usually some tension simmering? What is it like in your family now? Can and do you play well together?

Parents don't impose this point of view on their kids deliberately, of course. But when they're caught up in a hostile corporate takeover, or dealing with the financial stresses of a big medical bill that insurance didn't cover, or feeling trapped in a crummy marriage, there simply aren't very many "fun" feelings to share. When you're in a great mood, everything is funny. When you're in a bad mood, nothing is.

Depressed individuals are not well-known for their sense of humor. On the contrary, they seek out and expect only to find the things in life that are negative and serious. They unintentionally look for the things that confirm and reinforce their mood. So fun seems superficial, humor seems a waste of time, and people who aren't equally serious are dispensable. Too bad, because part of what makes a family close is being able to enjoy each other. Being able to play and joke and laugh and act silly and do entertaining things together that *don't* require an existential analysis is some of the strongest glue that can hold a family together.

Milton H. Erickson, M.D., was a pioneering psychiatrist in his systemic perspective long before it became obvious to everyone else. Erickson once said, "If you look over the lives of happy, well-adjusted people, they haven't analyzed their childhood—and they're not going to." I think Erickson was right. Not only that, but he knew how to have *fun*.

The family atmosphere, or mood of the family, is a training context for later feelings. Depression is about thoughts and feelings, and more; the feelings that are generated and encouraged within the family are blueprints for later experiences as an individual and as a member of a larger family system. What are the feelings you help bring out in others? Can you be serious when it's time to be serious, and fun when it's time to be fun? Do you help create an atmosphere crackling with tension, or one that is a refuge from the stresses of life?

From each of the vignettes in this section on family atmosphere, you can see how the things that people say and do affect the others around them, for better or worse. If you want to create an atmosphere in your relationships with others that is conducive to closeness, warmth, safety, loyalty, and similar vital characteristics, it will require having the drive and skill to deliberately bring those traits into each interaction.

Family moods are inevitable; the variable is what *kind* of atmosphere and mood you *all* will take the responsibility to cocreate. You can be deliberate in making efforts to mobilize the resources to get your family interacting in ways that tend to bring out the best in each other, rather than letting things deteriorate into what might be a comfortable familiarity that lacks any real joy or closeness.

A WORD ABOUT FAMILY EXPECTATIONS

You may have noticed that there is a common underlying theme implicit in almost everything discussed in this chapter. Let's make it explicit: There are expectations operating in every family system about how people should act, feel, think, react, choose, and interpret events. These expectations may be communicated directly ("I expect you to get your homework done before you go out and play"), or they may be communicated indirectly ("Don't ever try and talk to me when I'm in a bad mood" is inferred from an angry verbal attack and hostile body language instead of through dialogue). I want to draw your attention to at least two dimensions of expectations: those held by your family of origin, and those you hold of your own family members.

What were the expectations of you that your parents raised you with? What were you supposed to do or be? How were you supposed to act? What were the things that were supposed to interest you and what were you supposed to do about them? What were the consequences when you did and didn't live up to their expectations? What expectations do you now have of your own children? How do you communicate to them your expectations? How do you think they feel about your expectations and what concerns, if any, do they have about not living up to them? How do you know?

Expectations are powerful forces in shaping mood and behavior. To defy someone's expectations and invite their anger or rejection is difficult when we all want and need approval from others. The detrimental effect to your self-image can be considerable when you try to live up to others' expectations and find you can't, or when you live up to their expectations and in so doing contradict your own. It's colloquially called *selling out*, and the price is often self-loathing.

High or low expectations play a significant role in determining the level of ambition in you and those around you. Aim too high, and it seems impossible, so why bother? Aim too low, and there's no real reward in it, so why bother?

Learning and thereby teaching how to establish realistic expectations is one of the major tasks of a healthy family system. With all that you now know about ambiguity, attributions, family mood and atmosphere, and the inevitability of saying something to others with everything you do, it is realistic to expect that you should continually define and redefine your expectations in order to reduce the probability of hand-me-down blues.

DID YOUR FAMILY MAKE YOU DEPRESSED?

This book is *not* about blaming parents for their depressed children. How can you blame people who are, in large part, a composite of what they learned from *their* parents and were shaped by the cultural forces of the era they grew up in? I have repeatedly stressed the distinction between intentions and outcomes. Parents who are lost in their own worlds (through alcoholism, mental illness, personal inadequacies, *whatever*) and are therefore oblivious to the detrimental effects they have on the rest of the people in their sphere of influence are clearly destructive. To have and use power so badly is an abuse of power.

Part of becoming an individual in your own right, however, is learning that you don't have to think in the same way as your parents or siblings. You don't have to interpret the ambiguities of life according to the same attributional style you were exposed to as a child. You don't have to accept others' expectations of you when they are inappropriate or at odds with who you are. (Counterbalance that point with the realization that you do have a responsibility to your family, meaning differences between you should get addressed and resolved respectfully and in a timely manner. But simple obedience is *not* a realistic expectation in adult relationships.) And, finally, you don't have to replicate a family atmosphere that is gloomy and tense.

You see, one of the big research findings about depression is that, contrary to popular misconception, depression isn't just about bad things happening to you in your life. Yes, research shows that kids who suffered the early loss of a parent or other traumas may be at higher risk for later depression. But, that is a statistical probability, not a statement of destiny.

What I'm interested in are all those children who suffered a loss or trauma and *didn't* become depressed. I want to know why they didn't and learn what it is about their coping styles that insulated them from depression. And now that I and many researchers and clinicians have spent about a quarter of a century asking those kinds of critical questions, we've come to know many of the answers.

The foremost thing to understand is that *it isn't what happens that puts you or your family at risk for depression. It's much more about how you interpret and react to what happens.* If you take a negative event personally (internal attribution), believe it can never change (stable attribution) and that it will ruin your whole life, marriage, or career (global attribution), then you are at high risk for depression and have a lower probability of it lifting quickly. *Those styles of thinking preceded the negative event, however, and so by the time something bad happens, your patterns already had you at risk.*

Throughout your life span as an individual, and the life span of your family, many bad things will happen, just as they do for everyone. No one escapes the hurts of life: People we love die, our friends betray us, our bodies age, our investments go belly-up. If you learned, or are inadvertently teaching your own children, ineffective ways to think about the ambiguities and the hurts of life, then getting overwhelmed and depressed is an unfortunate but predictable response. You'll learn in part III that there are specific things you can learn to do that will help reduce the likelihood of hand-me-down blues.

Remember Sandy from this chapter's opening vignette? You may want to reread the vignette now in light of all you have learned about ambiguity and projection. Sandy, and all of the Sandys of the world like her, can change. She can read books like *Hand-Me-Down Blues* and she can get help and learn that her depressogenic responses aren't genetically programmed, gender-mandated, or culturally inevitable. She can take the many examples offered here and learn to choose different and better responses to the repetitive situations of life.

Sandy's son can change, too. He may have grown up and reached adulthood with a mother who never seemed to have patience or affection for him, but he can transcend the limitations of his mother (and father, too) by learning the skills *now* he never had occasion to learn before. He can learn to build trust and intimacy, he can learn to curtail self-criticism for honest mistakes, and he can learn to take action in his own behalf. Simply put, his future doesn't have to be more of the same.

Neither does yours.

It isn't your childhood that causes depression. It isn't unconscious conflicts about your right to be happy or residual guilt over having done something wrong. Depression is caused by many factors, including how you think, talk to yourself through your thoughts, interact with your loved ones and friends, interpret the meanings of your life experiences, and find fun and goodness in a world that offers all kinds of positive possibilities.

Did you *learn* depression from your family? Maybe. But this is one family legacy you *don't* have to carry on.

A SUMMARY OF KEY POINTS

- When people face ambiguity, they make *projections*, i.e., interpretations about the meaning and cause of whatever is going on. These projections hold the potential to be depressing when they lead us to believe hurtful things that may, in fact, be untrue.
- Depression is itself an ambiguous stimulus, hence the different perspectives about what causes it and the different treatment approaches as to what to do about it.
- Psychologists call the process of making meaning out of ambiguous events *attribution formation*. The style with which one makes attributions is patterned, meaning it is a fairly stable and repetitive style you respond with to various experiences over the course of your lifetime.
- Some attributional styles place a person at higher risk for depression than do others. Unless you identify your particular style, and those of your family members, and strive to identify and correct them when in error, they will continue to hold the potential to trigger depressive episodes.
- There is a strong relationship between the attributional styles of parents and their children. It is as you would expect, since children learn much of their perspective about life experiences from their parents.
- Each family also has what is known as a family atmosphere, an emotional environment for the many interactions between family

members. The emotional environment you grow up in plays a strong role in your internal emotional environment now.

- Family atmospheres can be described in a number of different ways: positive or negative, friendly or hostile, cooperative or competitive, close or distant, calm or tense, and fun or serious.
- Family attributional styles and family atmosphere encompass the expectations we have for ourselves and our family. Having or learning to have realistic expectations is an important skill in order to avoid hurt and disappointment from unmet expectations that weren't realistic.
- Families may unintentionally provide a context for learning depression. Getting stuck in blaming others isn't the least bit helpful or self-empowering. Learning about the family patterns and choosing to actively do things differently and more skillfully are essential to breaking the legacy of hand-me-down blues.

Marriage and Depression

6

Nothing has a stronger influence on their children than the unlived lives of their parents.

Carl Jung

Rick and Gabrielle discussed the possibility of going into therapy for the purpose of "giving it another try." Only two months earlier, they had decided to separate after having been married for almost eight years. The separation was portrayed as a mutual decision; in fact, Gabrielle said "I guess separation is a good idea" right after Rick told her he didn't want to be with her anymore. (Not unlike quitting right after you've been fired.) She was deeply hurt that Rick wanted out, particularly since she was under the impression that things had been starting to improve. Yes, there were times she felt angry and hurt by Rick, and yes, she often wished things were a little different between them. Yes, she often felt trapped in a relationship that couldn't or wouldn't change, but hey, things can't always be perfect, right?

Gabrielle often withdrew emotionally from Rick, but she was sure it was because he just couldn't match her emotional depth. She saw him as lacking seriousness, and was frequently put off by his seeming indifference to analyzing the deeper meanings of life experiences. Many times they had argued about Gabrielle's tearing apart the simplest of things to understand their deeper meaning while Rick said he didn't want to do that because it would ruin his enjoyment of them. Gabrielle interpreted Rick's feelings as superficial, while Rick viewed Gabrielle as a killjoy. By the time they separated, Rick told her that he just didn't think she was in the same place in life as he was. He said, "Nothing I do can make you happy and I'm tired of trying. I'm tired of feeling inadequate, and I'm tired of not having any fun in life. Life doesn't have to be so damn hard. You make it hard and I just don't want to live that way." And then he left.

Gabrielle was miserable in Rick's absence. Her feelings were terribly jumbled: She was angry he left her, glad she didn't have to deal with the problems he posed to her way of being, lonely without him to hold her, relieved to be free of his intrusions, sad they wouldn't share their lives anymore, afraid to be alone, guilty she'd driven him away, furious he didn't accept her for who she was . . .

What stuck in Gabrielle's mind the most was Rick having said "Life doesn't have to be so damn hard." She wondered why at the very core of her being she didn't believe that. Life had always *been hard for her, and so she naturally assumed it would always be hard for others. She began to wonder why this was so and began a self-exploration unlike any she had ever undertaken before. She became immersed in examining what it means to be "deep" and "profound," and what it means to be* too *deep and* too *profound, at least in regard to enjoying some of the simpler pleasures in life.*

It didn't take long for Gabrielle to realize that her ability to see the cloud behind every silver lining was a gift of sorts, but not a particularly welcome gift in certain situations, especially where others were concerned. She reviewed all the times that she had attempted to engage Rick in serious discussions about not very serious subjects. A glaring example came to mind from a time when she asked Rick why he enjoyed watching The Simpsons *when it set such a poor example for children. Rick said it was funny and the writing was great and he didn't think it had to be sociologically significant or politically correct for him to enjoy it for what it was. At the time, Gabrielle thought he was an insensitive jerk. Now she was thinking he might be onto something. She thought of another example from when they went hiking. Rick was happily musing about the beauty and peacefulness of being in nature, and Gabrielle started in on the hole in the ozone and rain-forest depletion. She accused him of being in denial about ecological deterioration, and he shot back that if she couldn't enjoy places like this, then where could she enjoy being?*

A few more similar examples came up, and Gabrielle became overwhelmed with the realization that she really had driven Rick away through her moodiness, self-absorption, and holier-than-thou attitude that she was "deep and sensitive" and so very few others were. Gabrielle was overrun with self-recriminations. She had to see Rick and share what she was coming to realize. She called and asked him to come over, and after a slight hesitation, he said okay. When she finished her tearful monologue, describing all she was realizing triggered by Rick's simple statement to her about her making life so hard, she saw the tears in Rick's eyes. She waited, then he finally spoke. Rick described in almost painful detail all the times he had tried to engage Gabrielle in lighthearted pursuits. He described how every interaction seemed like it had to be deep and from the heart. He liked that at times, but he also wanted a partner who could be fun and silly and more easygoing more of the time. He described feeling guilty for deliberately shutting out any meaningful conversation with her out of a desire to punish her for having made more complicated so many conversations that should have been simple.

Gabrielle hadn't realized how much her despairing moods had directly affected Rick, nor how difficult she'd made it for him to talk to her openly about this issue. Gabrielle suddenly understood that her bad moods were more than that, and the word depression *thundered in her brain as he went on. Then she wondered if she could function in a marriage without contaminating it, and whether she would be a suitable mother. She thought it ironic when she realized that Rick was a better partner and likely to be a better parent than she, and how totally opposite an appraisal that was from all the years they'd been married.*

When Rick finished, he took her hand and said, "Honey, the things you're realizing now are the very things I've been trying to get across to you for eight years. I love you deeply, and I'm willing to go on with you if you want to try again. I want us to enjoy our lives together and that's the only way I'd want to continue our marriage. But I don't know if you can change, and neither do you. I don't know if I can change, either. I need to be much more understanding, and much more flexible in the way I relate to you. There are lots of things I think I should've done differently, but I wasn't really sure what *to do differently. Maybe we should see a professional. . . ."*

When two people come together to form a couple, a new system is born. Immediately, true to the basic premise of systems theory, the whole is greater than the sum of its parts. If you and I are in a relationship, there are two individual partners in the relationship. But how we interact with each other holds the potential to enhance or diminish you, me, or us. And as a new system that is inevitably part of an even larger system of extended family, community, nation, and culture, how we interact invariably affects even more than just us.

Building on last chapter's consideration of how your family of origin can contribute to depression, in this chapter I will explore the relationship between marriage and depression. Specifically, how does depression in either or both of the marital partners (with or without children) affect the quality of the marriage and the family atmosphere?

DEPRESSION SPREADS

Relationships, when they're going well, can provide the euphoria that is the "high on love" poets and romantics have been describing throughout history. But when they're going badly, relationships can be a living hell.

As we saw in the opening vignette, depression in one member of a relationship invariably affects the overall quality of the couple's interactions. The relationship itself may be a trigger for someone's depression, or the relationship may serve to keep the depression going by inadvertently reinforcing the kinds of perceptions and behaviors that created it to begin with. The latter situation is evident in the relationship of Rick and Gabrielle.

People can bring their history of depression into the marriage, building the relationship on a depressed foundation, just as Gabrielle did. They can become depressed during the marriage, for reasons that might have everything to do with the quality of the marriage itself, or for reasons that have nothing to do with the marriage but adversely affect it. Depression spreads. People can become depressed after the marriage breaks up, the consequences of suffering a devastating loss. What happens when someone wants to be married, or wants to succeed in having a good, healthy, long-term relationship and then he or she fails? How someone deals with the failure of a relationship (or failure of *any* sort, for that matter) tells you a great deal about whether depression is likely to take hold in that individual.

Consider Gabrielle and Rick as a perfect example. Their eight-year marriage was clearly an intimate, committed, relatively long-term one. However, neither Gabrielle or Rick had the kinds of skills necessary to keep the marriage on a healthy track. Gabrielle had relatively poor boundaries, so she didn't monitor herself, manage her moods effectively, or set appropriate limits in her interactions with Rick. She felt entitled to spread her doom and gloom anytime, anywhere. When Rick reacted negatively to what she viewed as her perceptiveness, she felt misunderstood, unappreciated, and second-rate. She felt hopeless about things improving and helpless to do anything about it, and so in recent years she didn't even try to change or improve their relationship. She gave up, withdrew into depression, and despaired over her misfortune to be trapped in a less-than-ideal relationship.

Rick didn't know how to deal effectively with Gabrielle's moodiness and her cycles of anger and withdrawal. He was critical of her style, though not really understanding much about it. Angry at her tendency to always see the negative in things, weighted down with how heavy life always was with her, he'd clam up and refuse to discuss matters or else he'd just pick up and leave. Rick's boundaries were just as ineffectual as Gabrielle's, but in a different way. If it wasn't fun, he didn't want to talk about it. If there was a problem, it wasn't his—it belonged to whomever noticed it, namely Gabrielle. Rarely to blame for any problems, minor or major, Rick had the luxury of living in a self-created world where he could pretty much do as he wished. Nice for him—but hardly a way to function in the context of a relationship where he and another person must be both responsive and responsible to each other if it is to be a good thing. Rick was tired of Gabrielle being so high-maintenance, and so he withdrew from her. Over time, he became less and less responsive or responsible to Gabrielle, thereby unwittingly reinforcing her depressing perception that she was trapped, hopeless, and helpless.

VARIATIONS ON A MARRIAGE AND FAMILY THEME

The American family is no longer represented by the unusually pleasant fictional family on the old show *Leave It to Beaver*. Such traditional nuclear families still exist, of course, but so do many other configurations: stepfamilies (blended families), single-parent families, commuter-marriage families, foster families, special-needs-children families, and on and on. When you look past the unique properties of a particular family system's structure, there are common, underlying denominators that predispose a system to function well—or not. Many of these will be discussed in this chapter specifically as they relate to marriage and depression, including: 1) preexisting beliefs about people and intimate relationships like living together or marriage (expectations about how things "should" be); 2) attributional styles evident in interpreting others' meanings in their words and deeds; 3) the ability to develop a "we" that transcends "you" and "me"; 4) the presence or absence of other specific relationship skills (such as the ability to critically assess your own and another person's characteristics, to take responsibility for your actions, to distinguish your wants from your needs, to set limits, and to self-correct the relationship when things begin to move in an undesirable direction.

The key underlying point throughout this chapter, of course, is that depression can preclude the development of the skills necessary to build and maintain healthy relationships and thereby reduce or even prevent the possibility of a successful relationship.

PREEXISTING BELIEFS ABOUT MARRIAGE AND HOW THINGS ''SHOULD'' BE

People's feelings about themselves and their marriage are determined to a great extent by how well the marriage lives up to their expectations. If the marriage provides the things they think it should, they will likely feel just fine about it. If not, they can easily feel trapped and become miserable when they conclude there is nothing they can do to improve things.

Men and women have some similar expectations about marriage, but some different ones, too. The relationship between your gender and your ideas about what should happen in a marriage falls into the realm of what social psychologists call gender roles. Let's consider them briefly, especially as they relate to differing rates of depression and differing expectations about marriage that may predispose one to depression.

GENDER, GENDER ROLES, AND DEPRESSION

Previously, I described the epidemiology (prevalence) of depression. In that discussion, I described what appears to be a marked difference in rates of depression according to gender. The best data consistently indicate that in the United States, *and* in other Western societies, women are likely to experience depression about twice as frequently as men. The gender issue is a complex one that is receiving increased attention for its potential to be a window through which to better see specific aspects of depression.

There are likely some biological factors that may account for women's higher rate of depression, and we can consider these first. These are, primarily, hormonal factors associated with the reproductive cycle. (For example, no man is going to experience postpartum depression or the mood shifts associated with a menstrual cycle.) They are potentially significant factors, yet it is interesting to note that research on this topic shows there were no significant gender differences in the rates of depression in many low-income, non-Western societies. Consequently, biology may not be an inevitable risk factor for depression. It is also interesting that one published study indicated that Jewish males had depression in the same prevalence as women (i.e., twice as frequently as other men), further suggesting a socialization factor operating in depression that is at least as strong as biological factors.

Systems thinking demands much more than a mere biological interpretation for something as complex as depression. In considering the relationship between gender, gender roles, and depression, the relevant question is this: What role does gender play in the phenomenon of depression relative to the context of marriage?

Socialization and Gender Roles. From the time you were born, you were exposed to strong social and cultural forces that shaped your perspective in countless ways. You were told directly and indirectly through modeling by your parents, television, billboards, teachers, *everyone,* what a boy or girl could and should do. You were taught that your gender created a continuum of possibilities and, likewise, impossibilities. (Even now, there are still gender "firsts" taking place: first woman at a military institute and first woman space shuttle commander are just a couple of examples.)

Those dos and don'ts according to gender are what are known as *gender roles.* No one fully escapes culturally assigned gender roles, not even the househusband or female CEO, for even when you "do your own thing," you are still inevitably being compared to what would be more typical or "normal" for your gender (e.g., "She's a great boss, for a woman").

The influence of cultural gender roles literally begins at birth, with the differential treatments of boy and girl babies. It continues throughout childhood, of course, but is most keenly felt by self-conscious adolescents. Up until adolescence, research suggests that boys are more likely to be depressed than girls. At adolescence, some early research showed that girls are more likely to be depressed than boys. Subsequent research, however, has shown that the apparent higher rates of depression in adolescent girls may be a result of the way the data were collected more than a true representation of higher depression in adolescent girls compared to boys. Further research is necessary to clarify the issue.

Regardless of what may actually be the case, the key issue remains that adolescent boys and girls are both laboring under the weight of parental, peer, and societal pressure to be a certain way. Is it unfair to pressure them? I don't think so—the expectations of others we interact with are inevitable. I think what *is* unfair, though, is not adequately preparing adolescents to critically think through whether the expectations they face from others are worth trying to live up to.

Women are typically socialized to be other-oriented. The message is often "You're not important—what you do for others is what defines you. Be a good daughter. Be a good wife. Be a good mother. If you're able to attract and marry the right man, you'll have it made. And remember, it's just as easy to fall in love with a rich man as a poor one." By emphasizing to a woman that she is incomplete without an attachment to others, independence isn't encouraged, nor is competitiveness. So she fantasizes about finding the right guy. (She looks for "Mr. Right" but may impatiently end up instead with "Mr. Right Now.")

Women read romance novels and watch romantic movies. Men read *Playboy* and fantasize about women they'd love to get to know (in the biblical sense) for about an hour. Women typically want a close, communicative, emotionally intimate relationship, but men usually want to accomplish something. Once he's married her, what else is there to accomplish in that arena? No wonder women later complain that "he changed" after they married! But did he really? Or did she mistakenly assume that his behavior in a dating context was an appropriate indication of what he would be like in a marriage?

Gender roles have changed over the years. Half a century ago, gender roles were far more specific; "This" is what a man does, "that" is what a woman does. With the rise of feminism in the sixties and its continuing influence came the push to redefine the roles of men and women. Men could be more emotionally expressive and family-oriented ("It's okay for you to be the one pushing the baby's carriage, Big Fella"), and women could be more competitive and competent ("Sure it's fine with me if you get a job outside the house and earn six figures, honey").

If making new and freer choices became socially acceptable over the last couple of decades, then why have the rates of depression gone up for men *and* women instead of down? If men could be more emotionally attuned and women didn't have to be economically dependent, shouldn't depression have *decreased?* No, and here are my ideas as to why.

The Blurring of Gender Roles. What used to be well-specified expectations for men and women might have been restrictive, even painfully so at times, but they were nonetheless *clear.* There was an unambiguous standard defining one's range of appropriate actions, and most people didn't have to (or even *want* to) examine them very carefully. If your mother is about sixty-five or older, go ask her, "Mom, how did you decide to have children?" She will probably look at you like you are nuts! She'll probably answer, "Decide? I didn't decide. You get married, you have kids." If you blew the sequence and started to have a child first (i.e., unplanned pregnancy), then you got married. But marriage and children were a package deal.

It's hard for many women these days to understand that simple, elegant response. Instead, they tend to engage in what is known as *historical revisionism,* applying current understandings and values to times past when such understandings and values did not exist. You might remember that in 1992, when Americans were celebrating the five-hundredth anniversary of Columbus discovering America, that there were protest marches and media pundits harping on the evils of Columbus—his ethnocentrism, imperialism, antihumanism, and genocidal, mercenary ways. That's an interesting viewpoint five hundred years of social evolution later, but to judge 1492 by 1992 standards is simply foolish.

The blurring of gender roles in our society created less clarity about what we're supposed to do as men and women. While for many people the new freedoms are inspiring and provide relief from rigid social expectations, for others the ambiguity creates a crisis: "Who am I and why am I here and what am I supposed to do and what if I can't figure it out and what if I do the wrong thing or something that screws me up and why won't anyone help me?" I have previously described ambiguity as a risk factor for depression to the extent that an individual—male *or* female—is unable to create his or her own clarity for personal life decisions. When you're not clear, making decisions—even seemingly simple ones—can be an overwhelming task.

Attributional Styles and Reading Others' Words and Deeds. One of the most frequently cited examples by comedians poking fun at male–female relationships is when a woman presents a problem that is bothering her to a man and he tries to help her solve it. She reacts angrily with, "I don't want you to tell me what to do. I just want you to listen to me!" This familiar interaction is particularly interesting from a depression standpoint: He wants to take action, while she simply wants to feel his empathy or sympathy. He gets angry she doesn't *do* something, while she gets angry and hurt that she's trapped in a relationship with an insensitive jerk who can't seem to understand her.

Men are socialized to take action, and they're generally less depressed. Women are socialized to be passive, and they're more depressed. These are response styles that extend beyond specific circumstances, which is why this type of interaction can occur repeatedly throughout the course of a relationship. As family systems theorist, author, and researcher Peggy Papp pointed out, "Women who lose their voice in relationships often become depressed, and the best antidote is being heard." I would add, "And after they've been heard, they would be wise to take some positive, corrective action." Awareness, expression, empathy, and action hold outstanding antidepressant value for *both* genders.

Attributions again play a critical role in depression through such interactions. She can easily attribute his action orientation as "emotional regression," "denial," or some other flaw that makes him unable to "just listen." He can easily attribute her seeming emotionalism to "weakness" or "just wallowing." From a systems perspective, each viewpoint is incomplete without the other; both make sense, to some degree. Feeling hurt or victimized without taking action *is* a reliable path to depression. Taking action without being emotionally "tuned-in" *is* lacking in focus and likely to lead to some undesirable consequences.

Beyond the quality of the adult relationship being affected, if there are children present who are learning from your example, what are they learning? The boys who grow up modeling the kind of behavior shown by the "action Dad" above might well learn to be inattentive and impatient listening to their partners express their feelings. Do they learn to devalue honest emotional expression while simply waiting for the "take action" part? Do they learn to keep their feelings to themselves and just try to solve the problem, and thereby virtually preclude true emotional intimacy through sensitive sharing from their relationships? Do the girls learn from modeling Mom that simply expressing their feelings is more important than taking corrective actions? Do they learn that they can't really expect men to understand them? Do they learn that it's reasonable to blame insensitive men when things aren't going well?

I am not much of a fan of those popular works that amplify gender differences by saying men and women are from different planets, or worse, universes. I'm suggesting instead that we consider how gender-based issues can predispose both men *and* women to depression. Rather than make a value-laden judgment about what's the better or right way to be as a man or woman, we can use the information we've acquired about gender differences and depression to reduce each person's vulnerability. While women may be more predisposed to depression for a variety of reasons, *once men and women get depressed they suffer equally,* as recent research shows. The goal is to prevent depression whenever possible, and manage it skillfully once it appears, whatever your gender, age, race, religion, socioeconomic status, or ethnic group.

People tend to form negative appraisals of their spouse's traits when they are depressed. A comment that would seem funny when you're in a good mood seems mean when you're in a bad mood. Your partner is being thrifty when you feel all right, but cheap when you're not. Your spouse may seem independent when you're not feeling needy, and distant when you are. This is how depression can play a significant role in the decision to divorce and split up the family. The nondepressed partner hasn't really changed—what has altered is the way he or she is perceived by the partner who is depressed.

YOU, ME, AND WE

At the beginning of this chapter, I talked about a couple as a system in its own right. When two people come together, there is a you, a me, and a we. For many people, the idea of merging into a "we" is a scary one: They fear they will lose themselves to the other person, and cease to be an individual in their own right. Can one person dominate another? Of course. It happens all the time. But as an adult in an equal relationship, another person can control you only to the extent that you let him or her. There are many different relationship skills that foster good feelings, the absence of which can foster very bad feelings. Maintaining good personal boundaries that help you adhere to your sense of self while getting close to someone is among the most vital skills to develop and bring into a marriage. If you don't already have such skills, you can learn them. They can go a long way toward preventing depression.

Part of creating a healthy context for a relationship that won't foster depression is evolving a sense of protectiveness about yourself, but also about your partner. Maintaining your boundaries is one side of the equation, but respecting your partner's is the other. The "we" can be much healthier and happier when both individuals are allowed to maintain their individual views and values in an atmosphere of respect and cooperation, as we saw in the last chapter.

One of the most critical contexts for "we" to surface in is in conflict situations. That is when it is especially important to find the balance between disagreeing and behaving respectfully toward your partner. One of the ways a partner in a marriage can get worn down into a state of helplessness and hopelessness is when his or her spouse regularly fights to win at all costs, damaging self-esteem and any sense of closeness in the process. From the last chapter, you can now more carefully consider the kind of relationship atmosphere you create. What do *you* do to help your partner feel safe? Accepted? Appreciated? Cooperated with? Remember, all behavior has message value. You can learn to be very deliberate in the loving messages you put out.

People say things like "You can't make someone feel loved if they don't feel lovable." To a limited extent that's true, but it's also true that unless you provide a loving environment, how *could* he or she feel it? One of the ways to make sure a "we" never develops is to separate the other person's problems from your list of concerns, effectively isolating him or her with a dismissive "It's your problem" as if you don't have to help support your partner in an effort to solve it. Simply put, if it affects you, it affects me, and us. Depression is far more likely to surface when someone feels isolated and alone in having to deal with their problems. Losing that sense of closeness or intimacy is a trigger for most people's bad feelings.

Intimate relationships are sensitive and vulnerable contexts where depression can grow. As the research indicates, both men and women feel the pain of loss when relationships fall apart. Having realistic expectations of your partner from the very beginning can save considerable grief later.

WHEN EXPECTATIONS AND REALITY COLLIDE

Consider a depressed woman named Valerie. Valerie has been living with a fellow named Eric for about six months, and she is in a constant state of agitation about their relationship. Eric is thirty years old and has a decent job as an accounts analyst at a stock brokerage firm. He is a quiet man, but has hobbies (plays racquetball and goes to sporting events) and friends that he likes to hang out with. Valerie sees him as a good guy. He seems to be low-pressure, accepting, nice, good-natured, socially presentable to her friends, but . . . but he doesn't open up and talk about his deeper feelings. Valerie wants and expects him to open up to her. At first she thought he was just guarded and slow to trust her, maybe from a previous breakup. But six months later, their interactions still went predictably along these lines: She'd greet him warmly and he'd reciprocate. He'd ask how she was, she'd ask how he was, and then they'd get ready to go out to dinner or wherever they were going, since Eric almost always wanted to go out somewhere. Later, Valerie would tell him about something important that went on in her life, good or bad. After Eric's initial response of "Cool" or "Bummer," she'd wait for him to probe her feelings more or even express his own. When he didn't do so, she probed herself for him, as if to prompt him as to how to ask insightful questions. Nope. Her frustration would build, anger would follow, and she'd blow up at him. He'd get hurt and confused, ask her what she wanted, and listen to her say, for the thousandth time, "Communication!" Eric thought they were communicating. There were words, voices, lips moving, and everything!

Valerie turned the situation against herself. She thought, "I must be too demanding. Isn't it enough that he's a nice, gentle guy with a steady job and good friends? He's into health and he treats me well and what else can I ask for? I must be really needy and demanding and, the truth is, I'm probably not even good enough for him. I'm not good enough now and I never will be. Maybe I'm punishing him because I'm afraid he'll leave me and I can fool myself into thinking it was my decision to end the relationship by pushing him away. . . ." Valerie's thoughts spun around like this endlessly, clinically called *rumination,* another core element of depression, and her despair grew as her thoughts continued to spin.

Valerie shows a gender-typical response in assuming a greater share of the responsibility for the quality of the relationship. Despite women having attained parity with men in a variety of ways, studies show that women still tend to feel more responsible than men do for the health of their relationships. Can you see how this perception increases the vulnerability to depression if the relationship falters?

Valerie's agitation and depression are a typical product of attribution errors. She faces the ambiguity of Eric's lack of communicativeness and attributes it to her being too demanding and not accepting enough. She hopelessly concludes she'll *never* be good enough. Valerie is operating on the faulty premise that if she digs deeply enough, she'll find the wealth of Eric's emotional self. Why does she assume, though, that there even *is* a deeper emotional self in Eric? Instead of blaming herself and feeling terrible that she's somehow not good enough, why doesn't it occur to her that maybe he doesn't even *have* a deeper self?

This is an example of how individual belief systems set people up for depression when their beliefs contradict reality. Instead of questioning or adjusting their beliefs to fit the facts, a fundamental skill in clear thinking, people are more likely to twist the facts to fit their beliefs. Valerie believes each person has deeper feelings and a soft core (unfortunately, she's read a lot of "inner child" books) that can be accessed in anybody if only you approach him or her in the right way. The truth is, though, that Eric isn't all that deep or complicated. His feelings are right on the surface, he tells you what he does or doesn't like, and he doesn't give issues much more thought than whether they're good or bad, interesting or dull. Meanwhile, Valerie keeps digging for more and is getting more frustrated, hurt, and depressed believing that "Eric doesn't trust me or love me or else he'd open up to me."

Is it reasonable for Valerie to want a partner who can communicate about more than who won the big game? Is it a legitimate need to have her partner engage with her on a deeper level? Yes. Is it up to her to make Eric a deeper thinker? No. Yet she blames herself and feels hurt, cheated, and depressed. She may be right to want a deeper relationship, and she's certainly free to pursue that desire. But look at who she's asking to fill that desire! A basic rule in *any* relationship is, "Don't ask for or expect to get from people things they don't have."

It's easy to see how negative feelings can fester and become depression when people find themselves in emotionally limited or damaging relationships. But all too often they've placed and then kept themselves there through misattributions and erroneous beliefs absorbed through family and cultural influences. In Valerie's case, she absorbed the popular idea that there is always some deeper self in everyone to explore and share as the basis for intimacy. As a result, she ignored the equally popular notion, certainly true in this case, that "what you see is what you get."

What about those situations where a person's expectations don't seem unrealistic? There are many times when someone is led to believe that his or her partner can meet those needs because he or she listens, professes to understand, and directly agrees to them. For example, he says, "Okay, I'll cut down on my drinking; I didn't know it was such a big deal for you," but he never actually does. Or, she says, "Okay, I won't bring so much work home with me and I'll spend more time with the family," but after a couple of weeks she's right back to working as long and as hard as ever.

In such situations, it *still* comes down to the issue of unrealistic expectations. Just because you tell me you can do something, should I believe you? Just because I've been disappointed by others who said similar things in the past and didn't do them, should I disbelieve you? Again we face ambiguity: How can I know what you are capable of in order to have realistic expectations of you? Developing realistic expectations for others represents a most worthwhile skill that holds great antidepressant potential.

People get attracted to each other, plan to marry and have a family on the basis of a few dates, good sex, and some global, mystical quality called chemistry. In short, they follow their feelings. Following your feelings, "listening to your heart," isn't a bad strategy *if* your feelings are accurately representing what's going on. But, far more often than not, feelings are deceptive. FEELINGS CAN LIE! You can feel someone is trustworthy who betrays you right after you go to bed together. You can think someone is really nice who turns out to be incredibly selfish and insensitive. FEELINGS CAN LIE! You can feel you have a need that is really just a wish. You can feel you're entitled to have your needs met and then ask someone to meet them who is utterly incapable because you mistakenly feel that "if he or she really cared, they'd do it." *A great deal of depression in marriage could be prevented if people would use their feelings as one measure of what's going on but also think critically and look for evidence in the other person's ongoing behavior that he or she can really be the kind of partner they want.*

The important point, of course, is that people come into dating and marital relationships with an established set of expectations about how things should be, and those expectations represent genuine risk factors for depression. If the expectations are met, depression isn't nearly as likely. If not, a chain reaction occurs that can easily culminate in depression.

The real art of making a marriage (or other committed relationship) a place of comfort instead of pain is *knowing* what you need, want, and expect, and to what degree the other person can meet those needs, wants, and expectations. Likewise, the other person has to know his or her needs, wants, and expectations, and have a realistic way to determine whether you're a worthwhile investment. I think premarital counseling can be an enormously valuable tool in facilitating this process. It's a shame that often the people who most need it don't take the steps to get it.

DEPRESSION IN MARRIAGE

There are those who would suggest marriage is an antiquated institution that preceded modern extended life spans, and that no one person can possibly meet your lifelong needs. I don't believe that for a second. If two people are self-aware, can realistically anticipate life changes, and can evolve a strong sense of "it's us dealing with life" rather than "it's you against me," two people can usually (not always, of course) transcend the problems life hands them and enjoy the gifts it provides.

A deep and committed love can provide the foundation for optimism and the strength of knowing that whatever you face in life, good or bad, you're attached to someone who will support and love you. Love has remarkable healing properties, and a healthy romance is an antidepressant far superior to any drug you can take.

We have now considered many of the factors that lead people to bring depression into marriage, ranging from family background to socialized but often unrealistic expectations and even the lack of specific skills in forming positive relationships. What about the situation where depression surfaces in one or both partners during the course of a marriage when neither one had ever been depressed before? What do we know about how one spouse's depression affects the other, nondepressed spouse? And, how does one spouse's depression affect the marriage in general, particularly when there are children involved?

The research about the relationship between marriage and depression makes it clear that when partners lose their ability to have fun together or enjoy each other's company, and when they only focus on the negatives (the bills, the work pressure, the things that need to be done around the house), the likelihood of depression increases. The evidence is that at least half the people who are diagnosed as depressed are having marital problems, and that at least half the people who seek therapy for marital problems are depressed. *Marital distress often precedes depression, marital conflict is highly predictive of later depression, and an increase in marital conflict related to other stressful life events is a most common trigger for depression.* Furthermore, when a depressed spouse recovers from a depressive episode, there is a higher risk for relapses when the person is living in a critical and negative environment.

Gender differences play a significant role here, too. Family therapist Peggy Papp and her colleagues began the Ackerman Institute's Depression in Context Project in 1991, studying the gender-based variables common to depression in men and women. Papp describes disruptions in a woman's closest relationships as the most common trigger for depression, while for men it is threats to his self-esteem, like being demoted or fired. The cultural mandates for a woman to connect and a man to achieve are *very* deeply ingrained. Interestingly, though, Papp notices that getting men more emotionally connected (more sensitive and responsive) to their wives reduces their depression. Independent of gender, *everyone* benefits from closer, healthier, more loving and respectful relationships.

There are few things as depressing as feeling trapped and lonely in a marriage. It should be exceedingly clear that keeping romance and love alive for a lifetime involves having realistic expectations and generally (but not always) a stronger sense of "us" than of either "you" or "me."

A DEPRESSED SPOUSE AND A SUFFERING MARRIAGE

Having considered how someone's family history, preexisting beliefs, expectations, and attributional style might serve as risk factors that predispose them to later episodes of depression, let's turn our attention now to what happens when depression erupts in the marriage.

Regardless of whether it is the husband or the wife who develops depression, the effects on the partner and the marriage can be devastating. Depression is characterized by passivity, hopelessness, and negativity. The helpful spouse naturally wants to push the depressed spouse a little by encouraging positive action, open communication, and participation in activities that will restore some semblance of his or her life before depression surfaced. As you can appreciate, when you try to mobilize your partner, someone you love and desperately want to see acting and feeling "normal" again, and all you meet is apathy and little in the way of meaningful responsiveness, the frustration level can rise quite quickly. This is one of the most difficult things about loving and wanting to support someone who is depressed: Despite your best efforts, your spouse can defeat your good intentions simply by doing *nothing*. He or she doesn't have to actively resist your help and do things to sabotage your attempts to help. All they have to do is not answer, not move, not make eye contact, not try.

Reactions are different when it's the first depressive episode than when it's the third or eighth. Depression has a relatively high rate of recurrence, and so multiple episodes are not uncommon. The support and under- standing a loving spouse might provide the first time around can easily fade with each additional episode.

Under normal circumstances, when someone is sick or suffers some disorder it elicits sympathy from others around him or her. People can, on a temporary basis, be wonderfully patient and empathetic, and make short-term sacrifices for the well-being of the loved one. But when an episode of depression goes on and on with no apparent relief in sight, only a bona fide saint can possibly remain patient and understanding indefinitely. The reality is that such difficult conditions wear on people, exhausting and frustrating them, and it has nothing to do at all with how much they did or didn't love the depressed person beforehand.

Consequently, what starts out as a disruptive and confusing depression that initially elicits appropriate concern and caring can soon elicit only resentment and withdrawal. Partners of depression sufferers who don't understand depression often form the erroneous conclusion that if their spouse really wanted to snap out of it, then all they'd have to do is "start acting normal." That is the equivalent of telling a depressed person to "cheer up!" It's technically correct, of course, since overcoming depression means cheering up. But telling someone to do that is only likely to make matters worse for the implicit accusation that "you're not trying." It is no wonder that family members and even psychotherapists who should know better often form the conclusion that the person must, at some level, actually enjoy the depression or be benefiting from it by receiving additional attention or indirect rewards. This is a cruel response of blaming the victim. When partners of depressed people catch themselves in the midst of their anger and frustration, normal feelings given the circumstances, they typically feel guilty and selfish, and can become quite self-critical. The result, unfortunately, can be depression.

While some spouses become overwhelmed and resentful, and withdraw from their depressed partners in an effort to save themselves from a similar fate, other spouses become caretakers. They adopt quite readily the role of being in charge of the depressed spouse, and take on the responsibility of getting him or her to doctor's appointments, administering medications, fluffing his or her pillows, and serving meals in bed. They try and elminate stress for their partner by quickly grabbing the phone when it rings to screen calls, or not asking the person to go places or do things they don't want to do. They may even go so far as to protect their depressed partner from any bad news or negativity, somehow fooling themselves into believing they can protect their fragile spouse from the realities of life. Is this a good thing to do? Generally not. Taking steps to reduce stress isn't a bad idea, but better for a spouse of a depressed person is to avoid saying and doing the things that reinforce helplessness and hopelessness, the key components of depression.

How the depressed person treats his or her spouse during depressive episodes is another critical factor in how the marriage fares. It is difficult, but necessary nonetheless, for the depressed spouse do as much as he or she can possibly do to protect other members of the family from the negative effects of feeling so badly. Leveling and telling the others in your family that you're hurting is essential. However, using your depression as permission to say mean and hurtful things to others either inadvertently or just to make them suffer, too, may be understandable ("misery loves company"), but is destructive and should not be tolerated by anyone. It is an obvious indication of lacking the skills to compartmentalize pain, and getting help to learn to do so is important for your family's well-being and for your own as well. There's no sense in adding more things to feel lousy about to the pile.

The key point, of course, is that if you're married and you have a family, then depression isn't only your problem. You have to be tuned-in to how your depression is affecting others, perhaps driving them away even though you don't intend to, or turning them into guardians and tasking them with trying to protect you from life. It's more important that you create and follow a treatment plan that will turn things around.

When the marriage suffers because of the depression of one or both partners, the issue that most often arises is the possibility of divorce. It comes up on both sides, too. Partners of depressed individuals can and do ask themselves, "Is this really the life I want? Do I want to live with someone who is a shell of his or her former self, not even knowing whether he or she will ever get back to normal? Do I want to become depressed, too, just by staying trapped in this painful marriage?" Partners who are themselcves depressed can and do ask themselves, "Is this really the life I want? Do I want to live with someone who is such a pain in the neck to be around? Wouldn't I be happier, wouldn't it be more fun and exciting, with a different partner, someone who was less this and more that? How much of my depression is about this marriage wearing on me, anyway?"

Thus a major life decision that can have profound consequences for husbands, wives, children, and families can be made at a time of peak frustration and unhappiness. Depression goes away, but the divorce decree stays. To make such an important and potentially life-changing decision on the basis of depression affecting one or both partners in the marriage is generally a bad idea. The first goal should be to get the depression resolved, and the next should be to address whatever damage might have been done to the marriage and the family during the low times.

A DEPRESSED SPOUSE AND A SUFFERING FAMILY

When the contagion of depression spreads, children tend to be every bit as vulnerable to catching it as spouses, perhaps even more so. The reactions are quite similar in children initially trying to be understanding and empathetic, and then becoming frustrated and resentful that their mom or dad just isn't there in the way they need him or her to be. As you know, depression tends to absorb people inside themselves, and consequently their level of awareness for others' needs, and their diminished available energy to meet those needs, can have a most detrimental impact on vulnerable others. Children are often especially vulnerable because they tend to take things personally anyway (called *egocentric thinking),* and because they have fewer personal resources on which to draw when they're so dependent on their parents for feedback and guidance. A child might well attribute his parent's depression to himself, particularly when the child tries to engage the parent in conversation or play and the parent is unresponsive due to the depression. A parent's detachment can easily be mistaken for indifference, and the child's erroneous and painful conclusion is that Mom or Dad doesn't love him. That core belief can generate a lifetime of feelings of being undeserving, inadequate, and unlovable—a particularly serious manifestation of hand-me-down blues.

Last chapter's discussion of family atmosphere is especially relevant here. If a child becomes burdened at a young age with having to cope with a parent's debilitating condition that doesn't seem to be anything more than an enduring, very bad mood, he can readily get absorbed in a view of life as both difficult and painful. The child has to make all kinds of personal sacrifices ("I can't ask Dad to come see me play baseball and I can't ask Mom to come to my school play,") and accommodations

("When you come home from school, first check and see how Mom's feeling before you tell her about whatever happened during the day to see if she's in the mood to hear about it"). When depression surfaces in the family, certain sacrifices and accommodations *may* realistically have to be made, but each concession to depression should be made carefully, lest it consume everyone.

Just as a well-meaning spouse can become a caretaker, so can a well-meaning child. It is often the case that a child discovers one of the roles that will get almost instant approval is the role of helper. Some clinicians call this the *parentified child,* for the child is taking on a role more appropriate to a spouse. The child takes on the responsibilities of a parent trying to keep the family together, and so he arranges meals, does errands, even handles aspects of the family business. While he gets positive feedback from either or both parents for being "such a fine little trooper when the chips are down," reinforcing the child's desire to stay in that role, his childhood quietly slips away. Such a child will be blessed with a well-developed sense of responsibility, and cursed with it, too, for all the lightheartedness and fun of youth he will never know.

Clearly the presence of depression in marriage is a powerful factor in shaping the quality of the marriage, and the reverse is true as well. In the next chapter, I will focus more on specific aspects of relationships between parents and children that lend themselves to hand-me-down blues.

A SUMMARY OF KEY POINTS

- Closeness and love are fundamental human needs, and when people have the comfort of good relationships, in general they do better in terms of quality of life. Consequently, a healthy marriage can serve as means of both prevention and treatment for depression.
- Conversely, the evidence is considerable that marital problems are a powerful factor in depression. Depression can be a trigger, a consequence, or simply a factor to consider in marital discord. Thus, wherever there is a depressed individual, there is likely to be someone else adversely affected. There are some compelling reasons why the depressed person's partner should be included in the treatment process.
- People come into marriage with a family history, and beliefs and

expectations that can put them at risk for depression in the marriage. These factors need to be identified and addressed skillfully if the marriage is to be a healthy one. Love isn't enough to compensate for the unexplored risk factors people bring to a marriage.

- Gender roles formed from family and cultural influences are a particularly powerful influence on men's and women's ideas of what to expect or demand from a marriage. Gender roles are less clear now than ever before. For many, the lack of clearly defined roles has led to dissatisfaction and even depression.

- One of the way men's and women's gender roles surface is in their differing rates of depression and the styles each gender stereotypically has in dealing with adversity. Men are generally socialized to be more action-oriented than women, which may seem to hinder communication at times but also serves to reduce depression.

- An important part of creating a healthy context for a relationship is evolving a sense of protectiveness, establishing a "we" that is sometimes more important than just "you" or "me." When you learn to think systemically, you recognize that the things you say and do affect others.

- People often have difficulty distinguishing what they want from others and what is realistic to expect from them. The times that partners in a marriage are most likely to be dissatisfied is when they have expectations that go unfulfilled. Falling in love with someone doesn't have to preclude thinking about them on a logical level, too.

- When depression surfaces in a marriage, it has a different but equally profound effect on the nondepressed spouse and family members. People might initially be supportive and empathetic, but they often withdraw after repeatedly failing in their efforts, giving up in frustration and anger.

- Often when depression surfaces in a marriage, if it persists or recurs frequently, one or both of the partners may think of divorce as the best option. Generally, divorce is turned to too quickly by too many when in fact the relationship can get back on a positive track with the right kind of attention to both depression and the relationship.

- Women and men are both reactive, albeit sometimes in different ways, to the stresses of marital discord. Letting a doctor drug your depressed spouse is *not* going to resolve the distress in your marriage when the distress is the result of unfulfilled expectations, unmet needs, poor communication, and perhaps even hostility.

• Children can be especially sensitive to the effects of a parent's depression, perhaps blaming themselves or assuming more adult responsibilities than they would otherwise have to if conditions were more normal. The effect can be profound in either case, another variation of hand-me-down blues.

Hand-Me-Down Blues

If there is anything that we wish to change in the child, we should first examine it and see whether it is not something that could better be changed in ourselves.

Carl Jung

By the time Roz and Lenny decided to divorce, considerable damage had already been done. Alex was only nine years old, but despite his young age he had been witness to some of the worst sides of human behavior and some of the most destructive actions that people can take against members of their own family. Alex had struggled for months with the harsh reality that his parents were too angry and spiteful to ever resolve their differences. He was sure a divorce would happen, and he couldn't decide if that was good or bad.

Alex truly didn't know what it was that had turned them into such angry, bitter people. Maybe if he listened more carefully to their arguments he'd find out, but he couldn't bring himself to stay anywhere near them when the two were together, much less when they were arguing. They had stopped trying to act like a family and go places and do things together a long time ago. Every once in a while, one or the other of his parents would seem to suddenly remember that Alex was alive and living with them and make a lame, obligatory offer to take him to a movie or out to eat. Even at those times, they were simply too internally preoccupied to notice that they'd already asked, "So, how's school?" several times earlier in their stilted conversation.

Alex spent more and more time alone in his room, wishing things were the way they used to be. Once, Roz came in and asked him why he was just sitting there and not going out to play on such a nice day. Alex slowly answered that he just didn't feel like it. Roz didn't ask anything further, an opportunity to engage with Alex lost. When she started to leave, Alex asked if she and Dad were ever going to be nice to each other again. A hard look came over her, and she started to say something, apparently thought the better of it, and left without answering. Another time, Alex asked his dad if he wished he'd never gotten married and had a son. Lenny looked at him sharply and seemed angry at the question, then softened when he seemed to realize its implication. All he said was, "Sometimes, son, things just don't work out the way you want them to." He didn't elaborate. Another opportunity to say something more personally meaningful to Alex was lost, leaving a confused nine-year-old to try and work it all out for himself.

Alex was trapped between parents too consumed by their own hurt and anger to notice his subtle changes. Besides spending less time playing and more time alone, Alex was clearly showing more signs of stress. He didn't want to have to get on the phone to talk to his grandparents, and when he did he gave one-word answers. He didn't laugh at jokes much anymore, and he grew much less curious about the world around him. He used to be very curious about all kinds of things. Now, when he was supposed to be doing his homework for school, he couldn't concentrate. Again, neither Roz nor Lenny noticed that when they'd check on him and then check on him again an hour later, he'd still be doing the same page of his math assignment. His schoolwork was suffering, he was clearly unhappy, and he was caving in under the realization that there was nothing he could do to change things.

Roz and Lenny sat him down one night and gave him their hastily rehearsed speech: "We love you but we don't love each other. We will always love you, but we can't live together anymore. We're not happy in our marriage. It's no one's fault, it's just the way it is. We've talked a lot about it and here's what we've decided. . . ." Alex had known this was coming, but he panicked nonetheless. He ran from the room, screamed, "You never loved me, why are you doing this to me?" slammed the door, and started throwing his things around his room. First Lenny went in and tried to console him and explain further that he still loved him, he'd still see him and spend time with him, he was his only son and would always be his son, and on and on. Alex never heard any of it, so enraged and hurt was he.

Lenny left, and then it was time for Roz to take a turn. She said he'd be with her, he'd still have his room in his house and go to the same school and have the same friends and things would pretty much be the same, just without

Dad and, after all, he was at work most of the time anyway, wasn't he? Alex pulled away from her touch and looked at her with a hostility she'd never before seen in his eyes. She backed out of his room and mumbled, "We'll talk again later, after you've had a chance to calm down."

Alex grew angrier, but eventually acquiesced to the inevitable. Weeks later, with Dad already gone and Mom regularly spewing attacks on how much he had screwed up her life and what a jerk he was, Alex couldn't take it anymore. Every day was filled with anger and more loneliness than he could bear. He couldn't remember the last time either of his parents had spontaneously told him they loved him and really been with him in an attentive, caring way.

Alex fantasized regularly about some miracle happening that could make things go back to happier times, but the universe didn't provide any. Instead, he was dragged into talking to the court-appointed family counselor, Mom's attorney, Dad's attorney, the court's family mediator, the court-appointed psychologist, the school counselor, and all the go-betweens who were each playing some part in getting the custody dispute that had begun on the road to resolution. Things went from bad to worse. Everybody pretended to ask him what he wanted as if it mattered, but it was clear no one was really listening. They'd each say some variation of "Gee, Alex, I know this must be hard for you, but . . ." Then they'd give some elaborate explanation that never made sense to him for why things were going the way they were and why he'd have to answer more questions from some other creep in a suit.

People were surprised Alex took the divorce so hard. They'd say stuff like "Oh, you'll get over it" and "It's hard at first, but it'll be better for everyone in the long run, including you." When Alex didn't seem to be getting over it as quickly as everyone thought he should, he was criticized: "Grow up, Alex. Be a man. Stop your pouting and whining. Life is hard sometimes, deal with it. Accept what you can't change." As far as Alex could tell, no one really understood what he was going through. He was growing ever more firm in his beliefs that no one tells the truth, no one could be trusted, no one really cared about him, and no one could do a damn thing to help him. Years later, unfortunately, he still felt that way. He'd just gotten much better at keeping those thoughts to himself. And as long as he did his homework and kept his grades decent, it seemed no one ever really asked what he thought, anyway.

DEPRESSED PARENTS RAISING CHILDREN

The most salient implication of hand-me-down blues is that *if you truly want to help children, help their parents.* The prevalence of depression is highest among those ages twenty-five to forty-four. The fastest-growing age group of depression sufferers are adolescents—the children of baby boomers. With both generations struggling with depression, how available can each be to the other in order to help? Parents, whose role is vital in shaping the worlds of their children, are too self-absorbed as they struggle with their own stresses, fears, doubts, isolation, sense of entitlement, and unfulfilled expectations, to be genuinely attuned to their children's needs.

For the purpose of this discussion, let's focus on a moderate picture of an American family. Let's assume neither Mom or Dad is violent, drug-addicted, seriously mentally ill, or abusive. Let's assume a pretty "normal" household setup—a modest home, working parents, kids in school, no major life dramas going on. But, let's also assume that Mom and/or Dad are among what I call the walking wounded. They do their jobs, pay their bills, do their chores, carry out their responsibilities; but they live in the colorless shadow of being depressed, even though no one seems to really notice it. Where does the depression in their children come from when things seem pretty normal?

To answer this all-important question, we can now elaborate on the complex and strong relationship between parents' attributional styles and that of their children. As you can recall from the discussion in chapter 5, an attributional style is the characteristic (patterned) manner in which an individual interprets and reacts to the various causal events in his or her life. Parents are the people most responsible for introducing the child to various life experiences, and as they do so they *inevitably* reveal their own values, perspectives, and biases. Thus, they model a style of thinking about and reacting to life experiences through their mere existence. Children cannot help but be influenced by their parents' style of living, and so it is no surprise that children evolve an attributional style that so closely parallels that of their parents. Unfortunately, too often that style predisposes the person, adult or child, to depression.

There are three specific characteristics of a person's attributional style that are most powerful in shaping viewpoint toward self and life experiences. These were first described in simpler terms in chapter 5 as: 1) how personally you tend to take things, known as internal or external attributions; 2) how enduring you think conditions will be, known as stable or unstable attributions; and 3) how much of your life is affected by a particular event, known as global or specific attributions. Given their pivotal role in hand-me-down blues, we can now examine these patterns in greater detail as they apply to parents unwittingly passing on a depressive attributional style to their children.

INTERNAL/EXTERNAL ATTRIBUTIONS

David couldn't remember ever hearing his parents argue so ferociously. Even in his room with the door closed, and with them in their room with their door closed, he could hear his mom screaming "How could you?" to his dad, and his dad saying, "You're the one who let yourself go. Why is it my problem?" David wasn't even sure what the argument was about, but he knew better than to ask.

After that night, the tension in the house was so thick you could barely breathe being in the same room with either of them. And then Mom seemed to go crazy. She started exercising furiously and would eat hardly anything. David couldn't even have a normal conversation with her. While he ignored her unusual behavior, he knew something weird was going on, but he just didn't know what. One time when he mustered the courage to ask her, she pounced on him and told him it was none of his business. Dad said exactly the same thing to him when asked. David's worries about his mom increased along with her frenetic activity and extreme preoccupation with sudden and dramatic weight loss. After a while he couldn't sleep, couldn't concentrate on his schoolwork, and felt heavily burdened with the knowledge that something terrible was going on that no one would talk to him about. His immediate thought was that it must somehow be his fault, but straining his brain to figure out what he might have done left him only tired and still clueless.

When David's mom sank into a deeper despair than she could ever remember being in, a friend physically hauled her off to see a therapist. She was smart enough to let herself be hauled. When she told the therapist that she was devastated because she discovered that her husband had been seeing someone else, the therapist was quite sympathetic to her distress. When she added that it was her fault he'd strayed because she had gained some weight over the last few years, the therapist's sympathy turned to alarm.

The first attributional pattern you can learn to identify is the internal versus external attribution. When something happens, do you attribute it to yourself (internal) or do you attribute it to others or outside circumstances (external)? This attributional pattern is the one associated with *personalization*, i.e., whether you do or don't tend to take things personally even when they have nothing to do with you, just as David and his mom did in the above vignette. Consider three common examples in order to better understand the internal versus external attributional pattern.

After you read each one, identify whether the person in the example is demonstrating an internal or external attribution.

Example #1: Mom says to her daughter, "Hurry up—it's time to go to school. You'll miss the bus if you don't get moving." Her daughter continues to play and dawdle along as if she never heard Mom. Mom thinks to herself, "She must really have a lot of anger at me. She's so passive-aggressive in the way she defies me."

Example #2: A man gets put on probation at work along with a number of his coworkers for fudging their time cards. He explains to his wife, "I had to do it—everyone else was. They would've thought I was a wimp if I didn't. At least we're all in this together. It's not like I'm the only one."

Example #3: A woman explains to her husband why she has to give her brother a sizable amount of money. "I know he's always screwed up in the past, but I'm the only sister he has and if he wants to try and get a new business going, I think we should support his efforts. After all, if I had given him more money the last time he probably would have never gotten so stressed out and started drinking again and lost the business."

In the first example, Mom is attributing her daughter's behavior of playing and dawdling when she's supposed to be getting ready for school to anger at her that is being communicated passive-aggressively. *(Passive-*

aggressive is a common psychological term meaning anger that is indirectly communicated.) Mom's attribution is an *internal* one—she attributes her daughter's behavior to something about herself (the target of anger) and not about her daughter (who may just want to play).

In the second example, the man attributes his time-card-fudging behavior to the *external* environment—it's about what his coworkers "made" him do, not what he chose to do.

In the third example, the woman attributes her brother's past job failure and alcoholism to her inadequately funding him. She's feels his success is up to her, and so hers is an *internal* attribution.

I would hope that you already recognize that in each of the examples, the person made an attributional error. Daughter's dawdling is about daughter; Mom can certainly do some things to change her daughter's behavior, but not necessarily because it is directed at Mom personally. (It *might* be, but what facts are there to support or refute this projection?) The employee is blaming others (external attribution) for an action *he* chose to take. Ultimately, he is responsible for his own actions. (So are we all.) The wife is *not* responsible (despite her internal attribution) for her brother's finances, business decisions, stress management, or alcoholism.

Can you see how an attribution error can lead to depression? In the first example, you have a mom who might well come to believe her own daughter hates her—hardly a comforting, self-esteem-building, relation-ship-enhancing perspective. In the second example, you have a man who doesn't take responsibility for himself, blames others, and likely drives honest and responsible people away. He'll likely see himself as the victim of their insensitivity, and either get angrier and more explosive or more sullen and withdrawn. In the third example, you have a woman whose self-esteem will, to a significant extent, rise and fall with how her brother does, since she has assumed responsibility for his success. It's hard to feel you're in control of your life when you are out of control of the things that affect you. Depression feeds on situations such as these.

STABLE/UNSTABLE ATTRIBUTIONS

When Mack lost his job at the plant, he was inconsolable. He had worked there for twenty-seven years, building a career that took him from front line assembly to midlevel management. He knew the plant's operations inside out, and he was a solid performer. But when the plant was taken over by a big conglomerate, the more senior and therefore more expensive employees were given their walking papers.

Mack knew it was coming weeks before he was let go, but he had hoped and prayed that somehow company loyalty and an outstanding track record would save his job. He had always believed that there was more to business than money—that it was at least as much about people, too. When his hopes were dashed, Mack went home and went to bed, a behavior most unusual for him in previous times of stress. His wife, Betty, and son, Mack, Jr., were surprised but understanding.

A week later, Mack was still in bed. He hadn't shaved, had only showered once or twice that entire week, eaten next to nothing, and was mute in response to the polite queries and concerns from Mack, Jr., and Betty.

A month later, little had changed. Mack got up occasionally and shuffled from one room to the next, but he was clearly off in another world. Betty handled the family business herself now, not wanting to trouble Mack with mundane things like the mortgage and the latest aplliance to go on the blink. Mack, Jr., gave him a wide berth, avoiding all but the most necessary and polite superficial exchanges.

Betty and Mack, Jr., deliberated frequently as to what they could do to try to get Mack to address his obvious anguish. Betty decided to broach the subject directly; that approach hadn't been tried yet, out of the hope Mack would open up on his own. He didn't, of course, so Betty decided to say something to lift his spirits. In one such exchange, Betty made the mistake of saying quite optimistically, "There'll be another job for you, Mack." There was fury in his eyes and voice when he said, in a shout of a whisper, "There will never be another job for me. I lost everything and I'll never get it back. I'm fifty-two years old, unemployed and unemployable, and you know it. I'm as good as dead, so don't tell me that crap."

The second attributional pattern to consider is the stable versus unstable attribution. This refers to the person's perceptions regarding whether the current circumstances are going to continue (stable attribution) or are going to end (unstable attribution). The perceived relative *permanence* of a circumstance profoundly influences some of the most critical aspects of depression. The value of a *realistic hopefulness* about the future in recovering from depression cannot be overstated; hope motivates people to try rather than just give up, and hope keeps one involved rather than withdrawn. Stable attributions reflect an attitude that "things will never change." Consider the following examples and see if you can identify whether the person in the example is demonstrating a stable or unstable attribution.

Example #1: A single mother of two daughters is jilted by her boyfriend of one year. He tells her he loves her but isn't *in love* with her, and he wants to find a woman closer to his ideal of what he wants in a partner. Hurt, angry, and missing him, she breaks down in front of her daughters and tearfully says, "Don't ever let yourself be vulnerable to men. They are selfish and not to be trusted. I swear to you, I'll never fall in love again."

Example #2: A boy is waiting for his dad to pick him up for their weekend visitation together. The divorce only occurred a couple of months ago, and visitation has no comfortable or natural feel to it yet. Wishing the nightmare were over and that his parents would find a way to get back together, he thinks, "Maybe if I talk to them again and tell them how much I hate this, this time they'll listen and we can be a family again."

Example #3: A teenage couple is passionately involved in a "forbidden love" because he's black and she's white. Neither feels capable of telling their parents about their feelings for the other, fearful it would lead to rejection, beatings, or worse. They decide that if they can't be together, they don't want to live at all. Their intertwined bodies are found in the nearby woods two days later.

In the first example, the woman attributes her emotional pain to being vulnerable to men. When she says she will *never* let herself be vulnerable again, she is envisioning (and quite possibly creating) a permanent absence of men and romance in her future. Hers is a *stable attribution* that she will always feel this way—hurt, betrayed, and forever needing to keep vigilant against caring about a man.

In the second example, the boy has the classic wish of a broken family reunited. He holds an *unstable attribution,* believing that if he approaches things in the "right" way, he may be able to get his family back together again. He views the situation as changeable, and he is hopeful as a result. The problem, of course, is that the actual variables that determine the probability of his parents reuniting are unknown to him. In this context, hopefulness hurts.

In the third example, two passionate young lovers share the tragic perspective that nothing will change that would ever allow them to be together. Their *stable attribution* tells them it is hopeless and way beyond their abilities to cope with the pain of that despair. In this context, hopelessness is fatal.

There is no other single factor that is more influential in determining who gets depressed, whether they recover partially or completely, quickly or slowly, and whether they relapse than the factor of expectancy. Expectancy refers to your view of the future in regard to the specific situations that concern you. If you believe you can change, your family can change, and things can improve, then you are much more likely to expend meaningful effort in that direction. If, on the other hand, your expectancy is negative, i.e., that nothing can change or improve, then the natural consequence of your negative expectancy is to give up, withdraw apathetically, and say "Why bother? Nothing will make a difference in this crazy family."

Negative expectancy is a core component of depression. Only about 20 percent to 25 percent of depression sufferers bother to seek professional help, even though help is readily available and is quite likely to benefit them. If you or a family member has resisted getting help, even self-help, because of negative expectancy, it's time to realize that this is part of the disorder. It's a viewpoint, *not* a fact, and a very limited viewpoint at that.

When a family system experiences a crisis or a problem of some sort, like an accident or disease in one or more of its members, do people view this as a permanent change or a temporary episode? The position the family takes at such times is a strong predictor of whether the family will cave in or cope. People can too easily forget that bad times are generally transient—they don't last for very long. It's equally true about good times, and that's the point: Life is forever handing each of us good and not-so-good times, and the idea, of course, is to try and maximize the good times and minimize the bad times. This requires skill. The family can show strength in dealing with problems directly and solving them, thereby demonstrating to all that bad times don't last forever; or the family can cave in and disintegrate into warring factions that undermine each other's ability to cope and in the process make hurtful decisions that are sure to only make matters worse. The healthiest families recognize and live with the principle that "This, too, shall pass." You may not have realized it until now, but that is a strong statement of positive expectancy.

As you are learning, unrealistic positive expectancy (as in the boy wishing for a reunited family) can also be a path into depression. The relationship between the quality of your expectations—for your future, your children, your marriage, *whatever*—and what actually happens in your life is a powerful factor in the absence or presence of depression, and so must be carefully considered.

GLOBAL/SPECIFIC ATTRIBUTIONS

Marsha was more rushed than usual, which is hard to imagine given the frantic pace at which she typically moved through life. She had a thousand errands to do that day, somehow to be made to fit around her long day on the job. But Eddie seemed to move ever slower the more she asked him to hurry up and get ready for school, and traffic seemed to follow his example. Marsha didn't say much to Eddie on the ride to school that morning, but Eddie's nonstop, good-natured chatter made it clear he either didn't notice or didn't care. Eddie was only five, but he was already a worldly little guy. Marsha loved him beyond words, but this morning he was an impediment to the rapid progress she hoped to make on her errand list. Nevertheless, Marsha kept her impatient feelings to herself, dropped him off without incident, and went on her way.

The day got worse in terms of the pressures mounting on Marsha. She was assigned two new projects despite not having enough time for the ones she was already behind on, and she was dismayed when she realized she hadn't yet delivered the one she had completed days ago. Add that to the list of "must-do's" after work.

By the time she went to pick up Eddie, she was nothing short of frazzled. Only a few minutes into the ride, only minimally attentive to Eddie's description of his day, Marsha lapsed into ruminations about everything she had to do and became further overwhelmed. When Eddie began his chatter, Marsha went on "overload" and found herself screaming at Eddie with a vehemence that shocked both of them.

When Marsha was later recounting the story to her best friend, she couldn't stop crying. She remembers screaming at Eddie, but the only thing she actually recalls from whatever she yelled was something about him being obnoxious and demanding and a pain in the ass and how he should do her a favor and go live with his dad. She immediately saw in his eyes a deeply wounded expression that stabbed her in the heart, and no amount of desperate apologizing could take that look away. That image now haunted her and made her sink into a place inside herself that she didn't even know was there. She said to her friend, "Maybe he should live with his dad. I'm a terrible mother."

In this section, let's consider another attributional pattern, global versus specific attributions. I previously mentioned global thinking as a style of thought that correlates with depression for its tendency to overlook the salient details of situations, often to one's detriment. A global attribution indicates a view that encompasses everything; it is a *pervasive* "big picture" perspective that suggests "it is *all* this way." Marsha's conclusion that she is a terrible mother for having said something hurtful and careless in one particular interaction is a global self-condemnation, and as you can imagine, its impact on her self-image and mood is proportioned similarly. Such a thought instantly wipes out all the other things she has done over the years that were evidence of her being a wonderful mother. A specific attribution is a detail perspective that recognizes the many components of a bigger phenomenon. In Marsha's case, she could have concluded she is generally a fine mother, but that she really handled that one situation poorly. In the following examples, see if you can identify whether the relevant attribution is global or specific.

Example #1: A father is sitting with his kids at the breakfast table, reading the morning paper and smoking a cigarette over a cup of coffee. With each news item he reads, he shakes his head and angrily mutters, "What is this world coming to?" He continues to read and get more agitated, and finally yells loud enough for even his neighbors to hear, "This whole damn country is no good. Kids on drugs, politicians a bunch of slimeballs, people killing each other for a chunk of money that won't even last 'em a day. Being an American is nothing to be proud of, that's for damn sure."

Example #2: Billy tried out for the Little League team mostly because he wanted to please his parents. Both of them said they'd be proud of him for trying out, and that it would be good for him to be on a team since he had never played any team sports. He'd mostly engaged in solitary pursuits, like computer games and shooting pool. When Billy failed to make the team, he came home and said, "I guess Little League baseball isn't for me."

Example #3: A woman drove to work deeply enraged about the fight she'd had with her husband that morning. When the driver in front of her was a little slow getting going when the light turned green, she honked angrily. When the light changed from green to yellow, though she had plenty of room to stop—and she should have—instead she hit the gas and sped through the just-turned-red light. When she parked in the lot at work, she opened her car door so hard and fast that she made a small dent in the passenger side door of the next car. She thought nothing of it. When one of the colleagues greeted her with a cheerful, "Good morning," her snippy reply was, "Oh, shut up."

In the first example, the man gets so riled up reading specific news items of a negative nature that he forms a global attribution that *all* of America is "no damn good." Well, America has its share of problems, but it also has an even greater share of wonderful things. To say *all* of something as diverse and complex as a country is bad (*or* good) is a global representation that clearly lacks a more detailed, balanced, and realistic perspective.

In the second example, Billy tries out for Little League baseball and fails to make the team. Instead of a global self-condemnation (e.g., "I'm such a failure"), Billy makes a *specific attribution* to the effect that baseball may not be for him, but he is clear that his self-worth is *not* determined by whether he earns a place on a Little League team. He illustrates well that one can suffer a specific disappointment without being a failure as a person.

In the third example, the woman who is hurt and rage-filled over the morning fight with her husband lets her anger spill over into everything else she does. Her *global response* to a very specific situation is maladaptive and destructive. Instead of keeping her feelings tied to the situation with her husband, she responds (globally) angrily to the world, including other drivers and even a colleague at work.

"Going global" in your attributions naturally makes things much bigger than they really are. Instead of a husband and wife arguing about a specific issue, the whole marriage is on the line. Instead of having a bad day at work, the whole job stinks. Instead of one part of the movie being a little slow or confusing, the whole movie was rotten. Relevant to our earlier discussion, this insight might well give you a different view of television and ways it can inadvertently hurt some vulnerable people. First, the continuous stream of bad news about war, disease, crime, and so on can easily lead people to think the whole world is a terribly dangerous place. Second, how can people view bad times as temporary—a key to managing depression and maintaining optimism—if the news tells them every half hour how desperate the world situation is?

When you're dealing with such great magnitudes of perception, your feelings will naturally reflect it. Consider Marsha from this section's opening vignette. When she's already feeling overwhelmed with all she has to do, even a small irritant can seem huge because it is one more thing to have to handle added to a mountain of other things. Many of us experience this, but how she reacts to the additional stressor, in this case Eddie's nonstop chatter, is the key to good modeling or hand-me-down blues. Eddie gets blasted for some objectively pretty harmless stuff, and such an explosive reaction will surely have fallout for a long time to come. Will Eddie conclude he is unloved and unwanted? Will he feel afraid to ask for his mother's attention? Will he become terribly self-conscious about talking out of fear of rejection? Will he become withdrawn and depressed in the belief that he is so irritating that even his own mother doesn't like him? Of course, such conclusions on Eddie's part would be as global and distorted as Marsha concluding she is a terrible mother because of one careless and hurtful episode. Given the strong relationship between the attributional style of parents and their children, Eddie is at risk for forming such misattributions, and for depression as a result. How Marsha handles the stresses of life influences how Eddie sees life and helps determine how he will feel in his relationship with his mother.

Small disappointments will seem large, little bad moods will seem huge, short times of feeling lousy will seem to go on forever when one "goes global." In a culture that encourages global thinking, where image tends to count more than substance, is it any wonder that there are so many hypersensitive people who get hurt when they don't get what they feel entitled to? Furthermore, is it any wonder that there are so many people tired of being hypersensitive that they give up trying to be polite, thoughtful, or "politically correct," and lash out at those they perceive as getting treatment they don't deserve?

Building self-esteem, developing good marriages and good friendships, raising happy and well-adjusted children, and all the many other things that people want to do are not going to be accomplished through a global strategy. If you want to do any of those things, you have to understand and apply the specifics of sensible and effective approaches. A book like this can teach you *some* but not all of them.

When you listen to and identify the attributions in your own thinking and in the things your family members say to you about whatever happens to them, you can become empowered to *change the attributions when they are erroneous.*

It has been known for a long time that people in good relationships are less likely to experience depression. I believe one reason for that fact is because other people can provide alternative viewpoints, something people don't usually do for themselves. However, now that you know about ambiguity and attributions, you can skillfully push yourself to generate multiple, equally plausible explanations for events and thereby be less inclined to get stuck on a depressing line of thought. When you hear your spouse or child say, "I'm no good" when he or she fails at something, you can be quick to point out that a lack of success now says nothing about possible success later and that a lack of success in one area doesn't mean total failure. There will be many more examples, of course, of ways to intervene meaningfully for your family's benefit, but the attributional patterns of personalization (internal/external), permanence (stable/unstable), and pervasiveness (global/specific) in response to life expectations are absolutely *vital* to grasp if you are to do so.

PARENT/CHILD ATTRIBUTIONS

Parents don't generally realize they're teaching an attributional style to their children. On the contrary, they are most typically oblivious to it. If you go back to some of the earlier examples of attributional style, you'll see parents teaching explanatory styles to their children quite inadvertently. Did the father in one of the scenarios really want to teach his kids to be deeply negative about other people, emotionally reactive to newspapers, antipatriotic, and also global thinkers? Of course not. Did the mother in one of the scenarios really want to teach her daughter that when someone is doing something that bothers you (in this case, her daughter dawdling instead of getting ready for school), it's because he or she is unconsciously hostile, doing it passive-aggressively to hurt you, and therefore you should take it personally? Again, of course not. She doesn't realize that she's breeding suspicion about others' motives and teaching her daughter to look at simple things and make them complicated ("making mountains out of molehills"). The children of these particular parents, however, are at risk for adopting internal and global attributional styles. When life brings them pain, as it inevitably will, they'll be at risk for depression because they'll likely take the situation personally and believe it will ruin everything. *Mom and Dad, without realizing or intending it, modeled styles of thinking that their kids would inevitably absorb that would put them at risk for depression later.* You'll see what I mean if you go back to reread the other examples I gave and reconsider them from the standpoint of what a child would most likely absorb from his or her parent(s) in terms of attributional style.

THE PARENT-CHILD "DEGREE OF FIT"

Parents are caretakers, role models, and mentors. You've already learned about the way children interpret the Rorschach of life using patterns derived from their parents. Raising children is a challenge under *any* conditions, but trying to do so when internally absorbed and in distress makes a difficult job much harder. Consider what happens in the especially volatile mix of a "difficult" baby or child and a depressed parent. It isn't a pretty picture.

Researchers have analyzed the quality of interactions between depressed parents (primarily mothers, since more of the parent–child interaction typically involves them and they are statistically more likely to be depressed) and their children. Their findings highlight some of the specific ways children are likely to acquire hand-me-down blues. Some of their main discoveries include the following:

Depressed parents are more likely to withdraw when they meet resistance from children while trying to manage them. *The ongoing war for a clean room was coming to an end. Deborah was extremely battle-weary, and she knew that Bobby could wear her down and win the war simply by doing nothing. Over the years she had tried many different strategies: She argued, threatened, cajoled, bribed, ignored, and did everything else she could think to do to motivate him to put his million toys away. But now, for reasons that had nothing to do with her son, she was too depressed to care. She just didn't have the strength to ask a second time, and sometimes not even a first time. Her depression persisted for months, and during that time she noticed he was wearing dirty clothes, leaving home without telling her where he was going, and doing all kinds of things that if she were feeling better she'd jump on him for. But she wasn't up for the arguments, his back talk, his excuses, and so she let it all go. Her guilt about being a lousy mother was a powerful factor in keeping her depression going.*

Bobby wasn't learning the best of responses from his mother. She modeled for him that in the face of adversity, you can succumb to despair and just give up. He was also learning that if you just outlast people, you can get what you want. Will Bobby be the kind of person that is so insensitive to others they must pull away to protect themselves? And, if so, how will the further rejections he encounters affect his view of himself and life?

When a child is not immediately responsive to questions ("How was school today?") or compliant with demands ("Please go clean your room"), a depressed parent is far more likely to give up quickly than a nondepressed parent. Apparently, for the depressed parent who is already in distress, the additional burden of having to expend greater effort just to get a reply or a simple task done requires more energy than seems available. Thus, with no follow-through, the child may quickly learn the negative lesson that merely by being passive, outwaiting the parent past the initial demand, the demand soon disappears. From the child's point of view, the short-term focus becomes simply avoiding the immediate unpleasantness of doing some undesirable task. In essence, the child learns, "If you ignore it, it'll go away." The net result: a passive person whose ineffective response to the normal demands of life is avoidance, almost assuring that things will get worse, not better. Avoidance is rarely an effective strategy for getting problems solved. From a risk factor standpoint, such passivity is a place for depression to take root.

From the parent's perspective, the child is seen as difficult and disagreeable. As the parent gives up and retreats, you can be sure he or she isn't saying or thinking kind things. There is frustration, anger, and withdrawal on both sides of the interaction, but unless these are addressed skillfully by the parent, walls can get built between parent and child that may be difficult to ever dismantle, all because the depression got in the way of more effective responses than retreat.

Depressed parents are less able to compromise in disagreements with their children, tending to respond to even minor conflict situations with either harsh enforcement (yelling, threats of extreme punishment, verbal abuse, and even hitting) or by withdrawing completely and simply avoiding the confrontation. *Betsy was an avid fan of computer games. When she got home from school, she'd make a beeline to her room, and after that the only sounds you'd hear were the blips and sirens and explosions of whatever game she happened to be playing, mixed with an occasional expression of satisfaction or disappointment in a young girl's voice. Ron and Kate generally thought the games were harmless fun, but lately Kate had begun to think it would be better for Betsy to get out into the world more and develop a social network of friends her age to have fun with. Kate mused that perhaps Betsy could accomplish that and thereby succeed in ways she herself hadn't. Kate understood isolation and solitary pursuits like computer games all too well. She had never had much of a social life, and avoided Ron's efforts to cocreate one with her. She worried about whether she had passed on a "social misfit" gene to Betsy, and instantly decided that she'd better push Betsy to get out of the house and participate in life.*

It seemed like a good idea at the time, but Betsy didn't go for it at all. A major fight erupted when Kate said, "No more computer games. Get a life." Betsy said, "I don't want to do what you want—I want to do what I want." Kate was enraged, walked over to the computer, and shocked herself and Betsy, too, when she grabbed it and hurled it out the window, trailing all kinds of wires and parts as it disappeared. Betsy looked at her with rage, but said nothing. They didn't talk to each other for over a week after that episode.

The dichotomous (all-or-none) thinking that generally leads to extreme behavior of one type or another is often modeled by depressed individuals in normal conflict situations.

As discussed earlier, conflict is normal; wherever there are rules, boundaries, and individual preferences, there will inevitably be some conflict. Conflict situations require greater effort on the part of the parties involved—the effort it takes to stick to the issue at hand and resolve it respectfully and without either party "losing face." A child may be made to comply with your wishes yet still have his or her feelings acknowledged and respected if the parent takes the time to communicate some variation of "You're not going to get your way, and you might be mad about it, but I'm the parent here. I love you, but you can't always get what you want."

If you're depressed and already emotionally fragile and volatile, the effort required to think rationally and manage a dispute skillfully may seem too demanding. Additionally, if a parent interprets his or her child as being difficult on purpose, and thereby takes his or her behavior personally (internal attribution), there is an additional tendency to either lash out verbally or physically, or passively retreat from the difficulties. From such interactions, the child learns nothing about how to resolve differences deliberately and respectfully—he or she only learns to either blow up or give up. If hitting is employed, the additional unwanted lesson is that violence is an acceptable means to vent anger or obtain compliance from others. What about the issue of spanking? The occasional swat to the behind in children *under age six* is not unreasonable. Beware, however, that what is potentially instructive in young children can be self-esteem damaging in older children. A child punished in this way feels and truly is helpless to escape the hurtful circumstances, and such helplessness is fertile ground for the seeds of depression. Violence against children teaches all the worst things about human relationships.

Depressed parents tend to personalize and pathologize normal attempts at independence. *Caroline had known since she was a young girl that she wanted to be a doctor. A lot of children say they want to be doctors, but Caroline really meant it. She had a compassion for people's pain at a level far beyond her years, and she was blessed with the academic gifts necessary to succeed in medical school. Now that it was time to send out her applications to universities with strong premedical programs, it was quite clear to her that wherever she got in, it wasn't going to be in the same city as her parents lived. She knew her mom would understand, but she dreaded trying to explain to her dad—again—why she'd be leaving home to attend college. Telling him months ago that it was a good possibility she'd be going had filled him with a* *despair that was quite familiar to her from many similar episodes over the years. He seemed so fragile to her. Telling him now that it was all but certain she was going away would damn near kill him.*

Caroline wondered whether it was selfish for her to pursue her dream of being a doctor when it would hurt her dad, but only for a moment. She prepared herself for the difficult interaction, and when the time came to show him the acceptance letter, she told him in the gentlest way she knew how that she was leaving home to pursue her education and career goals. His first reaction, which she had accurately predicted and prepared for, was to attack her as selfish and disloyal. She'd heard that same attack on her so many times over the years, any time she wanted to go somewhere or do something he didn't want her to. After his anger passed, he visibly sunk inside himself and said, "You leave us nothing. Nothing." She felt guilty when she had the sarcastic thought, "Maybe now he'll get a life."

Let's consider the process of *differentiation*, the normal developmental process of evolving your unique sense of self—your existence as an independent human being with your own thoughts, feelings, wishes, values, preferences, and other self-defining attributes. When a child explores and eventually discovers his or her own unique wants and needs, there is an opportunity to either celebrate that emerging individuality or to try and squash it. If you're depressed and you want to avoid conflict because it is too stressful and demanding for you to handle, you may end up pushing for conformity. It's easier for you, but certainly not for your child. If you interpret others' different preferences as a rejection of your own—an internal attribution that implies they're choosing differently because they don't like or respect you ("If he loved me he wouldn't do that"), your depression will distort the true meaning of others' right to choose in ways different from you. It takes a "cooler head" to prevail over situations where your wishes, hopes, or expectations aren't being honored (you wanted her to play soccer, but she wants to take an astronomy course) in order to see the choice as a personal one, *not* a rejection of you. The parents who take it personally when their children begin to make independent choices almost force their children into either an outright hostile rebellion or, if the child sees the situation as hopeless, a depressed resignation into apathy. There is a fine line between encouraging obedience and conformity and quelling a healthy sense of independence.

Depressed parents speak less to their children, engaging with them less frequently even during routine activities such as preparing a meal. *It was the Saturday morning routine at the Horton home. Dad and Robbie would do yard work, while Mom and Kathy would do laundry and housecleaning. Robbie was always envious of Kathy, because she got to have fun while she did chores. He could often hear his mom and sister laughing, even from the far side of the property, and when he did he often glanced at his dad. He wondered if it ever made him smile to hear their laughter the way it did him. It never seemed to. He'd see his dad's furrowed forehead, the perspiration on his face, and the familiar faraway look that told Robbie he was somewhere else in his thoughts, as usual. The scowl that was etched on his face discouraged Robbie from asking where he was, but Robbie always wondered nonetheless. As Robbie got older, he began to wonder how two such opposite people as his parents got together. His dad was all work and utterly humorless. His mom was all fun and games. He wished he understood his dad, and what it would take to please him. No matter how many chores he did, or how quickly he worked, or how many good grades he brought home, his dad just didn't have anything much to say to him. It hurt.*

Children thrive on closeness. They thrive on being able to ask all the questions they have and receive patient, substantial answers. They thrive on sharing experiences, whether it's playing or taking neighborhood walks together. When a parent is detached, too internally absorbed to be responsive to the child much less to initiate interactions, the message is a strong one that says "leave me alone." Children tend to personalize such things ("Why doesn't Mommy love me?") and blame themselves ("It's my fault my daddy doesn't come visit me"), a phenomenon well-known as the egocentricity of childhood—the self-centered perception that everything in life revolves around you. Kids even blame themselves for being abused; in fact, it is a common theme in working with adults who were abused as children that they *still* blame themselves (for not fighting back, running away, or telling Mom). It makes quite a difference in a child's self-esteem to feel loved and not just tolerated.

Perhaps most important about the ability to engage with children on an ongoing basis is the ability to ask questions and prompt critical thinking. If you want to teach good social skills, empathy, flexibility in thinking, and other vital antidepressant skills for living life well, even the most mundane interactions have outstanding teaching potential.

The opportunity to interact on an ongoing basis is how closeness or intimacy is achieved in *any* relationship. People have created the illusion for themselves in our fast-paced world that they can talk to a friend once a month (or once a year) and still be "close." While the sentiment can certainly be real, by being uninvolved in the significant details from the everyday life of the person, you can only get so close.

Depressed parents tend to make more negative comments when they do speak. *Right after dinner each night, the nonnegotiable mandate was that Andie and her mom would do the cleanup together. They had established a rhythm in doing so over the years, Andie washing the dishes, her mom drying them and putting them away. Mom had always said this was some of their "quality time" together, but Andie sure didn't see it that way. On the contrary, she dreaded it. Andie had long ago learned to deflect the usual questions like, "How was school today?" because no matter what she decided was safe enough to share, it would rarely turn out to be. Her mom had a knack for always finding something to nitpick about. Generally, Andie tried to keep the focus of their conversation on her mom's job and friends. At least when Mom criticized her friends or complained about her boss there wasn't anything Andie had to do about it but listen. If Andie tried to interject something positive, Mom would actually get angry and tell her that she was just as lacking in empathy as her father. No wonder her dad fell asleep every night on the couch and he and her mom were hardly ever alone together anymore. Andie was sure that as soon as she was old enough, she'd get away from these people. For now, she'd just suffer in silence and complain to her friends and anybody else who would listen. It didn't seem to occur to Andie that, in doing so, she was becoming more and more her mother's daughter.*

Depression tends to lead one to focus more on what's wrong than right. One of the tools people use who are *not* prone to depression is specific attributions, discussed earlier. A specific attribution represents an ability to respond to one aspect of something without necessarily responding to all of it. If you have a bad morning, you have a bad *morning*. It doesn't mean "the whole day is shot." In interactions between children and their depressed parents, the depressed parents end up focusing on the one thing the child didn't do so well, comment on it, and leave the child with the global impression that what he or she did was without any positive value at all. So, a child cleans his or her room, and instead of praising the child's efforts, Mom and Dad criticize the one part of the closet where things aren't quite as neatly stacked as they could be. Do you know how many kids get criticized and even punished for bringing home a *B*-plus instead of an *A*?

A reliable path to depression is to believe that no matter what you do, it isn't good enough. Parents mistakenly think, "Why should I reward my kid for doing what he's supposed to?" (They seem to forget they expect their bosses to give them annual raises, Christmas bonuses, and verbal praise for jobs well done!) Or, they worry about spoiling their children. Many parents, though, are simply oblivious to recognizing the daily opportunities to offer positive feedback—about the child *and* about life— to the child who is at the very beginning of evolving both a self-concept and a view of life.

Any parent can squash a child's motivation to even try, and generate the very hopelessness that underlies depression, just by failing to notice and amplify the positive. Parents can provide criticism, of course, to help a child be realistic about him or herself, but it has to be given sparingly (not over trivial things) and with a motivating push to "do it again but this time do something different." Whenever possible, which is almost all the time, it is best to emphasize the positive.

Depressed parents are generally less skilled in talking to their children about their feelings, especially negative feelings. *Josh had tried out for the school play. He was one of the three boys vying for the main character's part, and he was earnest in his desire to get it. He tried to remind himself of what his dad had said, that it was just a junior high school play and that it was no big deal. But he was aware at a deeper level that this was just a feeble attempt to try and prevent his utter devastation if he didn't get the part. Utter devastation seemed like the only possibility to Josh if the unthinkable happened.*

Well, the unthinkable happened. He didn't get the part. And, as he predicted, he felt destroyed. He was sure everyone in the entire seventh grade thought he was a loser. By the time he got home, the tears were welling up in him so powerfully that he barely made it through the front door before he exploded into crying. His dad instantly knew what was wrong, and just said, "Bad break. There'll be another time." Josh wanted to kill him for his "oh, well" attitude.

His mother came up to his room, but her response was as empty as his dad's. She lived in a state of constant disappointment as far as Josh could tell; whereas his dad had at least said, "Go for it!" his mom said, "Don't do it, Josh. You won't get the part, and then you'll be miserable." She thought she was being helpful, but she was just being her usual negative, hopeless, depressed self. He was so tired of her always discouraging him. Now here she was sitting across from him with that look that said "See? I told you so." For a moment, Josh thought she was going to actually try and say something empathetic and supportive, but all that came out was a sigh. For all her experience with her depression, she was still clueless as to how to talk to him about anything that really mattered to him.

When people get wrapped up in their feelings, good or bad, it's often hard to give a name to or describe those feelings beyond giving global labels or descriptions. Much of what happens in therapy, of course, is creating a context in which people strive to and can give voice to feelings they've never before had to organize and express. The very process of putting your feelings into a framework of meaning can provide deeper understandings of the interplay between the different parts of your self, and between yourself and your environment.

One of the key tasks in the evolution of any person's identity is learning about yourself: learning about your feelings and what triggers them, learning to open up to your fantasies, learning to recognize your strengths, your vulnerabilities, and your style for living life. Learning the less comfortable, but ever-present, emotions like fear, anger, and sadness is as vital as learning how to manage more positive feelings, like happiness, attraction, and playfulness.

Parents are guides to one's inner world. But if they are depressed, unable to recognize and effectively short-circuit the triggers for their own dark moods, and are unable to explain what's wrong or problem-solve what to do about it, then their children do not have a guide to help them deal with those feelings. Negative emotions are inevitable; how you learn to manage them is a strong factor in how much or little they will influence your overall life experience. If you never learn to deal effectively with your negative emotions, the likelihood is to get overwhelmed by such feelings, mislabel them or yourself negatively ("I'm a screwed-up loser"), and feel helpless to do anything constructive in response to them.

The relationship between parents and children is reciprocal. Just as depressed parents influence the quality of their children's lives, so do depressed children influence the lives of their parents.

DEPRESSED CHILDREN RAISING PARENTS

Up until a few short years ago, the mental health profession didn't even recognize childhood depression as a potential problem, much less a reality. The assumption was that a child's personality isn't sufficiently formed yet to allow for so deep and complex an experience as depression. Tell *that* to the parents of newborns that are already showing some signs of depression. (Yes, that can happen. But it doesn't mean depression is inevitable if the environment doesn't create a context for its further development.)

As you now know, in a family system each person affects every other person. Just as a depressed spouse can skew the marriage and the family in a negative direction, so can a child's depression adversely affect the marriage and the family. In any of the vignettes in this chapter featuring unhappy children, you can easily see how one parent might blame the other for having tainted the child, particularly if one spouse seems to be a more obviously negative influence. In this final section of the chapter, let's consider what nondepressed parents can do when their child is depressed.

The very first thing to appreciate is that children's depression shares one very important feature with that of adults. The child's attributional style is established early on and serves as a foundation for how he or she assimilates life experiences. Thus, by the time depression strikes, the predisposing perspectives have usually been there for some time. As you will see in the next section, this represents a preventive opportunity.

What is different about children's depression, once it surfaces, compared to adults'? Younger children usually don't have the insight or the words to say much more than "I'm sad." Sometimes they can't even say that much, and all that comes out is "I don't feel well" or "My tummy hurts." Here is an ambiguity that represents a potential hazard if too much or not enough is read into it. Is it something at school? Is it the visitation schedule or the residuals of the divorce? Is it having to adjust to a new stepparent, or having to share you with a new stepfamily? Or is it the flu? You can raise countless possibilities in your imagination, but without some direct feedback you're merely guessing. Throwing guesses about what's wrong at a child, especially an adolescent, usually makes him or her feel even more poorly understood if your guesses are wrong. Your positive intentions aren't perceived as such.

The first distinction to make about your child's depression is this: Might it merely be a transient bad mood, or is it more enduring than that? Again, you must be careful to try to read it as accurately as possible. If the child's dejection and withdrawal lasts more than a few days, it's a legitimate basis for concern (not alarm). Regression (inappropriate childish, even infantile behavior), withdrawal from routine interactions, and "acting out" behaviors (such as throwing tantrums, damaging things, skipping school, abusing drugs or alcohol) are all potentially serious warnings signs suggesting something is going on. Direct questioning in a caring manner will work sometimes, but it may just generate anger and silence. Less direct methods are often more useful, such as going on errands together and thereby creating a context for discussion to "spontaneously" occur.

The key is this: Time matters. Don't wait! Many depressive episodes will simply go away by themselves, a phenomenon called *spontaneous remission* in the clinical literature. More likely, though, is that depression won't magically go away by itself. Even if there is a spontaneous remission, the chance of a relapse is far greater without intervention because nothing new was learned to prevent one. So, taking some definitive, progressive action is definitely the thing to do.

An even more compelling reason to take action is that, although most people who suffer a depressive episode fully recover, a significant percentage (10 to 20 percent) do not. An acute episode, which should be a temporary phenomenon, may instead become a chronic, enduring disorder. This is exactly what happened to Alex, the nine-year-old whose parents divorced in this chapter's opening vignette. Everyone thought Alex would and should recover from the trauma of his family breaking up, but he really never did. His parents were too self-absorbed in their own hurt and anger, and though that may be quite understandable, it certainly left Alex out in the cold, psychologically speaking. (Whenever divorces happen, I worry the most for the children. Adults have life experiences and other resources to draw upon to get the help they need. Children are dependent on their parents, and if the parents aren't attentive for whatever reason, they can end up essentially alone and struggling.)

Alex formed the global attributions that nobody tells the truth, nobody understands, nobody could be trusted, nobody cares, and nobody could help. He formed these painful overgeneralizations about people and about life, and well beyond just his hurt with his parents at the moment, these became predictions about his future relationships as well. It is depressing to go through life feeling as though you can only play defense against the world.

It's terribly frustrating to want to help someone you care so much about who seems, at least on the surface, not to want any help. Now you know, though, that a sense of hopelessness generates the apparent apathy and is a core component of depression. Don't let your depressed children raise you to be a quitter. Don't let their anger or their silence lead you to give up on them. Don't let their moodiness cause you to get wrapped up in guilt that you (globally) screwed up their lives. Stay connected even in small ways—a message on their answering machine, a note on their bed, an E-mail on their computer, *whatever*. Feelings have to be acknowledged, and circumstances have to be created to understand and resolve them. The most important point is that a child's depression, just as *any* family member's, provokes certain feelings in you. Care must be taken to remain connected to the person in distress, and not disengage from him or her out of frustration or anger.

Much more will be said in the next (and last) section of the book about things you can actively do to reduce and even prevent hand-me-down blues. What you now know, though, are many of the specific ways parents unwittingly pass depression on to their children, despite their best intentions. Such information is crucial to developing a good game plan for building a healthy, depression-free family.

A SUMMARY OF KEY POINTS

- Parents can unwittingly transmit depression to their children in a variety of ways, primarily through the attributional style which is always being modeled by a parent in the ways he or she interprets and reacts to everyday life experiences.

- Attributional styles can be characterized according to three main criteria: internal/external, stable/unstable, and global/specific.
- An internal attribution involves seeing yourself as the cause of an event, while an external attribution involves seeing someone or something else as the cause. Self-blame when things go wrong is typical of depression sufferers, even when such self-blame isn't reasonable or appropriate for the circumstances.
- A stable attribution means believing things will never change. An unstable attribution involves the perception that circumstances are temporary. Stable attributions can be the basis for hopelessness when a person assumes things will *always* be terrible, even though circumstances can and will change, especially if sensible action is taken to improve things.
- A global attribution is all encompassing, affecting *everything*. A specific attribution limits the influence of the event to just one particular area. Global attributions can be especially depressing when it seems *everything* is going wrong.
- In research into depressed parents' style of relating to their children that might later affect them adversely, a number of detrimental patterns were identified. These include withdrawing from their children when the children are difficult, difficulty reaching compromises, personalizing and pathologizing normal attempts at independence, engaging less frequently with their children and when doing so focusing more on the negatives, and difficulty talking about their feelings, especially negative ones.
- Just as parents' depression can affect children, so can a child's depression affect the parents. Staying connected to the child and not withdrawing out of frustration or anger are critical to creating an environment in which the depression can be resolved.

PART III

Treating and Preventing Hand-Me-Down Blues

Building Family Strengths

In every child who is born, no matter what circumstances, and of no matter what parents, the potentiality of the human race is born again.

James Agee

Paul Simmons enjoyed the travel his job as a manager required of him a couple of days each month. The travel was local, driving to other branch offices, none of which were further than about a hundred miles away. He'd spend the day, but was virtually never away overnight. He liked that because family time was his first priority.

One fine sunny southern California day, Paul was enjoying an easy drive along the same freeway he had driven many times before. This time, though, while relaxing and singing along to some of his favorite rock 'n 'roll tunes, lightning struck: A huge truck spilled over the center divide and came straight at him. With a fraction of a second to react, Paul's frantic attempt to get out of harm's way failed. The truck plowed into his car and shredded it into a pile of nearly unrecognizable metallic confetti. No one who witnessed the accident or saw the wreckage thought anyone could possibly survive destruction of such magnitude. When the police, and then the ambulance, arrived just minutes later, the sad and knowing looks silently passed between the officers and paramedics spoke eloquently about yet another freeway accident fatality. But their assumption was happily premature, for Paul was still alive. That surprise recognition sparked the paramedics into high-speed action; as soon as he was freed from the twisted metal, he was piled into the ambulance and they were gone in an instant, siren blaring.

Head trauma, internal bleeding, ruptured spleen, lacerated kidneys, broken bones, all frightening physical evidence of the violence he'd endured. Remarkably, though, he was still alive. Paul had extensive emergency surgery, and was kept together with all the life-sustaining glue and paper clips the medical staff could provide. Paul was in a coma, in critical condition, and no one felt comfortable predicting his chances of recovery.

Rachel Simmons was at work when she received the call about Paul's accident. Rachel was almost always the calm, rational type—but not this time. She panicked, she hyperventilated, she screamed, she became hysterical. Whomever she spoke to was apparently quite experienced in such fragile encounters, because she calmed Rachel down into a frame of mind where she could at least listen and follow directions. She called her mom, who rushed right over and picked her up, and the two drove the distance to the hospital. Rachel asked her dad to pick up the kids from school and take care of them until . . . until what? She didn't know. First priority was get to the hospital. Everything else could wait.

The ninety-minute drive to the hospital provided Rachel with plenty of time to imagine the worst over and over again. By the time they pulled up to the hospital, Rachel was in a barely controlled frenzy. She wanted to see Paul right away, but all kinds of people—doctors, nurses, admissions officers—were far more interested in asking questions than giving her access to Paul. When she finally got into the critical care unit and saw him bandaged nearly everywhere and hooked up to a thousand tubes protruding from every possible place, her terror became overwhelming. No matter how tightly her mother held her, there was simply no consoling her. Her crying was from a pain so deep her whole body shook. She didn't remember fainting, of course, but awoke to find herself on a hospital gurney with her mother on one side and a nurse on the other. She heard herself say she'd be okay, but her words didn't fool anyone, least of all herself.

Somehow, Rachel managed to maintain a bedside vigil. During the day, she sat at the foot of Paul's bed. At night, she slept in a chair. Her mother brought her daily changes of clothes and a welcome shoulder to lean and cry on. A few days later that felt like years off her life, Rachel was startled out of a reverie by Paul saying "Hi" in a weak, scratchy voice. She immediately jumped up and went to his side. She had rehearsed for this moment, and planned to tell him what had happened and what would happen in a clear voice with dry eyes. The rehearsals didn't work. She cried hard and in-between the tears she oriented him to where he was and why. All Paul could do was close his eyes again and drift off.

Paul was in the hospital for almost four months. Rachel brought the kids,

Peter and Renee, to see their dad as often as she could. She thought they would ask a thousand questions she wouldn't be able to answer, especially after seeing their dad for the first couple of times, but she was surprised at how silent and preoccupied they were instead. That didn't change much over time, either. Renee, age thirteen, was a little more inquisitive, occasionally asking some pointed "What if?" questions. Peter, age nine, was silently attentive to the goings-on, but couldn't or wouldn't discuss it directly.

When Paul was finally allowed to go home, he was barely able to walk and talk. He did so very slowly. He slept a lot, was in pain a lot, and Rachel wondered for the millionth time whether he would ever be normal again. She was pushed to her limits with all the new responsibilities for Paul's basic care, and even though her mom and dad helped out a lot, the burdens of aiding Paul's recovery while still struggling to hold the family together were rapidly overloading Rachel's ability to cope.

Some weeks later, Peter's third-grade teacher called. She expressed her concerns about Paul's recovery and offered Rachel her best wishes. Then she described some new behaviors Peter was manifesting that were not, in her words, "appropriate." He was often inattentive in class, unresponsive to direct questions, socially isolative during free times, and hostile when other children tried to engage in play with him. She said she understood the family stresses arising from Paul's accident, but she thought Peter should be coping better than he was. Rachel experienced the teacher's observations as criticism, and instantly felt guilty that she'd been so much less attentive to Peter lately. She vowed to be more attentive to him. She was thankful that Renee was so helpful, attentive, and quick to offer her mom help. Then all of a sudden she wondered if that was her way of being upset, and the thought scared her.

* * *

Two years and a painful rehabilitation process later, Paul is mostly physically recovered, a miracle. He has some residual chronic pain, but he can and does walk, drive, do chores, and play golf. He has more than a few scars, both physical and emotional, but he's alive, a fact he still appreciates several times per hour.

The echoes of the accident are still being heard, though. Rachel is distant and polite in relating to Paul, and is constantly on the lookout for signs that Paul isn't the same guy he was before the accident. Each confirming sign is taken as evidence that the marriage is doomed to either mediocrity or divorce. Peter is still a tight-lipped boy, and whatever he's thinking doesn't seem positive. He spends a lot of time alone in his room playing computer games. Renee is hardly ever home. She's a cheerleader at her high school, she's on this club and that team, and somehow manages to keep all the extracurricular balls she's juggling in the air. But she has an aura of sadness about her that Rachel hopes will eventually just go away.

Paul went to see a family therapist first. He mostly felt just fine, and was soon going back to work. He was spending more time with the kids and they seemed to enjoy it, and he was doing more of the things around the house he'd always done. But he knew Rachel was traumatized by the episode and he couldn't seem to get her to stop treating him like he was still a fragile bundle of bandages and tubes. Could he change her perceptions by himself?

Paul did a very wise thing for his family. He created the opportunity for them to all see a family therapist. He created a safe place for everyone to hear and be heard, and to revise their trauma-based views of life and each other now that the trauma itself was over. The therapy context provided a safe place designed for such sensitive interactions, and what couldn't be said at home soon spilled out. What started out as awkward for them all quickly evolved into a series of discussions, hugs, and reaffirmations of love and caring that brought down the walls each had built around himself to contain their fears and grief.

Paul, Rachel, Renee, and Peter went through hell. They're back now, and they're stronger as a family than ever.

This chapter is about families facing life, sharing its inevitable joys and sorrows, and how the very mechanisms families use to respond to whatever life throws at them, as well as what they *choose* to bring into their lives, can open or close the door to depression. When I say as I did earlier that *all* people face hardship, it's implicit that all families do, too. How does the manner in which a family deals with life experiences, good and bad, either predispose its members to depression or insulate them from it?

No one should have to experience the kind of life-threatening trauma Paul went through in his car accident. But an accident of this magnitude is a powerful way to illustrate how a family may be forced to face a major crisis together, and the reality is that this sort of thing happens all too often. Whether the crisis is an accident and life-threatening injury, a terminal disease, the death of a loved one, the loss of a job, or any one of countless other ways to be traumatized in life, is less important than how the crisis is dealt with. There is perhaps no clearer and more poignant way to demonstrate the key difference between individualistic and systemic perspectives than to look at crises that ensnare everyone in the family, each in a different way. Wife Rachel, Daughter Renee, and Son Peter were each affected personally and deeply by Paul's accident and long recovery. Paul's parents, Rachel's parents, Paul's and Rachel's employers and friends, Peter's and Renee's friends and even their teachers all felt the ripple effects of the accident either directly or indirectly. When the consequences of Paul's accident are so clearly spread over so many people's lives, how can we possibly reduce such an event to an individual problem and then attempt to treat it on that severely limited basis? Likewise, is it any more realistic to think that someone can be devastated by depression and it's only that unfortunate person's problem?

From time to time I've talked about the concept of risk factors for depression. A risk factor, as you know, is any factor that increases your chances of some particular phenomenon (such as a disease or an accident) occurring. For example, smoking cigarettes increases the risk of developing lung cancer, and driving after drinking increases the risk of injury or death in a car accident. Risk factors for depression include a sense of hopelessness about the future, feeling helpless to change negative circumstances, a history of abuse, early losses of significant others such as parents, poor problem-solving skills, a genetic predisposition to depression, the presence of marital and family discord, the presence of coexisting medical disorders, and a tendency to make misattributions or engage in distorted thinking. There are other risk factors as well beyond these most common ones.

In the largest sense, life is a risk factor. It's not unlike the old joke that says the leading cause of divorce is marriage. If you have health, you run the risk of getting sick or injured. If you have a job, you run the risk of losing it. If you love someone, you run the risk of losing that person to death, disease, or a breakup. The risks of life do not hide themselves from us. Every day, we see on television and read in the newspapers of the consequences, good and bad, of choices people make, and of life-changing forces that strike from out of the blue.

In facing the trials and tribulations of life, it helps to have a strong foundation of good problem-solving skills and the support of a close-knit family. Families can provide for many of the most basic needs we have, as we will see in the next section.

THE FUNCTIONS OF FAMILIES

As you learned in chapter 3, from a family systems perspective depression is often a reflection at an individual level of something that is being handled poorly in the larger social context. In this chapter's opening vignette about the Simmons family, Rachel and Paul's son, Peter, was manifesting some common childhood symptoms of depression, clearly reflecting what was going on in his family at the time. Their daughter, Renee, went the other direction in her behavior but also manifested a common response to depressing circumstances—channeling all the emotional difficulties into "busywork." She was apparently striving to achieve more and more in order to keep busy enough to not have to think much about what was really going on. (In fact, this can be a positive way of coping, but it is a coping strategy nonetheless.) Rachel's depression was more directly expressed in her ability to verbalize her despair and channel it in the direction of taking care of Paul. So the entire Simmons family was in a state of great distress, wishing and striving to get things back to normal. In family systems terms, the tendency of the system to strive to maintain a balance is called *homeostasis.* The balance of the Simmons's family life was established before Paul's accident, and efforts were made collectively to restore it. The pull toward maintaining an existing balance, *even if it's an unhealthy one,* is part of what makes trying to introduce changes into the family system potentially difficult. The principle of homeostasis provides an important glimpse into why even positive changes are not necessarily readily accepted and incorporated.

With its usual homeostasis disrupted, the Simmons family environment didn't have its previous feel of being a safe, comfortable place for everyone, through no fault of anyone in particular. But the primary function of a family is to provide safety for its members. Families must provide a safe haven in which love, acceptance, acknowledgment, good boundaries, respect, and all the other elements of emotional safety are readily available. Physical safety is an obvious necessity as well. The most critical functions of the family in this regard are the abilities to *insulate* its members from both internal and external threats as best it can and to *empower* its members to manage realistically those internal and external threats. *Much of the depression that occurs in individuals and families could be prevented if people would grasp the principle that only families can insulate and empower their members to deal skillfully with the realities of our complicated lives.* Families are perhaps the only potential safe haven for its members learning the relevant lessons. However, far too many people remain oblivious to what they could be creating in their families that would substantially reduce the likelihood of family members sinking into despair and giving up on a full, rich life. If this pattern persists, it is painfully obvious that the rates of depression will continue to rise and strike ever-younger targets. Furthermore, when depressed parents are themselves struggling to cope, how available can they be to organize the relevant teachings for their children? This issue will be explored more fully later in this chapter. Now let us consider further the family system's abilities to insulate and empower its members.

DEPRESSION AND EXTERNAL THREATS TO THE FAMILY

Previously I have talked about many of the specific catalysts for depression that are evident in our cultural milieu, such as the premiums placed on individual immediate gratification and less so on social responsibility, an increased reliance on technology, and the devaluing of social relationships. These and many other cultural influences represent genuine external threats to the family, predisposing it to depression if ensnared by them.

Let's go from global to specific in considering this point. Drug abuse is a huge and still-growing problem. Young children, junior high school age and even younger, are not only drinking alcohol, but are trying hard drugs as well. Children are still having children at an incredible rate, particularly when you realize no other industrialized society has as high a rate of unplanned, unwanted teen pregnancies as America. There have never been as many obese, unhealthy, inactive children as there are right now.

They lie around watching television, working and playing on computers, and their parents are actually thankful to have these ever-present electronic baby-sitters. More than a hundred thousand children go to school each day armed with guns. Children face gangs and threats of violence on a far too regular basis. The media, television in particular, is training young soon-to-be independent consumers with an income to feel entitled to have what they want and to want it all.

These and too many other such daily realities represent external threats to the welfare of the American family. These threats are real, they are ever-present, and they are hooks in the stream of life that can snag you even when you don't bite on them directly. Mary Pipher, in her book *The Shelter of Each Other,* makes a valuable observation when she says that we used to know who our adversaries were: anything that might hurt our family. It might be the weather (drought or floods), poverty, famine, unscrupulous business competitors, or the enemies of our country. The family provided an "us" in the "us" versus "them" dramas of life.

And now who are our enemies? It isn't quite so clear anymore. When people aren't sure who they should be struggling against, they often aim at and even hit the wrong target. Who is the enemy? Whoever does whatever they choose just because they *can,* and not because they *should.* Whoever does damage, actively or passively, and feels indifferent about it.

You can't directly control the drugs that are brought into the country nor the ones that are manufactured here. You can't directly control what is on television tonight, and you can't directly control how other families raise their children. You can't even directly control who your kids talk to or what they are encouraged to do.

You *can* try and minimize the negative influences, and you *can* teach skills for reducing their vulnerability, and thereby insulate your family from the external threats to its integrity. But, as soon as anyone leaves home for a mere trip to the grocery store, the influence of the outside world is felt. The key point is that you cannot control the external threats, *nor do you need to*—if your family is empowered to deal with them skillfully.

Safety isn't out there in the world. There are things you can do to make your family safer, of course, but safety is primarily in your own ability to anticipate and prevent hurtful circumstances whenever possible and to resolve them skillfully when they do arise, as they inevitably will. Depressed people often exaggerate what is hurtful. They see danger where lesser concern would be more reasonable. They see rejection where others would see polite neutrality. They see major setbacks where others would see only mild disappointment.

Rachel Simmons became fearful for her family after Paul's accident. She was enormously overprotective, fearful to let Renee or Peter of out her sight, especially terrified if their plans included being in a car. What is the effect of a parent's world view on his or her children? What did Rachel's perceptions about external threats communicate to the children about how they should cope with her fears and their own as well? Rachel didn't strive to introduce her children to the world and its many wondrous possibilities. She strived to keep them safe at home. Depression like Rachel's can cripple people as readily as an accident.

DEPRESSION AND INTERNAL THREATS TO THE FAMILY

Internal threats are those factors that destabilize families from within. These include death of a parent or child, debilitating and painful disease, trauma such as accidents or abuse (physical, sexual, emotional) by family members, job loss and economic hardship, public humiliation, family members leaving (moving away, divorces) and new ones arriving (marriages, births), and aging and diminished capacities. These, and many others like them, are powerful threats to the integrity of a family: Will the family unite and cope, or fragment and disintegrate under the pressure?

As significant as disease, death, and other such serious problems are, how they are managed is controlled by the rules governing the family system. There are rules for defining who takes charge, when and how decisions are made, who has a say in what goes on, whether discussion will be allowed or mere compliance is required, and on and on. *The primary threat to the family isn't external—it's internal.* It's the lack of necessary skills in communicating, problem-solving, and developing and following an organized, effective way to respond to life's demands. It's the inability of the family to establish clear rules for its own conduct and expectations about how those rules are to be absorbed and internalized by each member. This is the essence of the "us" in the "us" versus "them" paradigm.

I'm sure some readers will ask, "Do we really need a 'conflict model' of us versus them in order for the family to function?" I believe the answer is yes for several reasons. First, what makes for family cohesiveness is a sharing of common values and goals. Second, we naturally grow closer to others when we face a common threat or enemy. Third, conflict isn't to be avoided even if we try to avoid it. Conflict is as inevitable as two people's differing views. The relevant issue is how they address their inevitable differences. Fourth, loyalty isn't inspired in anyone unless there is a shared perception that "this (in this case, the family) is greater than any one of us." *Commitment to the "we" that transcends "you" and "me" is the critical component of how people learn personal and social responsibility.*

ANTIDEPRESSANT FAMILY RELATIONSHIP SKILLS

Throughout this book, I clearly encourage a skill-building approach to enhancing family systems in order to alleviate existing depression and prevent later episodes. In the families I treat, I frequently still get surprised at what is lacking in their interactions that seems so obvious to me yet remains hidden from the family members themselves. Mom and Dad don't understand why their children are so angry because, after all, didn't they get every comfort simply handed to them? Mom and Dad don't understand why the kids are so demanding of their attention because, after all, didn't they take a vacation together just a couple of months ago? "Jeez! How needy can they be?" The kids don't understand why Mom and Dad are so angry that they had a wild party while they were out of town because after all, didn't Mom and Dad say it was important for them to have friends? Such scenarios sound silly in a way, but they come up in treatment routinely.

Without critical thinking skills and specific relationship skills, people's family relationships are much more likely be a breeding ground for despair and depression. Many of these specific skills will be described here. Learning these skills so that you can overcome depression and so that others in your family can model them and thereby reduce and even prevent their depression is powerful reason to take them seriously. Additional resources mentioned in the appendices and the bibliography section of this book can be strong allies in your efforts to learn them—for your sake, for the sake of your children, and for the sake of your family.

CRITICAL THINKING SKILLS
Let's start with the skills in critical thinking:

Projections and Ambiguity. In my clinical trainings for mental health professionals, I often say that the basis for human anguish is *when people think hurtful things and then make the mistake of believing themselves.* You have now learned about the ambiguities of life and how the quality of your projections in response to them can place you at risk for depression. Learning to distinguish between facts and inferences and how your feelings can deceive you into believing something that isn't really true is a vital skill to master. Dealing with adversity by reminding yourself that it's transient and that, however devastating it may now seem, your life encompasses more than that, is the perspective of resilience. Learning to think clearly, without the errors of jumping to conclusions minus sufficent information, seeing things in all-or-none terms that aren't really so extreme, taking things too personally, and so forth, may well be the most important antidepressant skill of all. How can parents teach critical thinking skills to their children? Consider this example of good parents at work.

Hiking along on our way to Angel's Landing in Zion National Park a few months ago with my best friends, Wendy and Richard, and their seven-year-old daughter, Megan, my wife, Diane, and I were once again impressed with the quality of interaction between Megan and her parents. Throughout the entire time we were hiking that day, Wendy and Richard modeled for all of us how well Megan could be engaged in critical thinking and problem-solving by asking lots of "What if?" and "What do you think?" questions. Such questions can teach a child at an early age to take far more into account than merely his or her feelings or imaginings.

Wendy and Richard would ask questions like "What if I slipped and

fell down a ravine and couldn't walk? How would you help me? What if
Dad was bitten by a snake? What should we do first, and then what next?
Why do you think they tell us to stay on the marked trail and not go off
anyplace else? Why do you think they tell us to carry water with us? How
do you suppose animals that live here get the water they need? Why do
you think animals come out more in the morning and evening than
during the day?" We all asked Megan many such questions and used
them as a teaching vehicle about safety in state parks, the rhythms of
nature, and, more important, as a teaching vehicle of critical thinking
skills. The questions did *not* frighten Megan or make her anxious. On the
contrary, she felt like she knew or could learn what to do under all kinds
of possible conditions. She can start to distinguish a huge ecosystem, the
park, from the specifics of the creatures that live there and the specific
conditions that occur there. She can't control whether there's a landslide
while we hike, and she knows one is *very* unlikely, but she feels like she
knows what to do if all the adults were hurt or unable to help her for some
reason.

We continue to have lots of "What if?" and "How come?" discussions
with Megan about all kinds of things: strangers, other kids in her first-
grade class, teachers and other adults in authority, rules in games, ways to
treat others, and on and on. She's only seven years old, but already makes
inferences and develops understandings that many adults I know haven't
yet accomplished!

Megan isn't an anomaly, wonderfully special though she is to me. She's
only seven and there are many things she hasn't been and shouldn't yet be
exposed to. But, as I have stressed throughout this book, it isn't what
happens in a person's life that is the trigger for depression as much as it is
the way he or she learns to interpret and respond to it. Megan's parents
deliberately model critical, flexible thinking. They model anticipating
problems and responding to them insightfully with the goals of preventing and solving them if possible. They model expressing feelings but not
making them the sole basis for making decisions. They model the
perspective that things sometimes happen for no apparent reason (good
and bad things) and that taking things personally is not always reasonable.
They model that difficulties come and go, and hard times won't last
forever. (Neither will good times.) They model and actively teach lots of

wonderful skills that will continue to develop and will last Megan a lifetime. These are skills any parents can and should be teaching if they want to prevent depression. Sinking into depression as a result of a lack of ability to think critically and problem-solve skillfully is a tragedy. *The specific things people need to learn to relate well and think critically are not nearly as likely to be taught anywhere else than in the safe haven of home.*

Leveling About Depression. Leveling means being honest with yourself and your family that you're dealing with depression; and, leveling also means you can be clear in modeling to others that when something you or they are doing isn't particularly effective, that you or they are willing to take responsibility for it and do something constructive about it. (Doing something constructive about it it is what my previous book, *Breaking the Patterns of Depression,* is meant to help you do.) *You or the depressed person you care about has to be careful not to model giving up (helplessness) or passively accepting depression as if it is inevitable (hopelessness). It isn't.*

Leveling also means that you can be honest with your children by helping them understand, at whatever level is appropriate for their age, that you're not feeling too great right now, but you will again soon and you're actively striving to do so. Children certainly don't need all the details (keep your boundaries!) but they do need to know they're not responsible for your difficulties or those of their depressed parent. As you now know, what makes this important is that children are sensitive to the mood of the home, and when things aren't quite right, they tend to blame themselves. Go out of your way to assure them it's nothing they've done. Do your best to interact with them in patient and affectionate ways, hard as that may often seem, or encourage their depressed parent(s) to strive to deal with the children without depression infecting their relationship.

COMPARTMENTALIZATION SKILLS

No family is perfect, nor does it have to be. One of the greatest family strengths is the ability to *compartmentalize.* Compartmentalization means being able to distinguish a single part from the greater whole. I may not like one aspect of you or your behavior, but does that justify devaluing *all* of you? Few things in life are simply all or none, yet the tendency to see things in extreme terms is typical of depression sufferers. It's a well-known cognitive distortion known as *dichotomous* or all-or-none thinking. Some things *are* all-or-none (you're pregnant or you're not), but most things are not, a principle you already know from the earlier discussion regarding ambiguity.

Compartmentalization as a family skill means being able to have an argument about something and then being able to set it aside and still enjoy each other over dinner. It means not liking the person your kid is dating and still being polite, and not criticizing *all* of his or her decision-making just because you don't like *this* decision. It means others can be irritated by that very annoying habit you have and still love you deeply. It means not treating a part of a person as if it is all of the person. You're more than your job, more than your marriage, more than any one aspect of yourself.

Compartmentalization also means setting aside your depression as best you can, walling it off so it doesn't leak into your every interaction. Despite the popular cultural cliches to "let it all hang out," "be genuine," "do what you feel," and what I think is the worst of them, "be fully present in the moment," parents—*all* people for that matter—have a tremendous social responsibility. Going around spewing negativity and hurling toxic feelings at people with no regard for their feelings, the appropriateness of the circumstances, or other potentially negative consequences, is both harmful and unnecessary. You have a right to your feelings, but you don't have a right to impose them on others. You have a right to be depressed, but you don't have a right to be oblivious to its effects on those who depend on you.

If it's another member of the family whom you're concerned about, it's important to be able to discuss sensitively but directly the effect his or her depression is having on others. It may seem like an extra burden for the depressed person to carry by having to be more sensitive to others at a difficult and usually self-absorbed time. However, there is an opportunity through such discussions to motivate others to get help sooner and to prevent important relationships from getting permanently damaged during a temporary episode.

Bear in mind, depression is temporary; it will, in all probability, eventually go away, especially if you are sensible in learning to manage it skillfully. Even if you can't seem to see it as temporary because you're in the thick of it, keep the idea close to you that it will pass. However, the negative effects of the depression, ranging from merely neglecting others to directly hurting them by lashing out in pain can be felt for a lot longer than the length of the depression itself.

When what you're doing isn't working, *do something else.* Can't do it yourself? You don't have to. When you don't know what to do, it helps to talk to someone who does. For example, at the University of Miami Medical School, an innovative program led by Dr. Tiffany Field provides "interaction coaching" for depressed mothers striving to be better mothers so that their depression won't harm their children. I love that idea! The depressed mother wears an earpiece receiver, and while she plays with the child in an observation room a coach instructs her on ways to improve the quality of interaction between her and her child. Dr. Field says, "Even though the mother is battling depression, she has to be actively involved in suppressing its effects on her child." Agreed. I'll reiterate a point I made previously—you are more than your feelings. You have the ability to choose what you do and don't say, and what you do and don't do. *If you feel you don't have the kind of control it takes to separate your internal feeling state from the way you treat your children, then that is a strong clue you need to speak to a professional—and soon.*

Compartmentalization is not the same as repressing your feelings or being in denial. You can and should be aware of your feelings; they can and should be acknowledged and dealt with realistically and in a timely way. They just shouldn't be acted out on others.

Getting out of the "I'm a Victim of My Family" Mentality

Unfortunately, people have been conditioned by our culture to identify themselves as victims, a tendency unwittingly amplified by the mental health profession in its zeal to help the "underdog." The result is that people don't recognize their own power, much less how to use it skillfully. Sometimes it goes beyond merely silly and is truly absurd. While on a teaching trip to Milwaukee, I spotted an ad in the paper for a "recovery" group seeking new members that could identify themselves as "Adult Children of Affluent Parents." Victims of wealth? Gimme a break! What about Adult Children of Alcoholics? When exactly does someone ever outgrow *that* label? How can we empower people by teaching them to think of themselves as victims? Why teach people to (globally) define themselves according to only one aspect of themselves, like a habit or belief? Aren't people *more* than their parentage, *more* than their history, *more* than their feelings, *more* than their genes, *more* than *any* one aspect of themselves?

Since our culture encourages global thinking, as discussed in chapter 4, how are people to develop the compartmentalization skills that allow family unity and loyalty? Even therapists who should know better have bandied about the exceedingly global label *dysfunctional family*, and made it a part of standard English. ("Hi. I'm Mary. I come from a dysfunctional family." Everyone nods their heads in deep understanding in response.) It's a pity. The term *dysfunctional family* is so global as to be meaningless. Worse, it prevents helpful compartmentalization. It prevents a critical analysis in which you differentiate what was hurtful from what was helpful in your family of origin by portraying it as globally bad. Was there *nothing* valuable in your family? The term *dysfunctional family* even prevents eventually learning to think of the hurtful things that may have existed then as potentially helpful now. When one finally takes the responsibility to go out and actively learn (or perhaps, unlearn) what is necessary to live a deliberate and skillful life, one can more easily let go of the pains of the past. More than merely "making lemonade out of lemons," there is a deeper potential to learn to differentiate what has been from what can be—the essence of hopefulness. There is a deeper potential to distinguish what was once uncontrollable from all that is now possible—the very antithesis of helplessness. You are much, much more than just your history.

The necessarily active roles of parents in teaching social and cognitive skills to their children is an opportunity missed when parents see themselves as victims and are themselves struggling with depression. How available could Rachel Simmons, from the chapter's opening vignette, be for Peter and Renee when she was so mired in her own feelings of being overwhelmed at the enormity of what had happened? Parents who feel victimized by life not only set the emotional tone for the family, but set the parameters for what will and will not be experienced by the children. Experience is the most powerful and personal of teachers, and so the most rapid path of hand-me-down blues isn't through one's genes. It's through one's interactions. A stranger who *doesn't* share your genes can pass doom and gloom along every bit as readily as a relative.

No family is perfect any more than any individual could be. Furthermore, what you deemed perfect someone else thought of as only barely adequate. People often long for the perfect childhood they felt they were denied, even trapping themselves in the impossible and totally convoluted belief that "I won't be happy until my parents treat me better when I was a kid!"

In this respect, I want to dissuade you from thinking that you have to look backward in order to move forward with your life. Understanding what went on in your childhood that was far from perfect can too easily reinforce the notion that you are a victim of your family. Understanding your past may be helpful on some levels, but *not* the ones critical to overcoming depression. Coming to terms with what it means to have the choice about how you want to live from now on, and how you want to reshape your family's way of doing those things it may not do very well right now is the hallmark of maturity. Forever blaming others in your past for your problems and getting lost in the illusion that there's nothing you can do about the harm you think they caused you is a formula for failure. Take control and start doing something different, even just a little bit different, *today*.

Hopelessness and helplessness represent the "one-two punch" of depression. When a family system, through its very style of interaction between members, emphasizes that things can change and that *all* members are valuable, the one-two punch hits only air. The family can be a shield for the hard times and an inspiration and catalyst for the good times. A family shares a history, but it also shares a future. As far as depression goes, the latter generally matters more than the former. I think the best way to come to terms with a hurtful past is to get a really good future out of it. After all, the future hasn't happened yet.

CRITICAL RELATIONSHIP SKILLS

Being Responsible to Others. In the families that function best through good times and bad, there is an extraordinarily powerful shared recognition of a fundamental responsibility to each other. Not a responsibility *for* each other necessarily (although at critical times that may be true, too), but a responsibility *to* each other. It means all family members know intellectually and feel emotionally that there is a necessity to take others' feelings and wishes into account in choosing one's own course of action.

People will disagree, of course, and people will attempt to manipulate others to get their way. Naturally, each person must make choices for him- or herself, but not unfairly or destructively at the expense of those others it will affect.

Consider some common examples:

- Telling your brother you'll return to him by Friday that thing you borrowed last month and not following through is simply irresponsible, barring legitimate circumstances interfering. Deciding "he doesn't really need it" is making someone else's decisions for them while disregarding an agreement.
- Not returning your mom's phone call to you even days later because you just didn't feel like it is irresponsible. It discounts the other person for the sake of your personal convenience.
- Blaming others for bad choices you made ("Why'd you talk me into doing that?") is irresponsible. You are responsible for the choices you make. If you were misled or misinformed, that is another matter. If you chose to ignore relevant but undesirable information because it would dissuade you from doing what you wanted to do, it's still your choice and you're responsible for it.
- Cutting family members out of your life without an opportunity for achieving some resolution is irresponsible. Talking about matters may not lead to a resolution, but it allows for the possibility.
- Not discussing your concerns or reactions directly to someone who has offended you and striking back at him or her indirectly is irresponsible.
- Choosing to smoke may be your right, but to force your spouse and children to breathe your toxic fumes is terribly irresponsible. Why? Because you are deciding for others what risks they should endure because of your behavior.
- Deciding for others what they should think or feel is irresponsible. Treating people respectfully means letting them make their own decisions (as adults, not children). You may not agree, but acceptance is the starting point for you to decide what your response will be.

As you can see, the list of ways to be irresponsible and hurtful toward others is endless. Consider carefully how these issues are dealt with in *your* family.

The ability to deal with adversity, whether it is internal or external, in a united way requires each person to be responsible *for* themselves and responsible *to* the others they interact with. The times that overwhelm people and drive them into depression are when they feel isolated ("disconnected"), misunderstood, devalued, and unable to cope with the enormity of whatever they're struggling to deal with. When people don't have the support of family members who treat them respectfully even when they happen to disagree, people will be at the highest risk for depression.

Building Family Rituals. The various skills I'm describing throughout can neither exist or be taught in a vacuum. To build family strengths one must first build family cohesiveness—harnessing the forces that hold the family together as a unit.

Establishing family rituals is a means for building cohesiveness. *Family time can itself be an invaluable tool in preventing depression.* A recent study at Children's Hospital in Ohio indicated that families who had dinner together five nights a week had happier children who were much less prone to drug abuse than even those families who had dinner together three nights a week. Considerable research has reinforced the notion that, at least in some ways, more actual time together is at least as important as the quality of the time together. Once again, the value of close, healthy relationships as a buffer against depression is evident.

It's interesting how people who look back favorably on their childhoods inevitably remember the rituals of their families. They remember the family dinners, the holiday gatherings, the things that were special yet predictable. In general, people prefer predictability, at least where their emotional safety and comfort is at stake, as in their close emotional relationships. They want to be able to count on the reliability of significant others, they want people to do what they say they're going to do, and they want people to be clear about their intentions. It is no coincidence, therefore, that consistency counts for so much in people's emotional well-being.

Families can make rituals out of anything they choose. It is less important what the ritual is as its ability to be counted on as a reliable shared event. Simple rituals such as having dinner together or taking family vacations together are good ones. The more opportunity to spend time together in an atmosphere of caring, acceptance, and fun, the more valuable they will seem and the more fondly they will be remembered.

I have a particular ritual I like to encourage in the families I work with. It's clipping the "Dear Abby" and "Ann Landers" columns for the week and then having a family discussion about each of the letters that were published. Over time, the letters the advice columnists receive reflect almost every concern and problem that people have, and discussing them with your family and comparing what you'd advise versus what the "experts" advised is a valuable way to teach empathy, problem-solving skills, verbal skills in identifying and articulating feelings, and identifying differences in approaches that model more flexible thinking. And it's fun!

It takes clear boundaries and effective limit-setting to make family rituals work. Thus, from the time the children are very young, or from the earliest days of the marriage, it should be agreed to and then reinforced over the years that "this is what we do." It's not that exceptions should never be made, but it should be clear that the ritual transcends any one time it might prove difficult to maintain. If you don't strive to maintain the ritual, *whatever* it is, the kids will always have friends they'd rather play with or things they'd rather do instead of honoring family time. It is the parent's role to preserve precious family time for all.

Recognize and Use Your Personal Power to Do Something Different. There is considerable potential for harm to your self-esteem and that of others you interact with when you don't recognize your power (meaning capacity to influence) in the family system.

To prevent or manage depression in yourself and your family, each person must come to know what it means to have power, and not be allowed to sink into an unchallenged perception of helplessness. The best thing you can do for someone who is showing the apathy and behavior of someone who has started to give up is to use your power to lovingly but directly challenge his or her perceptions of hopelessness. Declare yourself a caring ally, declare your wish to help, and let your loved one know that as stymied as they might feel right now, there are options to consider. You can literally say some variation of "I see you hurting and I want to help. I care about you. You feel stuck, and it's apparent you're miserable and that you don't want to feel that way. Doing what you've been doing hasn't helped, so doing more of it doesn't seem like a very good idea. How about if together we try to figure out something to do that might make a difference?"

When you change one element of a system—one person's behavior—the others in the system will respond. Bringing home jokes instead of bad moods, rallying people to go to the park instead of sitting passively and watching yet another show on television, going over and giving a warm hug instead of some criticism, can break the vicious cycle of repetitive negative interactions.

Think of interactional sequences in your life that you can introduce something different into, and you will take the first step in preventing that helpless and trapped feeling from arising that is a frequent precursor to full-blown depression. More important, doing something different models flexibility in perceptions and actions, a potentially powerful preventive tool given how rigid the perception can be that "it *has* to be this way" even when "this way" hurts. Giving up goes hand in hand with feeling helpless and hopeless; experimenting with new behaviors and using yourself as a tool to bring out better and more beneficial responses in others is an unambiguous means for discovering, or *re*discovering, your power as a vital member of the family system.

Personal Boundaries, Roles, and Role Transitions. Being responsible to others, recognizing and using power sensitively and wisely, and getting out of the "I'm a victim of my family" mentality are all *vital* to preventing and managing depression. The underlying foundation for these skills is your sense of personal boundaries. In building family strengths, establishing and maintaining good boundaries with each other is critical. The lines you draw that you will simply not tolerate others stepping over, and defining what you will and will not let them say or do around you, represent your boundaries.

Developmental theorists talk about *differentiation*, the process of becoming an independent, unique individual. When children are not encouraged (or even allowed) to discover their individual and unique attributes, when thoughtless conformity is demanded regularly, when personal space is violated (such as when you can't even shower or go to the bathroom without people popping in on you), when the need for privacy is discouraged, and worst, when you violate or are violated by someone sexually, physically, or verbally abusing you on a regular basis, there's a very high probability that healthy boundaries are going to be absent. In the same way that "good fences make good neighbors," good boundaries can make a healthy family system in which people respect each other's needs and wants, even when they don't particularly understand or agree with them. Boundaries must be reciprocal to function, though; there is a need to have that sense of responsibility to each other shared if all are to honor the agreed-upon ways of dealing respectfully with each other.

Building family strengths involves building clearer, stronger, more family enhancing boundaries. Once you grasp the concept of boundaries, it can become easy to apply them equally well in totally different contexts, whether it's things like what we can and can't say to each other when we're angry (conflict management skills), defining what we will and won't watch on television, or what we will and won't allow as conversation topics at the dinner table.

Boundaries suggest roles. Roles in the family are defined by their boundaries. For example, if you're the family peacemaker, usually a self-assigned but readily reinforced role by others, it means that in that peacemaking role you can do "this" but you can't do "that." Roles and the boundaries that define those roles are not meant to be eternally rigid or never-changing. Roles change as people grow (or regress), as interests change, and as newly arising circumstances dictate. These role changes and redefinitions of boundaries are catalysts for the entire system to make adjustments, and the healthiest family systems are able to do exactly that.

Let's consider a couple of examples of how poor boundaries can lead to depression, and likewise, how good boundaries can prevent depression.

Example #1: *Marcy and Yvonne were competitive with each other for as long as anyone could remember. Only a year apart in age, they grew up wanting and competing for the same kinds of things, whether it was the attention of their parents, the approval of their peers, the bigger dish of ice cream, or the grades they got in school. As children, the sisters used to fight over the most trivial things, always jockeying for position. As they got older,* *the conflicts between them became less overt, but the feelings each had of wanting to win at the other's expense never went away. Now, as adults, they each had married and established their own households. Both were raised to believe that having a husband and family was more important than having a career of one's own. Yvonne married a man with a fine education and a career that held unlimited potential for financial success. Marcy married a good man with a good job, but it was just a job. Marcy told herself that happiness was more important than money, and that she was the better-off of the two because her husband was a much more down-to-earth, nice guy than Yvonne's humorless, pinstriped mate. But as Yvonne's life began to reflect greater financial success with a new and bigger house and a new and bigger car, Marcy found herself getting increasingly envious. She gradually stopped calling Yvonne, not wanting to hear her sister brag about her latest acquisition. She also found herself growing resentful of her husband and hating herself for it. The calm and self-satisfied feelings he had about himself that initially attracted her to him were now being seen as evidence of his passivity and lack of ambition. She found herself sniping at him for little things that never used to bother her, and he was clearly confused about why she seemed so angry and withdrawn lately. Marcy was growing ever more unhappy with her life and, to make matters worse, she knew she was doing it to herself with her childish envy of Yvonne.*

Marcy's boundaries were poor in this situation with Yvonne. Marcy chose to marry a man for reasons other than his income potential, but she let her competitive feelings from a lifetime of wanting to outdo her sister interfere with her marriage and ultimately her own happiness. Marcy had never come to terms with or outgrown the childish desire to win, even in contexts such as marital satisfaction that can't reasonably be viewed as competitions. Marcy needs help in getting her boundaries clear, defining her life in terms of what matters to her as an individual on her own merits, and not in comparison to anyone else, including her sister. There will always be people who are wealthier, better educated, better-looking, better experienced, better whatever, than we are. So what? Having good boundaries can protect you from making comparisons to others when the real challenge is how to become the best person you can be, regardless of others' choices or circumstances.

Example #2: *Cass lost her husband when Raymond was only six years old. She struggled to raise him as best she could and did an excellent job by everyone's accounting—except Raymond's. He was fifteen now, and he was spending less and less time at home with her; when he was home with her he always seemed so irritable. The more distant he became, the more Cass tried to engage him by saying and doing the things that had always worked when he was growing up, like taking him to a movie or out for ice cream. One night he got home later than he'd promised, and Cass went on an angry tirade that lasted far too long for the circumstances. All Raymond said in his defense was a quiet, "Mom, I'm sorry I was late, which was wrong, but quit talking to me like I'm a little boy. I'm not a kid anymore." Cass felt like he'd slapped her.*

That night, she tossed and turned but couldn't sleep. Raymond's simple statement kept ringing in her ears. The flash of insight occurred somewhere during the night, although Cass doesn't remember exactly when. The next morning, she asked Raymond if they could go out to breakfast together to talk, and he reluctantly agreed. Over breakfast, Cass said, "I thought a lot about what you said. I realized I have been treating you like you're still my little boy, and you're right, you're not my little boy. You're a young man now with your own interests and your own friends, and it's wrong for me to think that all I have to do is call you Ray-Ray and take you for an ice cream to get your unwavering attention. I'm really sorry, Raymond. I don't want to smother you or stop you from growing up. I just love you and want to be with you sometimes. Whaddya say?"

Raymond thought a long time before he replied. When he finally spoke, all he said was, "I love you, Mom. That's not going to change. But, yeah, I do want to talk about how I can

be around you without you calling me 'your little man,' ya
know what I mean?"

Cass may have had poor boundaries in the past in trying to keep
Raymond from outgrowing his childhood (accepting an inevitable transi-
tion), but she showed great maturity in realizing her error in dealing with
him, accepting responsibility for its inappropriateness, and creating an
avenue of discussion that could lead to correcting the problem between
them. Raymond also showed great maturity in giving his mother the
emotional reassurance she needed that he still loved her, and by keeping
the discussion on a solution-oriented track of how things might change
in the future instead of blaming her for her past mistakes in dealing
with him.

What could have been an ugly and depressing chapter in their lives,
featuring lots of anger, resentment, and withdrawal, was averted because
both maintained clarity about where the appropriate boundaries in their
relationship were.

Examples of the necessity of establishing and reestablishing good
boundaries in all relationships, but especially family relationships, are
endless. Your boundaries get tested a hundred times a day, and each
boundary violation holds the potential to victimize you or someone close
to you. Thus, the skill of knowing what is and is not controllable in order
to have realistic expectations about *whether* and *where* to invest your time
and energy is a vital skill to master. So often, depression arises when
people try to control the uncontrollable (such as aging, or death, or the
career your child chooses), or don't control what *could* be controlled (such
as what they say when they're angry, what they eat for lunch, or whether
they say "I love you" a lot to the people who most need to hear it). Both
aspects are evident in the above vignettes with Marcy and Yvonne, and
Cass and Raymond.

Expectations. At various times, I have talked about the influence of your
expectations on your experience. I've discussed how negative expectations
can fuel hopelessness and despair, and positive expectations can generate
hopefulness and motivation. In this context, I refer to the expectations
that you have of your family and whether they are realistic.

So often, the despair that people feel about their family is a product of having been let down or deeply disappointed in some way. They wanted support, and instead got criticism. They wanted acknowledgment, and instead were slighted. They wanted honesty, and instead got lies. They wanted closeness, but got emotional distance. The examples of the differences between what people wanted and what they got could go on indefinitely.

The critical issue for you to consider is this: How do you know whether an expectation, yours or a loved one's, is realistic? It is important to develop a sense of what is realistic to expect. For example, considerable disappointment and hurt could be prevented if a woman knew better than to ask her "man of few words" for lengthy and emotionally intimate discussions. (And, the reality is, he's *always* been a man of few words. She just *expected* that, over time, he'd change because of her continual encouragement to open up.)

Years ago it was fashionable to say "Don't have any expectations and you won't be disappointed." I don't believe it's a realistic expectation to have no expectations. People generally know what they want, or what they wish would happen under ideal conditions, but they get into trouble when they get attached to a particular outcome and ignore the information that indicates it isn't likely to happen. The idea isn't to have *no* expectations. The idea is to have realistic ones.

Hopelessness can be depressing. So can hopefulness. Believing that people you care about will change (stop drinking, stop using drugs, stop being violent) provides you with hope. But it is a common theme in therapy that the person has no intention of stopping their hurtful behavior, even saying as much, and the hopeful one sinks into ever deeper depression as a result of each new episode of disappointment. In such instances, hope is depressing.

Look for facts. Listen to what people actually tell you, and not just what you want to hear. Look at the relationship between what someone says and what he or she actually does. Until you really know someone, don't believe what he or she tells you, and don't disbelieve it, either. Observe. Learn about the person. Gather information about him or her in order to know what's realistic to expect. This applies every bit as much to members of your family as it does to someone you just met. People are people, and whether it's your mother, father, sister, brother, husband, wife, or child, he or she is a person first, with his or her own values, needs, motivations, and way of doing things. You can save yourself and your family considerable difficulty by being clear about each other's expectations. Talk about, and let others talk to you about, expectations. You (or they) may not like what you hear in response, but at least you can modify your expectations to be more realistic and prevent some disappointment, and even depression, later.

Rules and Conflict Management. Even when people are close, have good boundaries, level, compartmentalize, think clearly, and have realistic expectations, there will be disagreements between them. Other people will have interests you don't have, feelings you don't share, goals you don't value, beliefs you can't support, and they'll do things you simply don't like. Conflicts arise routinely in even the best of family relationships.

Anger can feed on itself, meaning it can evolve a momentum that carries it farther than it needs to go, possibly into dangerous territory where people say and do things in the heat of anger that they'll deeply regret. Throughout the book I have talked directly and indirectly about the need to have rules the family lives by: rules for how responsibilities are distributed, how communication is conducted, and how people express dissatisfaction, hurt, and anger.

Conflict management skills address the rules for how differences of opinion are handled. In the homes marred by violence or verbal abuse, the rule is a destructive "anything goes." Is there any way of demeaning or humiliating a person worse than to use violence to make the point? Or to call someone names that will stick far longer than whatever the point of the argument was?

In chapter 5, I discussed family atmosphere. I pointed out how critical it is to everyone's well-being to live in a safe environment, free of the threats of violence, abandonment, rejection, or humiliation. I talked then and also earlier in this chapter about how important it is to evolve and maintain a protective attitude toward all family members. It is hardest to do that when you're angry with that person, yet that is also the time that it will count for the most. When either or both of you are obviously angry, and you both strive to keep to the subject and not attack each other, there is a respectfulness evident that will last well after the argument is over. Communicating that the relationship's health ("we") matters more than winning this single argument ("me") is powerful. Keeping the boundaries clear about what is and is not acceptable behavior during an argument and maintaining the integrity of the relationship by honoring those boundaries is critical to having trust in each other. As soon as that trust is violated, it can be difficult to regain.

What are some good rules for conflict management? Honor people's right to be heard. Stick to the issue. Maintain the boundaries that define an agreeable disagreement. Don't use violence. Don't say anything you'll regret when the argument is over. Go do something on the light side together when the issue is resolved in order to affirm that the relationship goes on even after the argument is over. Don't threaten the continuation of the relationship with a family member. Do a follow-up soon after to check and see if there's anything left over still needing to be addressed. If something can't be immediately resolved, set a time to discuss it again and be there at the appointed time. If something can't be resolved at all, form an agreement as to how it will be handled respectfully, perhaps even using a mediator or a therapist to help work it out.

As relationships change, so must at least some of the rules of those relationships. One of the things that needs to be built into the rule system of any family is what the rules are for when and how to change the rules. That means setting up specific guidelines or observable signs that make it clear whether some plan of action you created is actually working. How will you know whether the new way we've decided to handle this issue is effective? How will we determine that it's time to stop doing this in the same old way and start doing it in some other way that might work better? The biggest challenge in life, as far as I can tell, is to continually adapt to changing circumstances in a meaningful way. Trying to preserve family traditions and at the same time trying to adjust to new or evolving circumstances often seem mutually exclusive. It takes skill to be able to sort out which things need to be changed and which things need to be left alone.

BE THE ANTIDEPRESSANT FAMILY

What are some of the helpful things you can do in your relationships with your children or spouse if they are depressed? In addition to all the ideas offered thus far, here are ten good possibilities to consider:

- Take prompt action to help. Don't wait. As stated earlier, time matters.
- Create a context for communication to occur. Whether it's through play, a shopping trip, or a drive to some distant place (suddenly needing to be visited), create the time and space that will make unhurried and uninterrupted talking possible.
- Listen nonjudgmentally. A sure way to end a conversation prematurely is to offer advice that wasn't asked for, offer judgments or reactions based on what *you* feel, or lapse into "when I was your age" stories with your child. Allow crying, swearing, or whatever else helps get out whatever is on your child or your spouse's mind before you start responding to it.
- Ask open-ended questions. Instead of asking questions that can be answered with just a yes or no, ask questions that get at the *process* of your child or spouse's thinking: "How did you know that? How do you know if what you're assuming is true? How will you feel when you find out you can do that?"
- Ask for other attributions for whatever has happened. You've now learned a few things about some of the qualities of depressed thinking—the self-blame, the belief that the pain will be permanent, the view that everything is ruined, not just one aspect of something. Gently ask some variation of "You seem to be assuming this . . . might there be some other explanation for this happening the way it did?" If he or she can't generate at least a couple more, then help out with some possibilities.
- Encourage activity. Physical activity is a natural antidepressant. Walking, running, tai chi, golf, tennis, weight lifting, gardening, swimming, hiking, *anything* that's physical has the potential to influence how long the depression will last and how severe it will get.
- Encourage frequent social contact. I believe that a primary reason people with a strong network of good friends are much less prone to depression is they provide a forum for exchanging views. When people are stuck inside their own heads, there is no opportunity for correction if ideas or perceptions are off. Also, closeness is a buffer— it helps to know you're liked, loved, appreciated. And socializing encourages getting out of yourself and into others. It works.
- Have fun. Unless you actively seek out opportunities for fun, they

will escape you. There are *always* problems to solve, tasks to do, obligations to meet. If you don't strive to keep fun a regular part of your life, it will go the way of the dinosaur.

- Encourage relaxation. Having fun isn't the same as being relaxed. Teaching children (and adults) how to spend quiet time with a relaxed focus on thinking straight is *vital.* It reduces anxiety, agitation, and rumination. It also teaches you that you have control over your own experience, countering that tendency toward helplessness. (In fact, I have created on audiotape program called *Focusing on Feeling Good* to facilitate learning these skills through direct experience. Further information is available in Appendix A.)

- Encourage self-care and personal responsibility. When people are depressed, they often stop caring for themselves. They sleep poorly, eat poorly, stop exercising, stop dressing well, stop socializing, stop doing the things they normally enjoy. The loss of pleasure in usual activities is called *anhedonia,* and it's a sure sign of depression. Self-blame or blaming others for one's feelings is a common but ineffective response. Personal responsibility ultimately comes down to saying to oneself, "This isn't where I want to be in my life, feeling this way. *It's up to me to do something different,* because doing things the same way will only yield more of what I don't want." I don't offer advice until someone says to me, "I know I need to do something different, but I don't know *what.*"

Dealing with a depressed child or spouse is never easy. But making comparisons to other families or others' kids, or wishing things weren't the way they are, only inhibits pursuing a timely and realistic plan of problem resolution. Depression can be resolved in the majority of cases, but not by simply wishing it would go away. When you strive to adapt your style and increase your sensitivity to the fact that your family member requires something extra from you, you'll likely discover how just a little extra can go a long way in creating a family system that really is a good place to be for *everyone.*

Let's focus our attention now on the issue of preventing depression in children.

An Ounce of Prevention . . .

Previously, I described my experience of going hiking with my wife and best friends, including their seven-year-old daughter, Megan. I described the way we engaged Megan in the process of critical thinking about her experiences there, and how we all do that with her in many different contexts. Megan is learning daily *how* to think, not merely *what* to think.

Following our time in Zion, I had another experience just a month later while on a teaching trip to the south of France. A married couple with children, from Germany, attended my clinical training, and at the end of one of the days the mother came up to me and related the story of how her five-year-old son had recently started school. His initial response was positive—he liked going. Several weeks into the school year, though, he got into a fight with another boy and was apparently deeply upset by the altercation. Now he was tearful each morning, reluctant to return to school. It required intensive work to get him to go again, and the effort didn't seem to be diminishing even though he did okay once he got there. His mother said she realized on the basis of what I had talked about that day that she could start to do something she hadn't done before: She could talk to him. She was good at offering him reassurances that he'd be fine, giving him hugs, wiping away his tears patiently and empathetically, but it never occurred to her to do more than that. She realized she needed to actively teach him to *think differently* about that experience, and to *think critically* enough to not overgeneralize from a single confrontation to the whole experience of school.

I'm glad she felt empowered by what she learned from me to go home and identify where her son's errors were so that she could strive to correct them. But I also find it frustrating that she didn't already think to do that. Do parents really listen to their children, and do they recognize opportunities to teach the relevant thinking skills that can reduce and even prevent depression? The rising rates of depression suggest they do not.

Two of the books I give my highest recommendation to are Daniel Goleman's book *Emotional Intelligence* and Martin Seligman's book *The Optimistic Child*. If I were Ruler of the Universe, these would be required readings before people would be allowed to have children. Both books emphasize an obvious truth: Being a smart person doesn't prevent one from making serious and potentially depressing errors in life.

In *Emotional Intelligence*, Goleman makes the point that merely having broad academic knowledge or above-average intelligence is not enough. We are not an entirely rational, fact-driven species. We are capable of rationality, but we are also capable of being highly emotional, irrational, inconsistent, and self-deceptive. People do foolish things and then rationalize them; for example, ever ask a smoker how he or she can smoke yet know at a purely rational level that it's poisonous to the body? The ability to organize and relate skillfully to your own emotions, to be aware of them but not governed by them when they are at odds with a greater goal, is the essence of emotional intelligence. Goleman cites some of the research that suggests early childhood experiences can "mold" the brain's emotional circuitry, predisposing children to depression that has been "wired-in" through experience. Goleman emphasizes the need to reverse the rising tide of childhood depression by actively teaching the various skills of emotional intelligence.

In *The Optimistic Child*, Martin Seligman documents the fact that teaching just some of the skills comprising emotional intelligence actually works in reducing and preventing depression. Furthermore, such skills also prevent many of the negative consequences of depression, including drug and alcohol abuse, unplanned teenage pregnancies, and dropping out of school.

Seligman and his colleagues began a longitudinal (long-term) research study to find out whether teaching practical skills to children in the areas of critical thinking, dispute resolution, and building optimism and self-confidence would make a positive difference in their lives. In what was called the Penn Depression Prevention Project, Seligman and his colleagues took on the task of "immunizing" children against depression. Seligman credits Dr. Jonas Salk, the brilliant scientist who developed the polio vaccine to immunize people against that dreaded disease, with the notion of a psychological immunization. To make a long, wonderful story short, Seligman demonstrated convincingly that you can teach children the very skills that will empower them to deal with life more intelligently and with less depression and far fewer self-destructive choices.

What are the skills of emotional intelligence? They have been woven throughout this book:

• recognizing and tolerating ambiguity without jumping to conclusions with no factual basis;

- discriminating what one merely thinks from what is actually true by gathering and weighing objective evidence;
- learning to differentiate between realistic and unrealistic expectations;
- learning what one is and is not responsible for;
- establishing and maintaining clear, healthy boundaries in relationship to oneself (defining standards of personal integrity) and in relationships with others (defining one's limits);
- controlling impulsive responses long enough to first establish clarity about what the goal of interaction is and how it may best be achieved rather than just reacting;
- having empathy for others and realizing they see and feel things differently as unique individuals;
- being able to generate multiple viewpoints to account for a given phenomenon (perceptual flexibility);
- recognizing and accepting one's uniqueness and honoring it assertively in the responsible and well-informed choices one makes;
- foresight, the ability to anticipate consequences and, if necessary, act preventively;
- stress management;
- adaptability to changing circumstances (behavioral and emotional flexibility).

As Seligman points out, helping children learn how to process their feelings and make decisions that reflect rationality and foresight also makes them better academic learners. It is difficult to concentrate, learn, and remember when depression blocks your path.

TEACH YOUR CHILDREN WELL

When children are taught that life doesn't "just happen," but that each choice yields a consequence, they are starting to learn critical thinking. When children are taught that to do anything well, there is a sequence of steps to follow, they can learn to think in more specific and less global terms. When children are taught to anticipate consequences and plan to succeed, they won't be so attracted to the impulsivity of the "now orientation" I described earlier in the book. When children are taught to think systemically in terms of multiple interacting components affecting whatever goes on, they will be less inclined to see things one-dimensionally or think the world revolves around them and whatever their "emotion du jour" is. When children are taught that there are often things more important than oneself at a given moment in time, they can begin to see the world from other viewpoints.

All of the skills of emotional intelligence contradict the popular psychology of "get in touch with your feelings," at least some of the time. It is growing ever clearer that if our children are to have a less depressed future, they will have to learn about all those times it will be important to "get *out* of touch with your feelings."

Parents can only teach what they know. You yourself must evolve the ability to turn off the television more often. You can instead turn on the regular family problem-solving meetings and frequent family discussions, and develop the family rituals that bind you to each other and thereby make it possible to immunize yourselves against the forces of popular (but depressing, in the long run) culture.

It's about the future of the family. You *can* reduce and prevent depression. The most powerful tools we have going for us are our minds and our closest relationships. The trick is learning to use them well.

A Summary of Key Points

- Hard times for the family represent times of elevated risk for depression; how hard times are managed is much more closely related to whether depression develops than the nature of the difficulty. You have to be very deliberate in making sure your family has the ability to face problems without disintegrating.
- Families are a basic biological necessity, and there are many things it must do well if it is to thrive. It must provide safety for its members as well as love, acceptance, acknowledgment, good boundaries, respect, and shared goals.
- The issue of safety is a particularly important one, since the absence of a safe family environment raises anxiety and leaves people poorly equipped to deal with internal and external threats to well-being.
- Depression is often a reflection at an individual level of something that is being handled poorly in the larger family system. Building skills such as thinking and relationship skills for managing life well can have a strong antidepressant effect.

- Critical thinking skills include distinguishing between facts and inferences, anticipating consequences of your actions, leveling, compartmentalizing, and letting go of the notion that you are a victim of your family.
- Critical relationship skills include being responsible to others, building family rituals, learning to use personal power wisely, establishing clear personal boundaries, having clear and realistic expectations for yourself and others, and managing conflicts respectfully.
- Having power means having the capacity to influence others. Whether you realize it or not, you have power in your family. There are many things you can actively do to minimize the likelihood of depression in your family, including taking timely action to address issues, facilitate communication of a nonjudgmental nature, and . . . having fun.
- Teaching children—and adults, too—the skills of what many call *emotional intelligence,* such as tolerating ambiguity and having foresight, has been shown to be valuable in not only reducing depression, but even preventing it. These skills are not likely to be developed much by watching television.

Redesigning and Rebuilding Families in Marital and Family Therapy

9

Symptoms usually appear when a person is in an impossible situation and is trying to break out of it . . . except in rare instances, a symptom cannot be cured without producing a basic change in the person's situation, which frees him to grow and develop.

Jay Haley

You have to do your own growing no matter how tall your grandfather was.
Abraham Lincoln

When Marie and Chuck started dating, each had been single for about a year. Chuck was divorced with a seven-year-old daughter, Holly. He shared custody with her mom, and had Holly with him on a visitation schedule of every other weekend and every Wednesday night. Marie was divorced with two children: Tommy, age eight, and Lynn, age six. She had full custody of the two. Marie and Chuck's engagement joke was, "We're cocreating an environment for consecutive children."

Marie and Chuck were now married only about six months, yet both were having serious second thoughts about the wisdom of their ever having gotten married. Each secretly wondered whether getting married was a "convenience thing" or maybe a reaction to the "I can't stand the dating scene" thing. In any event, neither was feeling good about how things had come together or, more accurately, how things hadn't come together. Both were feeling trapped, hopeless, and depressed. Here's how it came about.

Prior to getting married, Chuck and Marie dated steadily for a year. Both were slow and deliberate about getting into a new romance, and each was sensitive about bringing anyone home too quickly. Holly was slow to warm to Marie, but warm she eventually did. Tommy latched onto Chuck almost instantly, starved for male attention since his own dad couldn't quite seem to figure out how visitation worked. Lynn was a demanding child, but good-natured. She was slow in warming up to Chuck compared to her brother, but it didn't take her all that long. She was not averse to being this *daddy's little girl.*

For as long as Marie and Chuck dated, there was only the occasional "one big family"–type get-together, and everybody was fine. But from the moment Marie and Chuck decided to marry, buy a house together, and blend families, the kids became holy terrors in their own individual ways. Tommy was hitting the girls and stealing and breaking things. Lynn wouldn't sleep in her own room at night, fighting furiously at bedtime to sleep with Mom and this new guy she's been told is "okay to call 'Dad.'" Holly stopped doing the share of household chores she'd been assigned, and protested she "shouldn't have to clean up after two other kids that aren't even my real brother and sister." She alternated between ignoring them and glaring at them.

Marie and Chuck were perplexed. They scolded the kids, they attempted to reason with them, they held family discussions, and when results were not forthcoming their frustration led them to turn on each other, chastising one another for not handling the kids properly—that is, according to how they *would have done it. When each began to wonder aloud whether the marriage was a mistake, the anger flared. Fortunately, Marie's cooler head prevailed. She suggested that before things deteriorated any further, which both declared an unacceptable alternative, it was time to get professional help. Chuck was very reluctant to "air his dirty laundry to an outsider." To him, it felt like an admission of incompetence. Marie was able to impart a very sensible perspective: "What we're both trying to do is create a happy home for ourselves and our kids. But we're missing something, because it isn't working. Honey, should we really keep doing what we already know isn't working? Let's get some fresh perspective." Chuck set aside his reluctance and agreed that something needed to change. Since he didn't know what else to do, he hoped an experienced professional* would.

Getting everyone together to see the family therapist turned out to be the hardest part of the whole process. Once they were in her office, she asked each of them in turn to say some things about what they wanted from their family— what it would look like, how they would know if things were improving, what would be different in each other's behavior, and lots of other questions about what each could do better.

Chuck and Marie were surprised that the kids opened up so quickly in response to what seemed like questions for their imaginations. One of those questions was: "Suppose you woke up tomorrow and a miracle had happened while you were asleep and everything was changed and all the problems were solved. What would be different?" Chuck was especially pleased that he wasn't being blamed for being an insensitive jerk, while Marie was pleased it wasn't the old "the mother is always to blame" routine. Each family member was assigned very different ways to respond to the various troublesome kinds of interactions, and each was also given some homework (things like checklists to fill out or subjects to write about) to do in between sessions. Some of the assignments didn't really seem to make sense ("Why should I go lay down in Lynn's bed when she comes into mine?"), but lo and behold, they worked! Behaviors changed, some quickly and some slowly, but they changed, and a sense of family unity evolved that soon brought an end to any doubts Marie and Chuck had about whether they should have married. In retrospect, they talk about it as the "family's growing pains," and all the family members feel happier and more loved, even when dealing with the latest hassle of the day.

In this chapter, we will consider the subject of professional treatment of depression by mental health professionals. As illustrated in the above vignette, a skilled psychotherapist can be instrumental in getting the recovery show on the road. Depression is a paradoxical phenomenon in terms of treatment. On one hand, it can be *overdiagnosed* when every bad mood is interpreted as the sign of something serious needing to be fixed, because dismissing it as "normal" means being "in denial." (That's a common misinterpretation that follows the popular culture's "feel good all the time" philosophy.) On the other hand, and much more objectively true, depression is *underdiagnosed* in all those people who are actually depressed but don't know it. Depression can easily get masked by more evident medical or psychological problems, as discussed in the very first chapter. Even health-care professionals may miss the diagnosis, as appears to be the case roughly 50 percent of the time among physicians and 20 percent of the time among mental health professionals. Some professionals miss it because the person doesn't have the "classic" symptoms (such as sadness, excessive or inappropriate guilt, insomnia, and others described in chapter 1), and others miss it because they simply don't ask relevant diagnostic questions.

There are many other factors leading to the underdiagnosis of depression as well. Many depression sufferers don't complain about depression because they assume "it's just the way I am." They are what I have called previously the walking wounded, the people who get to work, raise families, and live their lives, though they do so in misery. In fact, only about a quarter of depression sufferers actually seek treatment because the prevailing but erroneous perception is "Why bother to seek therapy? Nobody can help me." As I discussed early on, the very hopelessness that is a primary symptom of the depression serves to prevent the depression sufferer from getting the help he or she needs. No complaints, no diagnosis, no treatment, no improvement.

Beyond underdiagnosis, there is also the very real problem of under-treatment. In fact, in January 1996, there was a gathering of professionals at the Consensus Conference on the Undertreatment of Depression, sponsored primarily by the National Depressive and Manic-Depressive Association, based in Chicago. It was an important meeting detailing some of the reasons for and implications of depression not being adequately treated.

Some of the undertreatment is caused by clinicians who do not track whether prescribed treatments are being followed or how people respond to the treatments. If patients do not do homework assignments given in therapy, or if they don't take prescribed medications because they don't like the associated side effects, then treatment is naturally unlikely to succeed, but *not* because it was incorrect or "bad." In general, more could be done to encourage depression sufferers to stay on track, particularly since low frustration tolerance for anything other than relatively instant cures is common in our society. Ultimately, no one can force compliance with a treatment plan, placing considerable responsibility on the client's shoulders.

Beyond doctors missing the diagnosis and patients not following prescribed treatments, a final component of the undertreatment problem is our health care system. Insurance and managed care companies share considerable blame for undertreating depression sufferers. They typically provide very poor mental health coverage to their subscribers, despite the substantial and still growing evidence that such coverage would serve to reduce health care costs by reducing many of the health problems directly and indirectly associated with depression: unnecessary but frequent trips to doctors with vague symptoms, alcoholism and substance abuse stemming from untreated depression, longer hospital stays and slower rates of recovery from heart attacks and strokes, and on and on. The research evidence for the effectiveness of psychotherapy in treating depression is substantial. Since the exceptionally narrow, reductionistic thinking only considers dollars in the short run, then denying people access to and severely limiting mental health insurance coverage makes a peculiar sort of sense. But look at the same issue systemically and with a wider-angle lens, and such policies are nothing short of stupid and cruel. The deep distress, the suffering, and the tens of thousand of deaths through suicide and violence each year *could* be prevented, if people could look a little farther than the short-term and if they'd stop looking for a magic pill for complex problems. There isn't one.

This is another paradox associated with depression in America: Despite the true depression sufferers being genuinely underdiagnosed and undertreated, the overprescription of antidepressants is a problem. It is unsettling to note that the United States has only about 5 percent of the world's population but consumes more than 75 percent of the world's Prozac. Many people now even refer to the drug quite casually as Vitamin P.

No depression expert I am aware of would ever suggest that depression is an *entirely* biological phenomenon that should *only* be treated chemically. If you were to go back and reconsider the lives of everyone I've described in all the case vignettes, you can see how depression had many causes, many appearances, many consequences, and many solutions. In this book, I choose to focus on *one* of the primary solutions: Family systems that can create a context for learning life skills, living well, and reducing and preventing depression.

In real world terms, a family systems perspective holds a greater chance to represent the multifaceted phenomenon of depression far more realistically than any single dimensional consideration. Marital and family therapists in particular tend to emphasize strongly the systemic perspective that I believe should be the mainstream viewpoint of depression.

WHAT IS MARITAL AND FAMILY THERAPY?

Family therapy is a generic label for any of a variety of approaches to treatment that all share one common denominator: The family system, rather than only individuals, is considered the fundamental focus of treatment. Family systems therapy is therefore a different style of therapy than more traditional individual therapy. Ideally, as many people as there are in the family system will get involved in the therapy. *The more people involved, the greater the opportunity to introduce positive shifts in the way they deal with each other that can result in everyone functioning better.* However, paradoxical as it may sound, family therapy can be done with individuals, if either necessary or desirable, by taking others' influences into account when mapping out potential solutions to problems.

The systemic perspective that emphasizes a much broader and more multidimensional view of problems can lead to a broad range of interventions that emphasize the *inter*personal as well as the *intra*personal. Thus, a focus on the quality of the marriage and the patterns of couple and family interaction is one fundamental avenue of consideration. Family systems therapists are far more interested in the question of how to change the negative or hurtful patterns of interaction between family members than they are in trying to find a scapegoat. "You made me do it" isn't an excuse that is likely to get much support from a systems-oriented therapist. The concept of circular causality—that behavior is typically both the cause *and* the effect, makes it undesirable and unnecessary to assign blame. (From a moral point of view, however, ascribing blame may be essential. People do need to be held accountable for their actions.)

Another key area of focus is on the quality of the relationships between parents and their children. Family-of-origin work examines how the family you grew up in shaped your personality, outlook, and style of interactions with others. *Genograms* are a common family therapy tool for exploring the intergenerational influences of one's predecessors. Genograms involve mapping family relationships and key events in the life of the family.

Marital and family therapy is obviously based on the indisputable evidence that positive and mutually satisfying relationships with your spouse and family can play an all-important role in reducing and even preventing depression.

GOALS OF MARITAL AND FAMILY THERAPY

As described earlier, marriages and families with even a single depressed member often have poor problem-solving and communication skills, high levels of tension with frequent conflicts, a lack of family cohesiveness or shared interests and goals, and a generally diminished ability to meet basic physical and emotional needs of its members. It may be abundantly clear to you by now that the popular cultural truism "Where there's a will, there's a way" is potentially dangerous in regard to depression. Thinking that people can overcome depression through sheer willpower if they are properly motivated is simply wrong. *No amount of positive motivation can compensate for a lack of relevant skills.*

Family systems therapy helps families become more resourceful in dealing with whatever changes or challenges they face. The emphasis in treatment is on building relevant skills to adapt and grow, changing with changing times. It's generally less important in systemic approaches to insightfully explain why things are the way they are, and more important to help people "do something different," i.e., take effective action to improve the family's ability to function in positive ways for everyone's benefit. Action is a cornerstone of family system approaches, since changes don't typically just happen. They come about when people start handling things differently.

Being happily married isn't merely about some global characteristic called chemistry. It isn't about fate, and it isn't about the luck of the draw. There are many skills that make good marriages possible, and the lack of these skills, likewise, assures a difficult if not outright destructive relationship. Similarly, being a good parent doesn't just happen merely because you were able to successfully reproduce. Being patient, loving, attentive, protective, inspiring, and all the other things parents have to be to even stand a ghost of a chance of raising well-adjusted and competent kids means having skills. Motivation without ability means little; the easiest defense for a job done poorly is, "Well, I *intended* to do better, but . . ."

By emphasizing the learning of specific skills and not just "sharing your feelings," although that is important, too, the active teaching of these skills and how they can be integrated into family interactions is a common focus of the various family therapy approaches. The kinds of skills that are taught as goals of therapy are all those that have been identified throughout the preceding chapters, such as critical thinking, assertiveness, empathy, recognizing and accepting responsibility, problem-solving, conflict resolution, building boundaries, value clarification, and so on. The therapy context is used to solve the marital and family problems presented, but more important is simultaneously teaching how to apply the principles used to solve current problems to future problems that may arise.

THE EFFECTIVENESS OF MARITAL AND FAMILY THERAPY

The field of marital and family therapy is a relatively young one. Throughout most of the history of psychotherapy, the emphasis was exclusively on individual treatment, as discussed in chapter 3. Only in the last two or three decades has really serious research been published documenting the effectiveness of performing psychotherapy from a family systems perspective.

The body of clinical literature on the subject of depression is *enormous*. As I documented in *Breaking the Patterns of Depression*, tens of thousands of research studies addressing various treatments for depression have now been done. Hundreds of thousands of patients have been followed over many years, carefully observing their rates of recovery, rates of relapse, the type, frequency, and intensity of the therapy they received, and other salient factors regarding the effectiveness of different treatment approaches.

The evidence is quite clear that two major avenues of treatment are viable for depression: psychotherapy and the use of antidepressant medications. They are *not* mutually exclusive approaches, and can easily be combined. The evidence is equally clear that each offers specific benefits. Psychotherapy can teach specific skills for how to reduce or even prevent depression, and it can yield a success rate that is approximately the same as medications (but without the side effects). Medications can often reduce serious symptoms of depression more quickly than therapy, and perhaps particularly so with more severe cases. However, the research evidence is unambiguous on this point: *Depression sufferers who only take medication, and do not receive psychotherapy, have a significantly higher rate of relapse.* Why? Simply put, without taking into account the other systemic variables affecting the individual's depression, the person will return to a system (family, job, community) that is still functioning as it always has. Unless the person is prepared to do something different in realistic and deliberate ways, he or she can easily get pushed back into the same "slot" he or she occupied previously—and suffer a predictable relapse.

The three psychotherapies with the greatest success rate for the treatment of depression are the interpersonal, cognitive, and behavioral therapies, discussed in chapter 1. Interpersonal psychotherapy focuses on relationships and emphasizes the teaching of specific relationship skills. It has a proven track record in successfully alleviating depression in the majority of people receiving such treatment. Its focus on relationships encompasses marital and family therapy, and while more research on specific marital and family approaches needs to be done, it is clear that the interpersonal focus is highly appropriate in treating depression. (You can do interpersonal therapy with individuals by focusing on their relation-ships and relationship skills, which is a different context for the methods than when you actually have both spouses or all the family members together in each of the sessions.)

Given all that has been said earlier about the relationship between marital satisfaction and lower rates of depression, and marital discord and higher rates of depression and relapses following recovery from depressive episodes, marital therapy is clearly a vital tool in treating depression systemically. Likewise, improving family atmosphere and providing the tools to enhance communication and problem-solving can translate into a viable means of recovery from depression. When each person's voice is heard, and victimization and dehumanization are alleviated, helplessness and hopelessness can give way to a new closeness and support that we now know directly reduces depression and its negative effects.

There are many aspects of the therapy process itself that have the potential to be therapeutic: accurate diagnosis, the communication and teaching skills of the therapist, specific techniques used, and the networking with additional outside resources (like support groups), to name just a few. What depressed patients actually report as perhaps being the most valuable aspect of therapy, however, is the relationship formed with the therapist. Having a skilled and knowledgeable person offering support and acceptance allows for the formation of what's known as a *therapeutic alliance*. It's the communication to the family and to its individual members that "I care, I'm on your side, I want to help, I want you to achieve what you came here to achieve." Boundaries are clear, trust is established, and goals are defined. The times that therapy is most likely to be successful, then, are those times that each member of the couple or family has that distinct sense that it's a true alliance: "us" against "the problem," rather than "you" against "me."

In creating the therapeutic alliance the therapist is also modeling how problems can be directly addressed, but without anger, blame, and forays into irrelevant side issues. Marital and family therapy provides a safe yet goal-directed context for learning the key interpersonal skills.

FINDING A MARITAL AND FAMILY THERAPIST

The great majority of states have licensure requirements regulating the practice of psychotherapy. Anyone who diagnoses and treats emotional and behavioral disorders is technically a psychotherapist. *Psychotherapist* is, therefore, a generic term that encompasses psychiatry, clinical psychology, clinical social work, and marital and family therapy. Someone may be a psychiatrist who, as a physician with a drug specialization, prescribes medications only and does little or no talking with the patient. Or someone may be a clinical psychologist who only does therapy with individuals but does not treat couples or families. Someone may be a marital and family therapist who focuses only on certain kinds of problems, such as depression or eating disorders, but not other sorts of things, like drug abuse. Can a psychiatrist (M.D.) do marital and family therapy? Yes. So can a clinical psychologist, clinical social worker, or marital and family therapist. It is less salient a factor what the specific degree is that the clinician holds, while the more salient factors are level of clinical skill and ways of approaching the treatment process.

When should you seek therapy? The answer is relatively straightforward: when you and your loved ones are in distress and you have no realistic plan for how to improve things or even just keep them from getting worse. When people are in danger of making foolish, self-destructive decisions that will likely lead from bad to worse, an objective outside influence can work wonders.

To be an intelligent consumer and shop carefully for a therapist at a time when you and your spouse or family are in distress is not easy. Yet shopping carefully for a good therapist is essential. Therapy is at least as much art as it is science, and consequently the skill level and range of clinical experiences possessed by a particular therapist are important factors to consider. At the very least, here are some of the key criteria for you to consider in seeking a therapist:

1. A referral from someone you trust is the best way to begin.

2. The therapist should be licensed by the state agency that regulates the practice of psychotherapy. Without a license, the therapist is not accountable in any way for the quality of his or her work. The license is hardly a guarantee of competence, but it does indicate a certain level of formal education and relevant clinical knowledge.

3. The therapist is experienced in treating the sort of problems you need help with.

4. The therapist can describe an approach to treatment he or she employs that is consistent with what is known to be effective. In the case of depression in the family, a therapist who is knowledgeable regarding antidepressant medications, cognitive, behavioral, and interpersonal therapies is *essential.*

5. The therapist is available for regular appointments.

6. The therapist is open, responsive, caring, and good at both listening and actively offering direction and new ways to approach things.

7. The therapist is able to offer information and perspective as well as facilitating a sense of safety in getting each family member to open up.

Once you decide to seek therapy, if you can't seem to obtain a good referral from friends or relatives you trust, then contact the various national organizations of professionals that can provide information to you about local practitioners. The American Association for Marriage and Family Therapy (AAMFT) is the most obvious place to start in your seeking a referral if you are looking for a therapist who will be the most likely to focus on marital and family issues regarding depression. The AAMFT address and phone number is found in appendix B along with the addresses and telephone numbers of other relevant organizations.

METHODS OF MARITAL AND FAMILY THERAPY

The typical goals of marital and family therapy for depression can be summarized succinctly:

1. Gaining the empathy and support of the nondepressed family members for the depressed family member(s). A little bit of understanding and compassion can go a long way!

2. Helping everyone in the family get a larger systemic perspective about the multidimensional nature of depression, and its multiple causes and potential treatments. It helps a lot when family members aren't offering their one-liners about their ideas of what's causing the problem. No one likes having their problems made out to be simple or trivial.

3. Increasing the focus on existing positive aspects of the marital and family relationships while striving to expand them and increase each member's satisfaction. Doing more of what works, more of what

people *do* like about the family is a valuable way to remind everyone that "it isn't *all* bad."

4. Identifying and building specific interpersonal and problem-solving skills that will meet the members' needs and increase their satisfaction with the marital and family environment. Instead of looking for blame, or who the "screw-up" is, the emphasis is on building the skills that will help interactions go more smoothly.

5. Striving to address and resolve specific issues and problems either leading up to depression or causing it. Getting everyone together to get focused on solving problems can create unity, teach new problem-solving skills, and build hopefulness.

6. Acknowledging and utilizing each person in the family as a part of the growth and recovery system. In good therapy, like a good family, everybody matters.

7. Defining common goals and encouraging working together in striving for them.

In the therapy process itself, a variety of methods can be used. These commonly include:

1. Assertiveness training.

2. Communication skills training (such as effective listening, making clear statements about reactions or preferences devoid of attacks or sarcasm, and open discussions of topics without rancor or manipulation).

3. Anger management skills (recognizing anger before it turns destructive, and expressing anger respectfully and appropriately).

4. Conflict resolution skills (sticking to and resolving conflictual issues).

5. Defining boundaries, expectations, and roles within relationships.

6. Coping skills in adjusting to inevitable transitions (births, deaths, job loss, kids moving out or in, etc.).

7. Intimacy and sexuality skills.

Specific techniques therapists typically employ include:

1. Providing factual information.

2. Practicing specific skills being taught in the sessions.

3. Doing written homework assignments that might enhance the learning of new skills.

4. Reading relevant books.

5. Watching relevant television programs and movies.

6. Trying out new behaviors in different situations in order to notice the changes they generate.

7. Role-playing different scenarios with others in order to learn new ways to handle them or to experience them from someone else's point of view.

8. Exaggerating ineffective behaviors or responses in order to make them less subtle and easier to recognize and abandon.

9. Identifying and keeping records of when things go well in order to discover how to do more of what works.

10. Providing a safe context simply to give voice to one's feelings and to receive empathy and support both as an individual and as a family member.

Therapy is *not* a context for mere complaining. It is *not* a context for blaming your parents or your genes. It is *not* a context for turning your quality of life over to someone else to fix, or a nice place to hang out while you passively wait for the medications to work. The common denominators of therapies that work are: 1) an emphasis on finding solutions, not just focusing on problems; 2) an emphasis on building skills, not just analyzing motives; 3) an emphasis on the future and how things could be, and not on the past and how things used to be; and 4) an emphasis on systemic, multidimensional thinking rather than simple cause–effect explanations.

Action is a defining characteristic of the therapies that are best for depression, rather than just passive reflection. During and after the process of therapy, the new skills are continually practiced, refined, adjusted, and readjusted. In recognizing that marital and family systems are dynamic and ever-changing, there should be no illusion that the same issues you face now will be the same ones you face later. Likewise, the new things you learn to say and do to others may not be the most useful things to continue saying and doing in the future. But, that's the whole point of understanding systems as dynamic, ever-changing entities. You learn to insightfully recognize that your own needs and interests change and also how to remain sensitive to the needs and interests of others around you. It means keeping communication open and checking in regularly with each other for sensitive feedback, allowing rather than fighting changes in yourself or others that may seem inconvenient to you and yet still be growthful.

This is how a marriage and a family can stay healthy even during periods of significant change. Circumstances may come and go, but as long as you have the fundamental skills described above, and the flexibility to adapt them in order to change with changing times, the family system can be a lifelong source of comfort and stability to all its members.

MARITAL AND FAMILY THERAPY FOR INDIVIDUALS

It may seem like an oxymoron to talk about marital and family therapy, which presupposes having at least two people involved in the process, for individuals. But, the reality is that, quite often, only one spouse or one person in the family is able or willing to seek therapy. Sometimes it's because of geographical separation (you live here, they live there), and sometimes it's because the other(s) simply refused to participate (they fear being blamed, they don't think anything can really change, they're too embarrassed about the problems to discuss them openly, they don't think the payoff will justify the effort, or the most likely of all the reasons, they think it's someone else's problem, not theirs).

THE POWER TO DO SOMETHING DIFFERENT

The primary benefit inherent in seeing problems from a systemic perspective is that you discover, or perhaps rediscover, that you have power. You have the power to change what you do, how you act, what you say, and how you react. Let me give you a simple yet common example. A woman named Maggie came to therapy feeling quite depressed. She felt utter despair about her marriage to a financially successful but emotionally detached man. They had no children. Maggie selflessly supported his climb up the career ladder, assuming (obviously incorrectly) that once he obtained some measure of economic comfort, he'd work less and be more involved in their marriage. That didn't happen. Now Maggie felt hurt, angry, abandoned, betrayed, and trapped.

Maggie's failing strategy was to keep telling her husband, Girard, how she felt. When Girard didn't respond in any meaningful way, she told him again, only louder. When he got annoyed and did nothing to change his way of relating to her, Maggie told him again, only louder and a lot more angrily. When Girard actually withdrew further, Maggie threw a tantrum—screaming, crying, and throwing things. She eventually concluded that divorce was her only option. She came to therapy to figure out how to cope with a divorce without becoming even more depressed than she already was.

When I asked Maggie if she truly wanted a divorce, she immediately replied, "Of course not. But I have no choice. I can't go on living in this lonely marriage." Her failing strategy had been to pursue, make demands, get angry, and make even more demands. This is *so* common a scenario: She pursues, he withdraws. Maggie and I set up a two-month experiment. What if she started leaving to go places when Girard got home, instead of dropping everything she was doing to try to be available to him? What if she started going places and doing things without him while dropping little tantalizing hints about what fun and interesting things she was doing that he was clearly not being invited to join? There was little to lose by running the experiment since she was already gearing up for a divorce.

The first couple of weeks went by with Maggie going out by herself for hours at a time and doing things she thought she'd enjoy. Girard's response was minimal at best. Maggie thought he actually seemed relieved to see her go when she went out. Girard's curiosity slowly grew, though, as to why she was so busy all of a sudden, and why she wasn't asking him to go along. Not only that, when Maggie was around, she was acting so suspiciously *nice*. She wasn't nagging him anymore or trying to make him change or trying to tell him how bad he made her feel. After about a month, Girard told her how distant he felt and worried that "maybe we're growing apart." He shocked her pleasantly when he suggested that "maybe we should try and do more things together." When Maggie didn't respond right away, and actually took some time to seem to contemplate his offer, he grew visibly concerned and said, "Don't you want be with me anymore?" *Now* she had some maneuvering ability to begin redefining their relationship.

This is a good example of how someone can go from hopelessness and despair to feeling good again. Maggie decided to actively do something different. She got out of the passive, helpless role in which she acted like a victim of her marriage. She was flexible enough to try a different way of dealing with Girard, and was patient enough to give her new approach time to work. Maggie didn't just do what she felt—she did what made sense to do in an emotionally charged situation. The quote from Jay Haley at the start of this chapter may seem even more insightful to you now in light of Maggie's experience.

Maggie's is an example of how one person can deliberately initiate a positive change in an ongoing relationship. *You do not control others, but you do influence them.* If you inadvertently cater to someone's depression, you can keep it going. If you deliberately introduce positive changes into the system that require others to change, their depression can change, too. What good therapy can do is to help you create a family context for the depression to abate. It can help you design sensible strategies for achieving—or restoring—a healthy balance to you and your family.

You can go from hand-me-down blues to hand-me-down cheer.

THE FUTURE OF YOUR FAMILY

The typical American family is nonexistent. There are *many* types of American families, each differing in form and content. But all families deal with the same sorts of underlying issues: getting and giving more love and attention, honoring a common family bond yet valuing each other's individual differences, managing pain and conflict, celebrating births and mourning deaths. And all the while, each member contributes to the sculpting of a family that is more than any single one of them.

These times of an ever-growing emphasis on the individual's right to choose are clearly not favorable to relationships. Relationships can only thrive when each member has the clear sense of being connected to something greater than him- or herself. Self-absorption is antithetical to good relationships and provides the fertile ground in which depression can grow. It is no coincidence that, as our society has developed the perspectives that families are expendable and that relationships are only valuable to the extent they are convenient, the rates of depression have steadily grown. It is sad yet easy to predict that the rates will continue to grow, unless people strive to rediscover and rebuild the family to be a place that insulates and empowers its members, unless people actively restructure their use of time to spend it together, no longer pretending it's family togetherness when all it really is is a collection of individuals who just happen to be in the same room watching the same television program, unless people take the time to listen to each other and exchange meaningful perspectives (depression doesn't infect people's souls nearly as often when they are able to get what's in their heads and hearts out into the daylight so even they can learn to see the holes in their logic), and unless people can discover that other people are as inevitable as our family is. The world will always include other people. Learning to value them and relate to them skillfully is a far more realistic and worthy goal than trying to hide from them.

You, the System

Your family is a system composed of multiple, interactional parts. So are *you*. You have many dimensions, moods, interests, talents, and strengths. You've come to learn here that you can influence your family by what you say and do. What you lead them to focus on influences what they experience. Likewise, what you focus on in *yourself* influences what *you* experience. When you focus on your feelings you have a very different experience than when you focus on your rational self or a goal that transcends your feelings. As a system in your own right, you can continue to develop all your parts, for all of them are valuable someplace, some time. "Growing" the different parts of your self is one way to assure that the roles you play in your life, your family, and your community are roles you can play well for your benefit and for the benefit of those you love and care about. Realize it or not, you are *already* connected in all kinds of ways.

You can strive to reduce, eliminate, and even prevent depression and thereby change the world of which you are a vital part . . . the world of your family.

A SUMMARY OF KEY POINTS

- Depression can paradoxically be overdiagnosed (when every bad mood is seen as a clinical sign) and underdiagnosed (when negative or ineffectual thought, behavior, and relationship problems are camouflaged or ignored by others).
- Hopelessness is a cornerstone of depression and leads people to give up trying to solve their problems or mistakenly assume that "no one can help me."
- Marital and family therapy encompass many different treatment approaches that share the common denominator of placing a strong emphasis on the recognition that symptoms and problems occur in a social context. The focus in these approaches is on recognizing and giving voice to the many influences that shape our responses, especially family influences.
- Good relationships don't just happen. They require care. Many disorders, depression included, can arise when important relationships go badly and the level of skill of the members isn't enough to improve things.
- Marital and family therapists typically emphasize the need for all members of a family system to express themselves and to learn key skills such as good communication, setting limits with others, and effective strategies for problem-solving and reducing conflicts.
- Being a marital and family therapist is less about academic degrees or credentials and more about holding a family systems viewpoint. When seeking a qualified psychotherapist for your marital and family concerns, you will need to do some shopping around. Any therapist you see should be appropriately educated, state-licensed to practice, and experienced with the kinds of problems you want help with. You can and should check on a clinician's qualifications even before setting up a first appointment.

Appendix: Sources of Help

AUDIOTAPE SUPPORT

I have created *Focusing on Feeling Good,* a series of self-help audiotapes for depression involving hypnotic methods of relaxing and focusing. They teach you to create feelings of comfort while you build a positive frame of mind in order to deal effectively with common problems associated with depression. These tapes can help you think more clearly and take appropriate action, and thereby better accomplish specific goals and resolve bothersome issues.

The tapes are listed below; each is titled according to the specific issue it addresses.

- *Depression as the Problem; Hypnosis as a Solution*
  (A discussion about how to overcome depression)
- *The Power of Vision*
  (Build positive expectations)
- *Try Again . . . But Do Something Different*
  (Manage life circumstances flexibly)
- *Is It In Your Control?*
  (Learning to control the controllable)
- *You're the Border Patrol*
  (Build self-defining boundaries)
- *Presumed Innocent But Feeling Guilty*
  (Resolve issues of guilt)
- *Good Night . . . And Sleep Well*
  (Curtail rumination and facilitate sleep)
- *Prevention Whenever Possible*
  (Integrate preventive learnings)

Price: All 8 topics on 4 audiotapes: $39.95 (plus shipping and handling)

For further information about these and my other audiotape programs, or to place an order, you can call, write, or fax:

Michael D. Yapko, Ph.D.
P.O. Box 234268
Leucadia, CA 92023-4268
(619) 259-7300
(760) 944-6368 Fax
e-mail: yapkom@aol.com

ORGANIZATIONAL SUPPORT

The following professional organizations can provide general information or specific referrals to assist you in your efforts to find a skilled psychotherapist.

American Association for Marriage and Family Therapy
1133 Fifteenth Street, N.W., Suite 300
Washington, D.C. 20005
(202) 452-0109

American Psychiatric Association
1400 K Street N.W.
Washington, D.C. 20005
(202) 682-6220

American Psychological Association
750 First Street N.E.
Washington, D.C. 20002
(202) 336-5800

Depression Awareness, Recognition and Treatment (D/ART)
National Institute of Mental Health
5600 Fishers Lane, Room 10-85, Dept. GL
Rockville, MD 20857
(800) 421-4211

National Association of Social Workers
750 First Street N.E.
Washington, D.C. 20002
(800) 638-8799

National Foundation for Depressive Illness
P.O. Box 2257
New York, NY 10116
(800) 248-4344

National Mental Health Association
1021 Prince Street
Alexandria, VA 22314
(800) 969-6642

INFORMATION ON THE INTERNET

Using the search words "depression" and "mental health" will lead you to more information and referrals than you can imagine. Listed below are some of the most relevant and helpful websites.

National Institute of Mental Health
www.nimh.nih.gov

National Mental Health Association
www.nmha.org

National Depressive and Manic-Depressive Association
www.ndmda.org

American Psychological Association Consumer Help Center
www.apa.org

Online Psychological Services
www.onlinepsych.com/treat/mh.htm

Psych Central
www.grohol.com

Nonprofit Directory on the Internet
www.idealist.org

Behavior Online
www.behavior.net

Dr. Ivan's Depression Central
www.psycom.net/depression.central

Mental Health Infosource
www.mhsource.com

Moodswing
www.moodswing.org

Internet Depression Resource List
www.execpc.com/~corbeau/

American Association for Marriage and Family Therapy
www.aamft.org

Michael D. Yapko, Ph.D.
www.yapko.com

Bibliography

American Psychiatric Association. *Diagnostic and Statistical Manual of Mental Disorders* (4th ed.). Washington, D.C.: American Psychiatric Association, 1994.

Andrews, Gavin, Gavin Stewart, Rae Allen, and A.S. Henderson. "The Genetics of Six Neurotic Disorders: A Twin Study," *Journal of Affective Disorders*, 19 (1990): 23–29.

Antonuccio, David, William Danton, and Garland DeNelsky. "Psychotherapy Versus Medication for Depression: Challenging the Conventional Wisdom with Data," *Professional Psychology: Research and Practice*, 26 no. 6 (1995): 574–585.

Appleton, William. *Prozac and the New Antidepressants*. New York: Plume/Penguin, 1997.

Apter, Terri. *The Confident Child: Emotional Coaching for the Crucial Decade–Ages Five to Fifteen*. New York: Norton, 1997.

Azar, Beth. "Environment Is Key to Serotonin Levels," *APA Monitor*, 28 no. 4 (April 1997): 26–29.

"Nature–nurture: Not Mutually Exclusive," *APA Monitor*, 28 no. 5 (May 1997): 1–28.

Barnett, Rosalind and Caryl Rivers. *She Works/He Works*. New York: Harper San Francisco, 1996.

Beach, Steven, Evelyn Sandeen, and K. Daniel O'Leary. *Depression in Marriage*. New York: Guilford, 1990.

Beardslee, William, Patricia Salt, Eve Versage, Tracy Gladstone, Ellen Wright, and Phyllis Rothberg. "Sustained Changes in Parents Receiving Preventive Interventions for Families with Depression," *American Journal of Psychiatry*, 54 no. 4 (1997): 510–515.

Beck, Aaron. *Love is Never Enough*. New York: HarperPerennial, 1988.

Beckham, E. Edward and William Leber (Eds.). *Handbook of Depression* (2nd ed.). New York: Norton, 1995.

Begley, Sharon. "Born Happy?" *Newsweek*, (October 14, 1996): 78–80.

Bell, Art. *The Quickening*. New Orleans: Paper Chase Press, 1997.

Birtchnell, John. "Negative Modes of Relating, Marital Quality, and Depression," *British Journal of Psychiatry*, 158 (1991): 648–657.

Bloomfield, Harold and Robert Cooper. *How to Be Safe in an Unsafe World*. New York: Crown, 1997.

Breggin, Peter and Ginger Breggin. *Talking Back to Prozac: What Doctors*

Aren't Telling You About Today's Most Controversial Drug. New York: St. Martin's, 1994.

Brugha, Traolach, Paul Bebbington, David Stretch, Brigid MacCarthy, and Til Wykes. "Predicting the Short-term Outcome of First Episodes and Recurrences of Clinical Depression: A Prospective Study of Life Events, Difficulties, and Social Support Networks," *Journal of Clinical Psychiatry,* 58 no. 7 (1997): 298–306.

Butler, Katy. "The Anatomy of Resilience," *Family Therapy Networker* 21 no. 2 (1997): 22–31.

Burns, David, Steven Sayers, and Karla Moras. "Intimate Relationships and Depression: Is There a Causal Connection?" *Journal of Consulting and Clinical Psychology,* 62 no. 5 (1994): 1033–1043.

Cadoret, Remi, Thomas O'Gorman, Ellen Heywood, and Ed Troughton. "Genetic and Environmental Factors in Major Depression," *Journal of Affective Disorders,* 9 (1985): 155–164.

Carter, Betty and Joan Peters. *Love, Honor, and Negotiate.* New York: Pocket Books, 1996.

Clarkin, John, Paul Pilkonis, and Kathryn Magrude. "Psychotherapy of Depression," *Archives of General Psychiatry,* 53 (1996): 717–723.

Compas, Bruce, Gerri Oppedisano, Jennifer Connor, Cynthia Gerhard, Beth Hinden, Thomas Achenbach, and Constance Hammen. "Gender Differences in Depressive Symptoms in Adolescence: Comparison of National Sample of Clinically Referred and Nonreferred Youths," *Journal of Consulting and Clinical Psychology,* 65 no. 4 (1997): 617–626.

Coontz, Stephanie. *The Way We Really Are: Coming to Terms with America's Changing Families.* New York: Basic Books, 1997.

———. *The Way We Never Were: American Families and the Nostalgia Trap.* New York: Basic Books, 1992.

Coyne, James, Susan Burchill, and William Stiles. "An interactional perspective on depression." In *Handbook of Social and Clinical Psychology: The Health Perspective* edited by C. Snyder and D. Forsyth, 327–344. New York: Regamon, 1991.

———and Margaret Calarco. "Effects of the Experience of Depression: Application of Focus Group and Survey Methodologies," *Psychiatry,* 58 (1995): 149–163.

Cross-national Collaborative Group. "The Changing Rate of Major

Depression: Cross-National Comparisons," *Journal of American Medical Association*, 268 (1992): 3098–3105.

Culbertson, Frances. "Depression and Gender," *American Psychologist*, 52 no. 1 (1997): 25–31.

Cytryn, Leon and Donald McKnew. *Growing Up Sad: Childhood Depression and Its Treatment.* New York: Norton, 1998.

Dash, Leon. *When Children Want Children: An Inside Look at the Crisis of Teenage Parenthood.* New York: Penguin, 1989.

DeVos, Dennis. *Rediscovering American Values: The Foundation of Our Freedom for the 21st Century.* New York: Dutton, 1997.

Downey, Geraldine and James Coyne. "Children of Depressed Parents: An Integrative Review," *Psychological Bulletin*, 108 (1990): 50–76.

Dubovsky, Steven. *Mind–Body Deceptions: The Psychosomatics of Everyday Life.* New York: Norton, 1997.

Duncan, Barry, Mark Hubble, and Scott Miller. *Psychotherapy with "Impossible Cases."* New York: Norton, 1997.

Duke, Marshall, Stephen Nowicki, and Elisabeth Martin. *Teaching Your Child the Language of Social Success.* Atlanta: Peachtree Publisher, 1996.

Dyer, James and Donna Giles. "Familial Influence in Unipolar Depression: Effects of Parental Cognitions and Social Adjustment on Adult Offspring," *Comprehensive Psychiatry*, 35 no. 4 (1994): 290–295.

Fassler, David and Lynne Dumas. *Help Me, I'm Sad.* New York: Viking, 1997.

Fisher, Seymour and Roger Greenberg. "Prescriptions for Happiness?" *Psychology Today*, 28 no. 5 (1995): 32–37.

Flan, Faye. "Happiness in the Genes? Recent Studies about Scientists," San Diego *Union-Tribune*, December 10, 1996.

Frank, Ellen, Jordan Karp, and A. John Rush. "Efficacy of Treatments for Major Depression," *Psychopharmacology Bulletin*, 29 no. 4 (1993): 457–475.

Franklin, Deborah. "Treat Depression with More Than Drugs." *Health*, (1997): 120–126.

Free, Kathleen, Ioulia Alechina, and Carolyn Zahn-Waxler. "Affective Language Between Depressed Mothers and Their Children: The Potential Impact of Psychotherapy," *Journal of the American Academy of Child and Adolescent Psychiatry*, 35 (1996): 783–790.

Glick, Ira (Ed.). *Treating Depression.* San Francisco: Jossey-Bass, 1995.

Golant, Mitch and Susan Golant. *What to Do When Someone You Love Is Depressed.* New York: Villard, 1996.

Goleman, Daniel. "The Happiness Gene: Seems Some Have it, Some Don't," San Diego *Union-Tribune,* July 24, 1996.

———. *Emotional Intelligence: Why It Can Matter More Than IQ.* New York: Bantam, 1995.

Greenberger, Dennis and Christina Padesky. *Mind over Mood.* New York: Guilford, 1995.

Gross, Martin. *The End of Sanity: Social and Cultural Madness in America.* New York: Avon, 1997.

Haley, Jay. "Therapy—A New Phenomenon." In *The Evolution of Psychotherapy,* edited by J. Zeig, 17–28. New York: Brunner/Mazel, 1987.

———(Ed.). *Conversations with Milton H. Erickson, M.D.: Changing Children and Families* (Vol. 3). New York: Triangle Press, 1985.

———. *Ordeal Therapy.* San Francisco: Jossey-Bass, 1984.

———. *Leaving Home.* New York: McGraw-Hill, 1980.

———. *Uncommon Therapy.* New York: Norton, 1973.

———. *Strategies of Psychotherapy.* New York: Grune & Stratton, 1963.

Healy, Jane. *Endangered Minds: Why Our Children Don't Think.* New York: Simon & Schuster, 1995.

Hendricks, Kathryn and Gay Hendricks. *The Conscious Heart: Seven Soul Choices That Create Your Relationship Destiny.* New York: Bantam, 1997.

Hendrix, Harville and Helen Hun. *Giving the Love That Heals: A Guide for Parents.* New York: Pocket Books, 1997.

———*Getting the Love You Want: A Guide for Couples.* New York: HarperPerennial, 1988.

Herbert, Wray. "Politics of Biology," *U.S. News and World Report* (April 21, 1997): 72–80.

Hooley, Jill and John Teasdale. "Predictors of Relapse in Unipolar Depressives: Expressed Emotion, Marital Distress, and Perceived Criticism." *Journal of Abnormal Psychology,* 98 (1989): 229–235.

Hyman, Irwin. *The Case Against Spanking: How to Discipline Your Child Without Hitting.* San Francisco: Jossey-Bass, 1997.

Jacobson, Neil, Amy Holtzworth-Munroe, and Karen Schmaling. "Marital Therapy and Spouse Involvement in the Treatment of Depression, Agoraphobia, and Alcoholism." *Journal of Consulting and Clinical Psychology,* 57 no. 1 (1989): 5–10.

Jamison, Kay. *An Unquiet Mind.* New York: Vintage Books, 1995.

Johnson, Sheri and Theodore Jacob. "Marital Interactions of Depressed Men and Women." *Journal of Consulting and Clinical Psychiatry,* 65 no. 1 (1997): 15–23.

Johnson, Lynn and Scott Miller. "Modification of Depression Risk Factors: A Solution-Focused Approach." *Psychotherapy,* 31 no. 2 (1994): 244–253.

Just, Nancy and Lauren Alloy. "The Response Styles Theory of Depression: Tests and Extension of the Theory." *Journal of American Psychology,* 106 no. 2 (1997): 224–229.

Kaelber, Charles, Douglas Moul, and Mary Farmer. "Epidemiology of Depression." In *Handbook of Depression,* edited by E. Beckman and W. Leber, 3–35. New York: Guilford Press, 1995.

Katz, Mark. *On Playing a Poor Hand Well.* New York: Norton, 1997.

Kender, Kenneth, Michael Neale, Ronald Kessler, Andrew Heath, and Lindon Eaves. "A Population-Based Twin Study of Major Depression in Women: The Impact of Varying Definitions of Illness," *Archives of General Psychiatry,* 49 (1992): 257–266.

Kessler, Ronald, Katherine McGonagle, Christopher Nelson, Michael Hughes, Marvin Swartz, and Dan Blazer. "Sex and Depression in the National Comorbidity Survey II: Cohort Effects," *Journal of Affective Disorders,* 30 (1994): 15–26.

Klerman, Gerald. "The Current Age of Youthful Melancholia: Evidence for Increase in Depression Among Adolescents and Young Adults," *British Journal of Psychiatry,* 152 (1988): 4–14.

———and Myrna Weissman. *New Applications of Interpersonal Therapy.* Washington, D.C.: American Psychiatric Association, 1993.

———and Myrna Weissman. "Increasing Rates of Depression," *Journal of the American Medical Association,* 261 no. 15 (1989): 2229–2235.

———and Myrna Weissman, Bruce Rounsaville, and Eve Chevron. *Interpersonal Psychotherapy of Depression.* New York: Basic Books, 1984.

Kornstein, Susan. "Gender Differences in Depression: Implications for Treatment," *Journal of Clinical Psychiatry,* 58 suppl. 15 (1997): 12–18.

Kramer, Peter. *Should You Leave?* New York: Scribner, 1997.

———. *Listening to Prozac.* New York: Penguin, 1993.

Lara, Marian, Julie Leader, and Daniel Klein. "The Association Between Social Support and Course of Depression: Is It Confounded with Personality?" *Journal of American Psychology,* 106 no. 3 (1997): 478–482.

Lewinsohn, Peter, Hyman Hops, Robert Roberts, John Seeley, and Judy Andrews. "Adolescent Psychopathology: I. Prevalence and Incidence of Depression and other *DSM-III-R* Disorders in High School Students," *Journal of Abnormal Psychology*, 102 no. 1 (1993): 133–144.

——, Rohde, Paul, John Seeley, and Hyman Hops. "Comorbidity of Unipolar Depression: I. Major Depression with Dysthymia," *Journal of Abnormal Psychology*, 100 no. 2 (1991): 205–213.

Levav, Itzhak, Robert Kohn, Jacqueline Golding, and Myrna Weissman. "Vulnerability of Jews to Affective Disorders." *American Journal of Psychiatry*, 154 no. 7 (1997): 941–947.

Lyons-Ruth, Karlen, David Connell, and Henry Grunebaum. "Infants at Social Risk: Maternal Depression and Family Support Services as Mediators of Infant Development and Security of Attachment," *Child Development*, 61 (1990): 85–98.

Mack, Dana. *The Assault on Parenthood: How Our Culture Undermines the Family.* New York: Simon & Schuster, 1997.

Markman, Howard, Scott Stanley, and Susan Blumberg. *Fighting for Your Marriage: Positive Steps for Preventing Divorce and Preserving a Lasting Love.* San Francisco: Jossey-Bass, 1994.

Marsh, Diane and Dale Johnson. "The Family Experience of Mental Illness: Implications for Intervention," *Professional Psychology: Research and Practices*, 28 no. 3 (1997): 229–237.

Mays, Mark and James Croake. *Treatment of Depression in Managed Care.* New York: Brunner/Mazel, 1997.

McGoldrick, Monica. *You Can Go Home Again: Reconnecting with Your Family.* New York: Norton, 1995.

McGrath, Ellen, Gwendolyn Keita, Bonnie Strickland, and Nancy Russo (Eds.). *Women and Depression: Risk Factors and Treatment Issues.* Washington, D.C.: American Psychological Association, 1990.

McGuffin, Peter, Randy Katz, and Joan Rutherford. "Nature, Nurture, and Depression: A Twin Study," *Psychological Medicine*, 21 (1991): 329–335.

McKay, Matthew, Patrick Fanning, and Kim Paleg. *Couple Skills: Making Your Relationship Work.* Oakland, CA: New Harbinger, 1994.

Meichenbaum, Donald. *A Clinical Handbook/Practical Therapist Manual for Assessing and Treating Adults with Post-Traumatic Stress Disorder.* Waterloo, Ontario: Institute Press, 1994.

———. "Evolution of Cognitive Behavior Therapy: Origins, Tenets, and Clinical Examples." In *The Evolution of Psychotherapy: The Second Conference,* edited by J. Zeig, 114–122. New York: Brunner/Mazel, 1992.

Michels, Robert. "Psychotherapeutic Approaches to the Treatment of Anxiety and Depressive Disorders." *Journal of Clinical Psychiatry,* 58 suppl. 13 (1997): 30–32.

Minuchin, Salvador and Michael Nichols. *Family Healing.* New York: The Free Press, 1993.

Mitchell, Angela and Kennise Herring. *What the Blues Is All About: Black Women Overcoming Stress and Depression.* New York: Perigee, 1998.

Mitchell, James. *For Shame: The Loss of Common Decency in American Culture.* New York: St. Martin's Press, 1997.

Mondimore, Francis. *Depression: The Mood Disease.* Baltimore: Johns Hopkins University Press, 1993.

Nolen-Hoeksema, Susan. *Sex Differences in Depression.* Stanford, CA: Stanford University Press, 1990.

———"Sex Differences in Unipolar Depression: Evidence and Theory," *Psychological Bulletin,* 101 no. 2 (1987): 259–282.

Nowicki, Stephen and Marshal Duke. *Helping the Child Who Doesn't Fit In.* Atlanta: Peachtree Publishers, 1992.

O'Connor, Richard. *Undoing Depression.* New York: Little, Brown & Company, 1997.

O'Leary, K. Daniel and Steven Beach. "Marital Therapy: A Viable Treatment for Depression and Marital Discord," *American Journal of Psychiatry,* 147 (1990): 183–186.

Page, Susan. *How One of You Can Bring the Two of You Together.* New York: Broadway Books, 1997.

Papp, Peggy. "Listening to the System," *Family Therapy Networker* 21 no. 1 (1997): 52–58.

Peterson, Christopher, Steven Maier, and Martin Seligman. *Learned Helplessness: A Theory for the Age of Personal Control.* New York: Oxford University Press, 1993.

Pine, Daniel, Patricia Cohen, Diana Gurley, Judith Brook, and Yuju Ma. "The Risk for Early-Adulthood Anxiety and Depressive Disorders in Adolescents with Anxiety and Depressive Disorders," *Archives of General Psychiatry,* 55 (1998): 56–64.

Pipher, Mary. *The Shelter of Each Other.* New York: Ballantine, 1996.

Prince, Stacey and Neil Jacobson. "Couple and Family Therapy for Depression." In *Handbook of Depression* (2nd ed.) edited by E. Beckham and W. Leber, 404–424. New York: Guilford, 1995.

Radke-Yarrow, Marian. *Risk and Protective Factors in the Development of Psychopathology.* Cambridge: Cambridge University Press, 1993.

Real, Terrence. *I Don't Want to Talk About It: Overcoming the Secret Legacy of Male Depression.* New York: Scribner, 1997.

Resnick, Stella. *The Pleasure Zone: Why We Resist Good Feelings and How to Let Go and Be Happy.* Berkeley, CA: Conari Press, 1997.

Rutter, Michael. "Nature-Nurture Integration," *American Psychologist,* 52 no. 4 (April 1997): 390.

Scarf, Maggie. *Intimate Worlds: How Families Thrive and Why They Fail.* New York: Ballantine, 1995.

Schorr, Lisbeth. *Common Purpose: Strengthening Families and Neighborhoods to Rebuild America.* New York: Doubleday, 1997.

Schuyler, Dean. *Taming the Tyrant: Treating Depressed Adults.* New York: Norton, 1998.

Schwartz, Jeffrey. *Brain Lock.* New York: Regan Books, 1996.

Seeman, Mary. "Psychopathology in Women and Men: Focus on Female Hormones," *American Journal of Psychiatry,* 154 (1997): 1641–1647.

Seligman, Martin. *The Optimistic Child.* Boston: Houghton-Mifflin, 1995.

———. *What You Can Change . . . and What You Can't.* New York: Alfred A. Knopf, 1993.

———. *Learned Optimism.* New York: Alfred A. Knopf, 1990.

Shamoo, Tonia and Philip Patros. *Helping Your Child Cope with Depression and Suicidal Thoughts.* San Francisco: Jossey-Bass, 1990.

Shapiro, Laura. "The Myth of Quality Time," *Newsweek* (May 12, 1997): 62–69.

Sheffield, Anne. *How You Can Survive When They're Depressed.* New York: Harmony Books, 1998.

Sherven, Judith and James Sniachowski. *The New Intimacy: Discovering the Magic at the Heart of Your Differences.* Deerfield Beach, FL: Health Communications, 1997.

Shimberg, Elaine. *Depression: What Families Should Know.* New York: Ballantine, 1991.

Shure, Myrna. *Raising a Thinking Child.* New York: Henry Holt, 1994.

Siever, Larry and William Frucht. *The New View of Self.* New York: MacMillan, 1997.

Simpson, H. Blair, John Nee, and Jean Endicott. "First Episode Major Depression: Few Sex Differences in Course." *Archives of General Psychiatry,* 54 (1997): 633–639.

Straus, Murray. *Beating the Devil Out of Them: Corporal Punishment in American Families.* San Francisco: Jossey-Bass, 1994.

Sullivan, Kieran and Thomas Bradbury. "Are Premarital Prevention Programs Reaching Couples at Risk for Marital Dysfunction?" *Journal of Consulting and Clinical Psychology,* 65 no. 1 (1997): 24–30.

Swartz, Holly and John Markowitz. "Interpersonal Psychotherapy." In *Treating Depression,* edited by I. Glick, 71–94. San Francisco: Jossey-Bass, 1995.

Thase, Michael and David Kupfer. "Recent Developments in the Pharmacotherapy of Mood Disorders." *Journal of Consulting and Clinical Psychology,* 64 no. 4 (1996): 646–659.

Tsuang, Ming and Stephen Faraone. *The Genetics of Mood Disorders.* Baltimore: Johns Hopkins University Press, 1990.

Wallerstein, Judith and Sandra Blakeslee. *The Good Marriage: How and Why Love Lasts.* New York: Warner, 1995.

Weiner-Davis, Michele. *Change Your Life and Everyone in It.* New York: Fireside, 1995.

Weissbourd, Richard. *The Vulnerable Child: What Really Hurts America's Children and What We Can Do about It.* Reading, PA: Addison-Wesley, 1996.

Weissman, Myrna, Virginia Warner, Priya Wickramaratne, Donna Moreau, and Mark Olfston. "Offspring of Depressed Parents: 10 Years Later." *Archives of General Psychiatry,* 54 (October 1997): 932–940.

———, Roger Bland, Peter Joyce, Stephen Newman, J. Elisabeth Wells, J, and Hans-Urich Wittchen. "Sex Differences in Rates of Depression: Cross-National perspectives," *Journal of Affective Disorders,* 29 (1993): 77–84.

Whybrow, Peter. *A Mood Apart.* New York: Basic Books, 1997.

Yapko, Michael. "Spotlight on Brief Therapy." In 1998 *Encyclopedia Britannica Medical and Health Annual,* (290–293). Chicago: Encyclopedia Britannica, 1997.

———. *Breaking the Patterns of Depression.* New York: Doubleday, 1997.

———. "Stronger Medicine," *Family Therapy Networker,* 21 no. 1 (1997): 42–47.

———. "Depression: Perspectives and Treatments." In 1997 *Encyclopedia Britannica Medical and Health Annual,* (287–291). Chicago: Encyclopedia Britannica, 1996.

———. *Essentials of Hypnosis.* New York: Brunner/Mazel, 1995.

———. "Hypnosis and depression." In *Handbook of Clinical Hypnosis,* edited by J. Rhue, S. Lynn, and I. Kirsch, 339–355. Washington, D.C.: American Psychological Association, 1993.

———. *Hypnosis and the Treatment of Depressions.* New York: Brunner/Mazel, 1992.

———. "A Therapy of Hope," *Family Therapy Networker,* 15 no. 3 (1991): 34–39.

———. *Trancework: An Introduction to the Practice of Clinical Hypnosis* (2nd ed.). New York: Brunner/Mazel, 1990.

———(Ed.). *Brief Therapy Approaches to Treating Anxiety and Depression.* New York: Brunner/Mazel, 1989.

———. *When Living Hurts: Directives for Treating Depression.* New York: Brunner/Mazel, 1988.

Young, Michael, Louis Fogg, William Scheftner, Jan Fawcett, Hayop Akiskal, and Jack Mase. "Stable Trait Components of Hopelessness: Baseline and Sensitivity to Depression." *Journal of Abnormal Psychology,* 105 no. 2 (1996): 155–165.

Zuckerman, Barry, Howard Bauchner, Steven Parker, and Howard Cabral. "Maternal Depressive Symptoms During Pregnancy, and Newborn Irritability," *Journal of Developmental and Behavioral Pediatrics,* 11 no. 4 (1990): 190–194.

Index